GENDER DIVERSITY AND LGBTQ INCLUSION IN K-12 SCHOOLS

This exploration of effective practices to support lesbian, gay, bisexual, trans-gender, queer (LGBTQ) and gender-diverse students in elementary, middle, and high school contexts focuses on curriculum, pedagogy, and school environment. Narratives and artwork from the field are framed by sociocultural and critical theory as well as research-based elaboration on the issues discussed. Applications of antidiscrimination law and policy, as well as learning skills like creativity, collaboration, and critical thinking help teachers tackle some of the most significant educational challenges of our time. The stories of real-world practices offer encouragement for building inclusive environments and enhancing social-emotional relationships among youth, families, and schools. *Gender Diversity and LGBTQ Inclusion in K-12 Schools* provides a helpful roadmap for educators hoping to create safe and empowering spaces for LGBTQ and gender-diverse students and families.

Sharon Verner Chappell is Associate Professor, Elementary and Bilingual Education Department, California State University Fullerton, USA.

Karyl E. Ketchum is Associate Professor, Women and Gender Studies Department and Queer Studies Minor Program, California State University Fullerton, USA.

Lisa Richardson is a recently retired Elementary School Teacher and School and Community Outreach Coordinator for South Orange County PFLAG, USA.

GENDER DIVERSITY AND LGBTQ INCLUSION IN K-12 SCHOOLS

A Guide to Supporting Students, Changing Lives

Sharon Verner Chappell, Karyl E. Ketchum, and Lisa Richardson

Routledge
Taylor & Francis Group

NEW YORK AND LONDON

First published 2018
by Routledge
711 Third Avenue, New York, NY 10017

and by Routledge
2 Park Square, Milton Park, Abingdon, Oxon, OX14 4RN

Routledge is an imprint of the Taylor & Francis Group, an informa business

© 2018 Taylor & Francis

The right of Sharon Verner Chappell, Karyl E. Ketchum, and Lisa
Richardson to be identified as authors of this work has been asserted
by them in accordance with sections 77 and 78 of the Copyright,
Designs and Patents Act 1988.

Library of Congress Cataloging-in-Publication Data
A catalog record for this title has been requested

ISBN: 978-1-138-04450-0 (hbk)
ISBN: 978-1-138-04451-7 (pbk)
ISBN: 978-1-315-17229-3 (ebk)

Typeset in Bembo
by codeMantra

To Taylor, you have taught me so much. You gave me the gift of opening my world to a community of warm, loving people and dear friends whom I would never have known. Walking beside you on your journey, I began my own. Through you, my eyes were opened to the incredible struggle that so many young people endure in school. It led me to my passion for creating school environments built upon embracing diversity and respecting one another. The gratitude and love I have for you are beyond measure.

—Mom

To Hail, my warrior daughter whose commitment to social justice, even at the age of 17, inspired so many around her and no one more than her mother. Your willingness to stand up for the rights of those who could not stand for themselves has provided me with one of my life's greatest models and proudest moments. You will always be my shining star. And to Christian "Glitch" Rodriguez, whose irrepressible smile will live forever in my heart.

—Karyl

To Gillian, whose smile radiates through me and shows me the possibilities in the world. You are my gender detective, the one who has an open heart and considers inclusion in your everyday thinking and action. The future is bright because of you. I love you.

—Mommy

CONTENTS

FOREWORD

sj Miller

Imagine you are a second-grade teacher who has just received your class roster for the new school year. You glance down at the names, genders, ages, and ethnicities to gain a sense of whom you will see on Monday morning at 8:10 am. You note these identifiers and start to prejudge, unknowingly, who you will greet, the types of icebreaker activities you will implement, and student groupings for subject matter activities. You then create a form for your students to fill in on the first day:

My name is: _____
My gender is: _____
My age is: _____
My ethnicity is: _____
My favorite subject is: _____
I'm really good at: _____
My favorite food is: _____

Monday morning comes. You welcome your students with a huge smile as they file quietly into desks arranged in pods of five. You go through the roster and call names. Students raise their hands when they recognize themselves and smile with that "first day, everything is great" smile. You then give them pencils and ask them to fill in their forms, so they can introduce themselves to their neighbors.

As you walk around saying hi to each child, you notice a student staring at the form. You see that they have filled in everything except "my name is" and "my gender is." The sweet, innocent face looks up at you. You crouch down, and you say, "Hi. Do you have a question?"

They say, "You called me Brighton when you called roll, but my name is Emily and I am girl." You listen to Emily say a bit more about herself and take a deep breath. You rewind in your mind back to when you were planning for class. You realize all of the presumptions you had made about *what you thought you knew* about your students.

Your pause helps you think of a careful, kind response. "Emily it's so nice to meet you. Welcome to the first day of second grade! I am so glad you're here." She smiles and returns to her form and with excitement writes "Emily" and "girl."

The interaction with Emily has been playing like a broken record in your mind all day. Later, when you have a moment to reflect, you realize that meeting Emily was a first for you. You decide at that moment that you want to learn as much as you can about supporting all of the Emilys and Brightons you will meet in your teaching career. You have questions about what to do, whom to ask, how to integrate gender identity topics into your classroom (and school), and how not to make assumptions about students' gender identities. You question why you hadn't received any tools in your teacher education programs or in your professional development sessions preparing for your first day teaching in the district.

The authors of this book, and stories of practice told by educators in each of the book's chapters, provide answers to these questions. This book addresses gender and LGBTQ diversity and inclusion in K-12 schooling environments, curricula, and pedagogy. Across these captivating and educative chapters, the authors take us on a journey of supporting students in self-determining their diverse gender identities and sexual orientations/desires. While we often see the pain and tragic consequences for our queer youth that can manifest in schools, this book provides a blueprint of preventative inclusion strategies for schooling in elementary, middle, and high school as well as in higher education.

At the time of this writing—in fact, last night—I read that Finn, an eighth-grade trans*[+] male, killed himself. Every time we lose an LGBTQ child or a student with a self-determined gender identity, we are complicit in not doing enough. The Finns, Emilys, and Brightons are ours to love and respect, and we are forever indebted to them for how they are rearchitecturing different social contexts. But our youth should not have to take their own lives to force social changes to happen. We must intentionally intervene in the statistic that says over 50% of trans* youth have attempted suicide by their twentieth birthday (Ybarra, Mitchell, & Kosciw, 2014). When our queer and gender nonbinary students are not present in school, everyone misses out on opportunities to impact and spatialize school and social change.

Every time someone laughs at a student because of their sexual orientation and/or gender identity, not only does it strengthen and give permission for different forms of queer-based violence, but it also feels like a nail going into the victim's body and makes it near to impossible for them to express their true identity. Now, think of that same body over a school day, a week, a month, or a year. Think of that body filled with nails for 12+ years of schooling. I cannot finish this thought—you do the math.

As educators commit themselves to this work, we will see decreases in bullying, harassment, dropping out, lowered grade point averages, truancy, mental health and substance abuse issues, homelessness, presence in foster care and group homes, pushout into the school-to-prison pipeline, *and* suicidal ideation. This book helps us to disrupt dangerous mind-sets and gaps in schooling contexts, curriculum, and pedagogy through concrete strategies. The book demonstrates how the schooling system can embrace policies and practices that shift beliefs about LGBT and gender identity topics from early on in schooling experiences. The authors are reshaping and changing how we can stop microaggressions and interrupt LGBT and gender identity-based violence. This book is part of a trajectory of time-sensitive solutions.

To ensure that this work is sustainable, as a collective, we can commit to closely working with others on shifting the conditions that have structured the schooling system that positions queer, trans★+, and gender nonbinary bodies as vulnerable. To truly envelop these students, this work will require commitments from various stakeholders, including students, teachers, administrators, staff and school personnel, anyone who has contact with youth, parents, communities, teacher education programs, deans, professors, preservice students, researchers, and policy-makers involved in schools. To truly commit to this work means we must first hear where others are coming from and enter into difficult and yet courageous conversations. To truly commit to this work means divesting from structures that reinforce and sustain queer and binary gendered privileges and living lives that embody and stay committed to eschewing heteronormative and cisgender privileges. When we participate in such a system and accept these logics as truths, we continue to strengthen ignorance about LGBT and gender identity topics.

While we do see some changes happening in schools that are inclusive of, and mindful to, the affirmation and recognition of queer, trans★+, and gender nonbinary bodies, cosmetic changes do little to help establish more fair and equitable schooling environments. Our work must look at root causes; ways to rehabilitate and then change exclusionary political, economic, and affective practices; and the subsequent conditions that have created injustice in the first place. As we stay committed to understanding how such bodies are commodified as a pathway to dive deeper into interrogating the beliefs, practices, and policies that have created "gender-typical" glass ceilings, schools can be transformed.

These authors show us the "how to"—now it is up to you all to *do*. Let Brighton, Emily, Finn, and the many others you will encounter be your guides. Listen to them, hear them, affirm them, and recognize them as you mediate opportunities for them to recognize themselves in the work. Ask yourselves what purpose does a form even serve? Ask, "Do I need forms?" And if you answer yes, think about how questions can essentialize and reposition gender norms, expressions, and identities. Take to heart the questions your students ask and let them push you to seek answers and solutions. Keep in the forefront of your mind that as we stand up and with them, and fight for their rights to experience human dignity, we pay back a debt for their courage. As you stay committed to this work, and develop new tools that do not use nails, I suspect that the next time you meet an Emily, you will be prepared to respond.

My hope is that many of the questions you had before reading this book have been answered and that you will now figure out solutions for the many others that surfaced.

Forever indebted to our queer, trans*+, and gender nonbinary youth.

sj Miller, PhD
Deputy Director, Center for Research on Equity in Teacher Education | Metropolitan Center for Research on Equity and the Transformation of Schools

Research Associate Professor | New York University | Steinhardt School of Culture, Education, and Human Development

References

Ybarra, M. L., Mitchell, K. J., & Kosciw, J. G. (2014). The relation between suicidal ideation and bullying victimization in a national sample of transgender and non-transgender adolescents. In P. Goldblum, D. Espelage, J. Chu, and B. Bognar (Eds.), *Youth suicide and bullying: Challenges and strategies for prevention and intervention* (pp. 134–147). New York: Oxford University Press.

PREFACE

The three primary authors come to writing this text through very different trajectories and have found together a shared, urgent commitment to the work of providing educators with a resource on the increasingly important goal of understanding gender identity, gender expression, biological sex, and sexuality in schools.

Dr. Sharon Chappell grew up passionate about feminist movements, reading about the stories of gender bending civil rights leaders like Amelia Bloomer and Amelia Earhart. She read *Ms. Magazine's* "Stories for Free Children" voraciously and remembers her first contact with Baby X, a story about a baby whose parents refused to gender them using the binary of she/he. Sharon struggled with gender roles and stereotypes as a teenager as well as her own questioning sexuality. At University of California, Berkeley, her majors, English Literature and Women's Studies, informed her developing activist educator identity about gender and sexuality, particularly in schools. She now facilitates professional development in Los Angeles and Orange County to build LGBTQ- and gender-inclusive schools in pre-K–12 grades.

The challenges faced by LGBT and queer students came into sharp focus for Dr. Karyl E. Ketchum when her daughter, after a move from a school in Northern California, attended school in Newport Beach California at Corona del Mar High School. Through a confluence of events, Karyl discovered that the environment her daughter was in at school was both blatantly misogynistic and dangerously homophobic—ideologies that, as you will learn in this text, always appear together to various degrees. This same confluence of events also attracted the attention of the American Civil Liberties Union of Southern California, who stepped in and filed a lawsuit on behalf of the women students and the LGBT students at the school. As part of the suit's settlement, the school agreed to extensive training. Dr. Ketchum witnessed firsthand the tremendous difference this training made for students and teachers. She also discovered that not a single one of the many teachers, principals, and superintendents she met during this time had received academic training in the many critical, intersecting facets of gender identity and sexuality in childhood and adolescence. This was the beginning of her commitment to the text that lies before you.

Elissa Richardson attended her first Parents and Friends of Lesbians and Gays (PFLAG) meeting after her son came out to her at age 16. After hearing stories of the torment and agony LGBTQ students around Orange County were experiencing and learning about her own son's struggles, she was compelled to take action. She began to make changes to the curriculum and strategies she used in her own classroom. After making changes to her program and creating a more accepting and gender-neutral classroom, she saw the incredibly positive effect that those changes had on all of her students. She became a speaker for the PFLAG Speaker's Bureau and an Outreach Coordinator. She now works with teachers, school counselors, and administrators, sharing her experiences and providing training and advocating for LGBTQ-inclusive curriculum and school environments. She is committed to changing the experiences of young people in schools and to advocating for the LGBTQ community.

All three contributors have experienced firsthand what a tremendous difference an understanding of such topics—and related understandings of lesbian, gay, bisexual, transgender, queer, and questioning identities—can make in school districts, on school campuses, and in the classroom.

And as educators ourselves, we understand through our own classrooms, research experiences, and relationships with students that such information can, and does, save lives.

This text brings together a unique combination of disciplines and ideas. It draws fluidly from best practices in education and pedagogical theory as well as from gender theory, cultural studies, and contemporary queer theory, among others. We believe that this combination makes for a powerful and exciting lens for our readers/educators in their practices with youth and families. Through the cross-pollination of these interdisciplinary ideas emerge productive new framings of educational spaces, learning goals, and a new understanding of the needs of all stake holders within our educational communities. We hope that this approach allows the text to translate into classroom practices that both transform and inspire.

In the interest of making the text as usable, affective, and expansive as possible, we solicited the stories and creative work of many teachers, school administrators, parents, and students, bringing together a group of voices and experiences that is intended to breathe life into the theories and ideas we share and into the very specific challenges faced by LGBTQIA students and educators. Working with this group of contributing story authors has been one of the greatest gifts of this project as we have been moved and renewed by their generosity and commitment to facing challenges of bias and discrimination with bravery, both in and outside of schools. By weaving their first-person accounts, poetry, and lyrics into the text of each chapter, we mean to create a kind of dialogue between the stories and the theories/concepts we discuss in order to illustrate how these might connect with the emotional lives and experiences of students.

The success of this project in many ways hinges on this dialogic relationship between theory and practice. After all, it is one thing to learn in the abstract through reading theory and often quite another to be able to apply these ideas in the immediacy of our relationships with students. In other words, through this strategy, we hope to move our readers fluidly from their head to their heart. Just as the piece included at the end of this preface makes clear, we often turn to the poetic and the personal when the words do not yet exist within us to trace a straight path to our ideas and feelings. We believe this is particularly effective when it comes to a book whose ultimate goal is to transform the relationships among students and educators. Though it's certainly the case that not all of our readers will be members of the LGBTQIA community, we still all share in the very human experiences of belonging, believing, and thriving or not.

In addition to including creative work, the book's form also emphasizes language and the importance of vocabulary. Even a single new word can open entire vistas of understanding. For example, when we learn the words that differentiate gender identity from biological sex, suddenly, the experiences of trans students make more sense: their biological sex does not align with their gender identity. Got it. We further believe that much of the struggle educators have had in the past with topics related to LGBTQIA students really is one of language; for example, when an imprecise language does not allow us to recognize the difference between gender and sexual orientation, we can misread issues of gender as being about sex—a topic many educators do not feel comfortable addressing. A more developed vocabulary, such as the one we propose within this text, goes some distance to providing more nuanced and accurate understandings, thereby freeing up ideas and approaches to integrating gender diversity and LGBTQ advocacy and inclusion in schools.

This text means to tackle some of the most significant and challenging educational issues of our time. In many ways, these ideas can be thought of as providing a bridge between historical and traditional ways of understanding schools, pedagogy, and students, and ways that have evolved at a particularly rapid pace throughout the latter half of the twentieth century. We see this evolution as inevitable. As a result of several factors, such as the role of technology and social media, students arrive in our schools and classrooms today with a variety of understandings regarding their own identities, aptitudes, and ways of engaging with each other and ideas. Education and educators are most effective when they understand these positionalities. Through the careful treatment of vocabulary and language, curriculum and pedagogy, and the school environment itself, we hope to set up a meeting ground for students and educators in which identities named and as yet unnamed within language—*potentials*—can be explored, honored, and strengthened in the interest of our increasingly diverse future.

"Song of Myself" by Veronika Shulman

In the narrative that follows, educator, activist and poet, Veronika Shulman explores the power of weaving the personal and political with the youth in her community organization, Get Lit Los Angeles.

I have learned so much from the youth of Get Lit.
I discovered my queerness alongside them and entangled with them, and we have taught each other how to love and how to live.

I came out when I was 23, and I started working at Get Lit when I was 24.
We are a youth empowerment organization that works with young storytellers all over Los Angeles, mostly aged 14–20, and emboldens them to process their own personal narratives through spoken word poetry and other related art forms (music, dance, etc.).

The poets have elevated the world of spoken word to a whole new medium, transforming what was an oral and amorphous tradition into a professional content studio where anthems and manifestos have been commissioned by the United Nations, performances have been requested by the White House, and kids from across the globe wait patiently on YouTube for their newest videos to go live. One poem, inspired by a Jay-Z song, has over 100 million views, ironically making it way more influential than the song that inspired it.

To manage communications and content for the organization has been a privilege, and I have learned so much from our brilliant youth.

I have also experienced my adolescence alongside them.

The first time I came out to a student at a café in Santa Monica, the words felt tender and uncooked in my mouth, like a runny egg. I wasn't sure they were even totally true. And yet, we were writing about LGBT history month, so I felt it only fair to say something of my inner journey, my quiet longing.

She came out to me right after.

We shared a moment of authentic vulnerability and queerness and then went on drinking our chai lattes.
It was the most sweaty and pure I had felt in months.
I will never forget the feeling of walking to my car after that writing session and feeling so naked, so just-showered, so salt-aired and natural.

Then I started to try on my newfound identity and venture to LA's pretty rad queer world of bars and nightclubs and DJs and art walks. I found a great, kind, lovely crowd of girls to hang with, and my favorite kids from Get Lit started following all of us on social media, longing to be part of it, if only in spirit.

A big part of me wished the poets could come out with us. Why do you have to be 21 to explore your sexuality?

Then, as we got closer, a few of the poets started to rely on me as a queer mentor of sorts, and I had no idea how to guide them…except to go by instinct. I tried to be calm and even-keeled, to listen to them and treat them as I would treat all of my closest family and friends, as others who I loved had treated me: as equals.

Generation Z kids explore their sexuality and gender in the most nuanced ways, both earthly and surreal, through experiments and experiences and art, and it has been incredibly inspiring.

One boy "came out as goth" to me one day as a kind of joke/commentary on people coming out as trans and playing with their gender. I could tell he was testing how chill I would be about it. I tried so hard to think of something clever. "Just remember," I advised, "goth isn't a binary. It's not just a switch that goes off. It's a spectrum and a transition. You don't have to decide just how goth you are in one day." He loved it. Sigh of relief. Maybe he thought I was cool.

Another one of our kids who I particularly adored was struggling with whether they were cool with their assigned birth gender or whether they should transition. I didn't know what to say. I told them it's OK to play around and change your mind too. Change your name, pick a nickname, choose little things. See how you feel. Try things on.

We all should do that. Life is all about self-evolution, and if we can't evolve or if others judge us for it, then that's a problem.

I told the teens that they would know deep down what was true, to listen to the voices they hear right when you wake up in the morning, before you put on makeup, before you brush your teeth. When they are still one with the earth and sky. I thought we should all change little things about ourselves. I told them that they were not alone.

Then the same kid told me as gently as they could that I really needed to find a girlfriend. That I wasn't as young as them and wasn't getting any younger. I was so embarrassed and tried to hide it. They were totally right. I started online dating that night. After all, I didn't want my sixteen-year-old best friend to think I was a loser! That was not an option.

In so many ways, I faked being okay with my queerness, and I faked a maturity around my sexuality for the sake of the poets. And the strange thing is that my fake self-love slowly faded into being true. I slowly began to feel truly queer, to feel so gay and love it, to feel okay not wearing makeup all the time, to feel okay feeling young and adolescent and hormonal, to feel wild and free.

I matured with the sage advice of my young friends. My online obsession with contemporary queer celebrities like Kristen Stewart gradually transformed into a real-life relationship with a real-life girl that looks and acts remarkably like Kristen Stewart. And unsurprisingly, hanging out with my real-life girlfriend is much more satisfying than looking at pictures of cool lesbians on Pinterest.

I started to grow up. And my queerness did too.

Queerness has become a very important and meaningful staple of Get Lit culture. Our community has become a space where queer youth can push the envelope of ideas of drag, femininity, masculinity, loudness, identity, togetherness, longing, and solitude through art and through friendship.

Two poets had brought the house down at an international poetry festival in Washington, D.C., with a poem called "Queerly Beloved" in which they talk about the "thing that has no name": their sexuality.

They say,

"Let's call it a palm tree…it sways with the wind.
No no, let's call it a telescope…it knows a star when it sees one."

No one had ever described my sexuality so eloquently. I don't think at this point, for example, that I would date a guy. I prefer to date girls. But what is gender, anyway? Why do I have to make such a strange arbitrary lifelong decision now?

I do not.
Life is so much more complex and surprising than that.
I realized that after listening to the kids.

They come to me for advice, yes, but I come to them too.
We teach each other and sprinkle each other with our own unique brands of fairy dust, our own knowledge and wisdom and magic. We are each experts in our own lives.

They are friends.
They are queer scholars.
They are fashion icons.
And they are prophets.

You are what you are.
You are greater than label, greater than stereotype, greater than gender or sexuality.

We have to rid ourselves of the high school bullies that live inside of all of us trying to tell us we are not worth it.
We are all vast and great.

I remember at one point looking around at my desk, my house, my friends, and thinking of that part of *James and the Giant Peach* in which the characters live in the peach but also eat from it, just scoop a piece of a wall and eat it right up when they're hungry, and they are happy in their cohesive little utopia.

I felt just like that and thought to myself, *This is real life.*

The world is loud and full of so many stories.
Who should we listen to?

Listen to the kids.
Listen to the poets.
They know more than we do…

ACKNOWLEDGMENTS

We wish to thank Monique Valle, California State University graduate student extraordinaire, for her tireless work editing this book. Her commitment to gender advocacy and knowledge of American Psychological Association (APA) formatting has made the completion of this book possible.

Thank you to all the brave story contributors to this book. Your passion and commitment to queer youth and families inspire us each day. Your stories will impact so many lives. This book is yours.

This book lives in the energy of queer youth, who refuse to give up and instead thrive as their authentic selves. You are the reason this book exists. The future is yours. The future is queer.

1

INTRODUCTION

Building Gender-Diverse and LGBTQ-Inclusive Schools

A preschool teacher tidies up her classroom, placing the toys and dress-up items in their locations and filling the paint canisters. While holding a "princess dress," she remembers casual talk between a few of her students that day. When one boy tried on the dress, another told him, "You can't wear that. It's pink. It's a dress, and you are a boy." Then two girls talked about being mommies to the baby dolls, and another girl said, "You can't be married. Only mommies and daddies get married." The teacher personally believes that all colors are for everyone, that her students can play many parts in their make-believe play, and that there are many ways to be a family. *How can I talk to the kids tomorrow about stereotypes and diversity? How can I encourage them to embrace each other's curiosities and interests in their play?*

A parent stands at the door to the school office and stares through the window at the familiar faces who had greeted him often during his older child's elementary school years. Now, his younger child is entering third grade, changing schools after years of harassment for being transgender. Summoning the courage, he twists the knob and opens the door, ready to register his son. The parent knows there are many state and federal laws that protect his son's gender identity and expression, but he has no idea how the administration will react when his son goes in the office and it all becomes real. *Will the school be safe, welcoming, and inclusive of us as a family with a child who is transgender?*

A middle school girl doodles in her notebook during math, glancing at the empty desk that should be occupied by her best friend but hasn't been for a week now. He had been in the drama club, and she hoped the club would help him feel better, less picked on. But every day, he would retreat to the school's theater in tears after being called derogatory names, and now, he's not coming to school. She texts him and lets her mind wander. The girl heard somewhere that there was something called a Gay–Straight Alliance (GSA). *Would starting a GSA at our school help my friend? If so, how do I get started, will other students want to join? Will I receive support from my teachers and my parents?*

A high school boy talks with his science fiction literature group about a story to choose for English class. He has been out for some time and supported by most everyone he knows. So, he suggests reading *We Are the Ants*, talking excitedly about the book's alien invasion plot and honest character relationships (he has started skimming the book). His group agrees, so they submit the title to their teacher. The teacher does a quick search and notices that the book has lesbian, gay, bisexual, transgender, and queer or questioning (LGBTQ) content. He imagines his email in-box filling with complaints from parents and asks the group to find some alternative titles, just in case. *How can I support my students' interests and lives in the face of controversy and concern?*

In all these examples, teachers, parents, and students grapple with the complexities of navigating LGBTQ identities and inclusions/exclusions at school. How will each one of them pursue the answers to their questions? How will the adults and youth in each situation respond to the actions they take? What resources and networks will help them in the face of challenges and resistance, and strengthen their confidence in becoming advocates and allies for LGBTQ youth at school? This book seeks to respond to such questions, providing a resource for teachers at all levels: elementary, middle, and high school.

Children and youth in US schools regularly experience discrimination directed toward their bodies; languages spoken; gender, racial and ethnic identity; perceived sexual orientation; national identity, immigration and documentation status and family diversity. In particular, bias-based bullying most often impacts LGBTQ youth, which sometimes leads to self-harm and disengagement from school (AERA, 2013). However, establishing safe, welcoming schools for LGBTQ youth and families can prevent this harm.

This book explores effective practices to support gender diversity and LGBTQ advocacy and inclusion in elementary, middle, and high school contexts, with a particular focus on curriculum, pedagogy, school environment, and applications of antidiscrimination law and policy and twenty-first-century learning skills of creativity, collaboration, and critical thinking. We include exemplary stories of educational practice that positively impact LGBTQ youth and families at school—approaches that include support from education professionals across community, school district, and teacher education programs. We also address the struggles and barriers experienced by LGBTQ youth and families in an effort to move toward improved conditions at school. As you read this book, we hope you will feel empowered to act in many ways:

- To learn more about LGBTQ youth and families
- To identify state and federal school-based laws and policies that support your allied advocacy work
- To evaluate curriculums and pedagogy in terms of their inclusivity and exclusivity based on gender and sexuality
- To prevent and intervene in bias, stereotyping, and discrimination when you observe it at school

- To proactively advocate for queer, gender-expansive, and transgender youth and families
- To support the pluralism and intersectionality of students' identities
- To set goals for yourself as an educator and advocate in this important work.

Building gender-diverse and LGBTQ-inclusive school environments enhances social-emotional relationships among children and youth, families, and school staff. Inclusive environments support overall wellness, academic achievement, and growth and development for *all* children and youth. Yet teachers need opportunities to learn how to proactively build safe, welcoming, and inclusive schools; how to intervene when they witness harassment; and how to include LGBTQ role models and contributions in the regular school curriculum. As you read, we hope that, as educators, advocates, and allies, you will feel empowered to act. We will address how to evaluate curriculum, pedagogy, and school environments, and how to identify personal/professional goals for taking allied actions as educators.

The book begins with an introduction to sociocultural and critical frameworks for understanding gender and sexual diversity, with a particular focus on gender nonconforming, transgender, and LGBTQ children and youth. We deconstruct naturalized binary-based norms and power structures that influence young people's identity construction and behaviors, reframing gender and sexuality on a pluralistic continuum or spectrum. We address the ways in which children experience bias-based bullying—teasing, harassment, and sometimes violence—about actual or perceived personal characteristics, such as their body shape/size, languages spoken, gender, race/ethnicity, perceived sexual orientation, or family structure (Buckel, 2000; California Safe Schools Coalition, 2016; Griffin & Ouellett, 2003; Prevent School Violence Illinois, 2017).

The book draws particular attention to the impact of bullying and discrimination on LGBTQ youth. For example, transgender youth are disproportionately at risk for harassment and violence. In a national survey of K-12 trans youth respondents, 78 percent experienced harassment, 35 percent experienced physical assault, 12 percent experienced sexual assault, and 15 percent said harassment was so bad it led them to leave school (Grant, Mottet, & Tanis, 2011). Disproportionately, bullying involves homophobic and gender-based teasing and slurs (Espelage, Basile, & Hamburger, 2012; Meyer, 2009; Poteat & Espelage, 2005; Poteat & Rivers, 2010), and occurs more frequently among LGBTQ youth in US schools than among those who identify as heterosexual (Espelage, Aragon, Birkett, & Koenig, 2008; Kosciw, Greytak, & Diaz, 2009). This book provides examples of school and community approaches to applying laws that protect against LGBTQ discrimination and bullying; ensuring the availability of resources for LGBTQ youth at school; and requiring the inclusion of contributions of diverse communities, including LGBTQ individuals, in the K-12 curriculum (A Project by the ACLU of California, My School My Rights Know Your Rights, 2017).

STATISTICS YOU SHOULD KNOW ABOUT GAY AND TRANSGENDER STUDENTS

Reliable estimates indicate that between 4% and 10% of the population is gay, which means that in a public school system of more than one million, like New York City's, there are at least 40,000 to 100,000 gay students.

Schools should be a young person's primary center for learning, growing, and building a foundation for success in the world. Growing up and getting through high school can be challenging for any student, but lesbian, gay, bisexual, transgender, and queer (LGBTQ) youth too often face additional obstacles of harassment, abuse, and violence. The statistics are astounding:

Academics

§ LGBTQ students at schools with comprehensive policies on bullying and harassment are much more likely to report harassment to school authorities who, in turn, were more likely to respond effectively.

§ LGBTQ students are twice as likely to say that they were not planning on completing high school or going on to college.

Health

§ Gay teens are 8.4 times more likely to report having attempted suicide and 5.9 times more likely to report high levels of depression compared with peers from families that reported no or low levels of family rejection.

§ LGBTQ youth who reported higher levels of family rejection during adolescence are three times more likely to use illegal drugs.

Family and Shelter

§ Half of gay males experience a negative parental reaction when they come out, and in 26 percent of these cases, the youth is thrown out of the home.

§ Studies indicate that between 25 percent and 50 percent of homeless youth are LGBTQ and on the streets because of their sexual orientation or gender identity.

§ LGBTQ youth are overrepresented in foster care, juvenile detention, and among homeless youth.

Harassment and Violence

§ Nearly one-fifth of students are physically assaulted because of their sexual orientation, and over one-tenth are physically assaulted because of their gender expression.

§ About two-thirds of LGBTQ students reported having been sexually harassed (e.g., sexual remarks made, being touched inappropriately) in school in the past year.

§ The average GPA (grade point average) for students who were frequently physically harassed because of their sexual orientation was half a grade lower than that of other students.

*Approximately 40 percent of homeless youth are LGBTQ

(PFLAG New York City, 2016)

This book is separated into sections by grade span across elementary, middle/ junior high, and high schools, anchored by personal narrative stories and artwork from the field, and framed by theory and research-based elaboration on the issues discussed in the chapters. Each chapter ends with discussion questions for the reader. Separating the book into sections based on educational setting allows readers to easily identify practices that directly apply to them and read beyond their settings for related strategies to anticipate what works when students come into their grade levels or leave them for future grades. Although we have separated the book into sections, we highly recommend that you read everything! There are many strategies and resources throughout the book that all readers can utilize.

We aim to inspire hope in teachers, other school professionals, community partners, and families; through stories of current safe, welcoming, and inclusive practices, we can envision how to improve our own schools and enhance social-emotional relationships among youth, families, and schools in dynamic ways. Anchoring the book in personal narratives about schools, teaching, and learning provides a basis for teacher development. Stories shape our world, helping us navigate problems, experiences, and ideas in our daily lives (Clandinin & Connelly, 2000; Goffman, 1974). Constructing stories about life and work experiences helps us examine society and ask questions about why things stay the same and why they change, particularly in the context of school (Clandinin & Connelly, 2000; Geertz, 1995). Often, stories portrayed in media and schoolbooks remain narrow (representing primarily majoritized populations) and stock (representing stereotypical expectations for the life experiences of particular affinity groups). In this way, the stories of minoritized LGBTQ youth and communities have remained concealed in schools, leaving students without exposure to a rich mosaic of perspectives and experiences of the world (Bell & Roberts, 2010; Cruz, 2002; Takaki, 2011).

The stories in this book excavate concealed experiences of gender-diverse and LGBTQ youth, families, and educators as we learn from counter-narratives that offer alternative viewpoints on the impact of power, injustice, and the othering of LGBTQ people (Anzaldúa, 2012; Bell & Roberts, 2010; Chappell & Chappell, 2015; hooks, 2013; Solórzano & Yosso, 2002). Through these counter-narratives, we hope to inspire you—teachers, school professionals, community partners, and families—so we may all become more inclusive in our practices to better support LGBTQ youth and families in our classrooms and schools.

Contexts for School-Based LGBTQ Inclusion and Advocacy

Whether we teach in the classroom or an out-of-school setting, lead a school, counsel young people, or are their parents and guardians, we have a profound influence on their growth and development, particularly their sense of self-worth. How we recognize or ignore, embrace or reject their identities matters. Young people's ways of seeing themselves and the world are socioculturally constructed through the communities in which they participate.

We focus on their identities as related to their gender and sexuality, particularly those identities that are LGBTQ. In most cultures globally, young people develop in relation to norms about what it means to be male and female, boy and girl, man and woman (Britzman, 1998; Butler, 1993; Carrera, Depalma, & Lameiras, 2012). Communities socialize and naturalize gender norms, often depending on hierarchical binaries that assign power and status to gender-conforming behaviors (Butler, 1993, 2004). These binary-based norms and power structures influence children's identity construction: how society presents definitions of *boy* and *girl* informs how children see themselves (or do not see themselves) as *male* or *female*, or otherwise gendered.

In the US culture, schools contribute to the conflation of biological sex, sexual orientation, and gender, communicating heteronormative expectations for children and their families. Children learn about what it means to be in a relationship, for example, through fairytale stories of princes finding their princesses, rituals like the Father/Daughter dance, and school forms that ask for the names of the student's mother and father. Peers discipline this conflation through comments about media and toy consumption; ways of acting, speaking, and dressing; acceptable topics of discussion; and types of play during recess, to name but a few. For boys/men, masculinity is recognized through stereotypical behaviors and is read—and misread—as evidence of heterosexuality and being straight. Femininity among girls/women is likewise assumed to be an indication of heterosexual orientation (Carrera et al., 2012; Depalma & Atkinson, 2009). More complex, fluid, and expansive identities; expressions; and attractions are subsumed or erased within these binary gender frameworks. The Gender Unicorn (see Figure 1.1), created by Transgender Student Educational Resources, illustrates a more nuanced vision of gender and sexuality,

FIGURE 1.1 "Gender Unicorn" by TSER (Trans Student Educational Resources).

including gender identity, gender expression, sex assigned at birth, physical attraction, and emotional attraction.

For the purposes of this book, we define *gender identity* as one's internal sense of self as male, female, or an identity between or outside these binary categories. It is formed through an individual's psychological and emotional relationships to femininity and masculinity as categories of identity. We define *gender expression* as a performative act meant and/or assumed to publicly establish an individual's relationship to femininity and masculinity, often built on societal gender assumptions (Miller, 2015). Gender expression is the outward presentation of gender signaled through a symbolic language of visual and auditory cues (Bilodeau & Renn, 2005). The gender identities of *transgender* individuals, for example, are not aligned with "biological sex assignment or societal expectations for gender expression as male or female [as associated with biological assignment]" (Bilodeau & Renn, 2005, p. 29). Further, gender identity is often situated on a *spectrum* or continuum and can be experienced as shifting and fluid depending on context, time and space, and relationships and activities. We point out that, within the individual, gender identity and expression are highly personal and, contrary to many cultural assumptions, vary widely. We define this constellation as *gender pluralism,* not only in terms of individual expression but also as institutionalized in spaces such as school classrooms and playgrounds (Davis, 2009; Monro, 2008).

IMPORTANT GENDER, SEXUALITY, AND LGBTQ DEFINITIONS

Ally: A term used to describe someone who is supportive of LGBTQ people. It encompasses non-LGBTQ allies as well as those within the LGBTQ community who support each other, e.g., a lesbian who is an ally to the bisexual community.

Asexual: A term used to describe individuals who do not experience sexual attraction.

Bisexual: A term used to describe individuals who are physically and emotionally attracted to both the opposite and same sexes.

Gay: A generic term used to describe individuals who are physically and emotionally attracted to someone of the same sex. Sometimes used just to refer to gay men. It has also been used as a derogatory slur to describe anything, anyone, or any behavior that does not meet the approval of an individual or a given group.

Gender: The socially constructed roles, behaviors, activities, and attributes that a given society considers appropriate for men and women. Gender varies between cultures and over time. There is broad variation in which individuals experience and express gender.

Gender binary: The idea that there are only two distinct and opposing genders (female/male).

Gender continuum/spectrum: The idea that gender identity and expression is often experienced through a continuum or spectrum.

Gender expansive: Conveys a wider, more flexible range of gender expression, with a range of interests and behaviors. Expanding beyond traditional gender stereotypes. It reinforces the notion that gender is not a binary but a continuum and that many children and adults express their gender in multiple and changing ways.

Gender expression: How one expresses their gender to the world (clothing, dress, mannerisms, speech).

Gender identity: How one feels inside. One's internal, deeply felt sense of being girl/woman, boy/man, somewhere in between, or outside these categories.

Gender nonconforming: A term used by the California Department of Education (CDE) to describe students whose gender expression does not fit into the socially constructed gender binary of male/female.

Heteronormative: The expectation that all individuals are heterosexual. Often expressed subtly through assumptions that everyone is, or will grow up to be, straight. Can also refer to the social, political, and economic system that supports and rewards heterosexuality and to the institutionalized belief that heterosexuality is the superior and singular mode of sexual organization for society.

Intersectionality: Describes the ways in which people's multiple identities are formed and forming in relation to systems of power and oppression. The whole of one's identity is complex and informed by component identities in relation to social institutions impacting those component identities.

Intersex: A general term used for a variety of conditions in which a person is born with a reproductive or sexual anatomy that doesn't seem to fit the typical definitions of female or male.

LGBTQ or LGBTQIA: Acronym for Lesbian, Gay, Bisexual, and Transgender. Q can stand for Questioning or Queer, I stands for Intersex, and A stands for Ally or Asexual. Also abbreviated as GLBT and LGBT.

Lesbian: A woman who is sexually and romantically attracted to other women.

Queer: Historically, a negative term for LGBT people. More recently reclaimed by some LGBT people to refer to themselves. Often used to reference a more flexible view of gender and/or sexuality. Some people still find the term offensive. Others use it as a more inclusive term that allows for more freedom of gender expression. Also used in academic fields, such as queer studies or queer pedagogy, indicating an interest in how norms and difference are constructed and maintained.

Queer theory: A theoretical approach to analyzing lived experiences used in academic fields like queer studies and queer pedagogy. This approach challenges either/or essentialist categories about gender and sexuality, and includes a critical and historically grounded inquiry into normative social and cultural processes.

Sex: One's biological and physical attributes—external genitalia, sex chromosomes, hormones, and internal reproductive structures—that are used to assign a sex at birth.

Sexual orientation: Who you are attracted to—physically, romantically, or emotionally. Current research indicates that sexual orientation exists along a continuum of emotional and sexual attractions and, in some cases, can change over the course of an individual's lifetime.

Transgender: An umbrella term that describes a wide range of identities, expressions, and experiences. It includes those whose gender assigned at birth does not match their internal sense of gender identity. A child who is transgender will often assert firmly, over time, that their gender identity is not that which was assigned at birth. They will often insist that they are in the wrong body. Not all gender nonconforming individuals consider themselves transgender. Some transgender individuals do not assert their identities until they are adults or even seniors.

Think about the first time you were encouraged, or perhaps even expected, to have a gender. How old were you? What did your gender mean to you? Did you think of yourself in relation to the binary of boy/girl? If so, was your identity formed in opposition to, or in relation to, the other gender? If you saw yourself as nonbinary—falling outside the prescripted male/female dichotomy—how did you navigate the world of gender binaries you experienced? What systems, ideas, values, and beliefs helped or hindered your gender identity development? Were you rewarded in some way for enacting a gendered identity, or were you in some way punished?

Now, think about your sexual identity. When did you first think about your emotional attraction to someone? Physical attraction? Did you identify as heterosexual, gay, pansexual, asexual, or something else altogether? What were your first memories of thinking about or interacting with someone who was gay? Was it a positive or negative experience? Was the experience influenced by social norms, assumptions, or even stereotypes about what it means to be gay?

These early experiences impact our dispositions as educators, school leaders, counselors, and parents/guardians. They impact the curriculum and pedagogy used in K-12 schools and in higher education during the preparation of school professionals. In the last 20 years, some efforts have been made to include and advocate for LGBTQ topics in education. These efforts sometimes include examining assumptions about heteronormative relationships; family composition; and binary-based gender, sex, and sexuality systems. These educational efforts also sometimes include identifying inclusion opportunities in the curriculum in which the contributions of LGBTQ individuals are recognized and nonbinary thinking about multicultural gender, culture, and family diversity is present. While we are now seeing these curriculum changes in a limited number of teacher training programs, they are by no means universal. Mainstream approaches in K-12, higher education preparation of school professionals, and school environments have too often remained hostile to gender nonconforming and gay youth and families (American Educational Research Association, 2017; Au, 2014; Davis & Kellinger, 2014; Flores, 2012; Malmquist, Gustavson, & Schmitt, 2013).

For example, recent approaches in US elementary teacher education have included teaching about gender socialization in child development, sexual orientation in relation to family diversity, and the impact of gender stereotypes on equitable classroom instruction (Curran, Chiarolli, & Davis, 2009; Depalma & Atkinson, 2006; Sanders, 1997). Most often, though, discussions of gender, sexuality, and LGBTQ communities occur in unique prerequisite courses on diversity in education or educational foundations, while these topics are less commonly integrated into subject matter preparation classes, such as social studies or language arts. And, unfortunately, within these contexts, such topics are still often framed through a normative/nonnormative binary model. However, subject matter courses can and should address the inclusion of gender and family diversity, such as through the contributions of LGBTQ individuals and communities as well as the role of LGBTQ struggles in civil rights in the regular curriculum (Flores, 2012, 2014; Hermann-Wilmarth, 2010; Naidoo, 2012; Phillips & Larson, 2012). Other approaches sometimes include discussing LGBTQ youth, family, and community experiences in relation to bias-bullying and bullying prevention programs (American Educational Research Association, 2017; Flores, 2014). While we argue for greater dispersion of these ideas throughout teacher education curriculums and particularly in subject matter preparation classes, we also assert that gender-related topics would be more productively, and practically, explored through continuum-based models, which more accurately reflect the complexities of identity.

Sometimes, teacher education courses draw upon feminist and queer theory to assist in supporting teachers in their deconstruction of gender socialization and the heteronormatization of relationships at schools (Depalma & Atkinson, 2006; Miller, 2016). These critical theories call for the deconstruction and dismantling of rigid gender norms, binaries, and hierarchies (Atkinson & Depalma, 2008; Flores, 2014; Miller, 2015, 2016; Renn, 2010; Sears, 2009). Yet, often, multiple subject teacher candidates express discomfort discussing LGBTQ-related topics, both in their preparation classroom and in K-8 settings—a discomfort that can be eased by increased discussion, resources, and strategies (Curran et al., 2009; Jennings & Sherwin, 2008; Walton, 2005). In some cases, simply having a clear understanding of the differences between sexual orientation and gender identity/expression goes some way toward easing teacher discomfort with these topics.

SNAPSHOT OF GENDER-INCLUSIVE SCHOOLS' PROFESSIONAL DEVELOPMENT

Increasingly, school districts are opting for professional development to assist teachers, administrators, and school staff in learning about gender diversity and LGBTQ inclusion as well as about how to support students in becoming more aware and inclusive themselves.

For an example of such supportive professional development, check out the film *Creating Gender Inclusive Schools*, directed by Jonathan Skurnik (2016). Here is a description:

What happens when you bring gender training to a public elementary school? In *Creating Gender Inclusive Schools*, the Peralta Elementary School in Oakland, CA, demonstrates the power of an open and honest conversation about gender.

The school brought in the staff of Gender Spectrum to provide training for teachers and administrators as well as an age-appropriate curriculum for students. During this step, everyone involved was empowered to look at their own personal confusion, bias, and feelings around gender.

Parents are brought into the mix next and add to the spirited discussion about creating a safe place for all children to be themselves. A week of classroom activities helps the students learn about gender, stereotyping, and bullying. Their insightful and intuitive discussions will open your eyes to how comfortable young people can be when given the opportunity to express their thoughts and feelings about gender.

Creating Gender Inclusive Schools demonstrates that it's not only possible but it's downright fun to train an entire public elementary school community to be inclusive of transgender and gender-expansive youth.

Creating Gender Inclusive Schools is one of four films in the Youth & Gender Media Project, which together demonstrate how to reach every member of a school community—students, teachers, parents, and administrators—to help them create educational settings that welcome all young people, regardless of where they fall on the spectrum of gender identity and expression.

Schools and school professional preparation programs have laws and policies in the USA that protect our efforts to make schools more safe, welcoming, and inclusive for LGBTQ youth and families (Welcoming Schools—A Project of the Human Rights Campaign Foundation, 2016, 2017). There are federal laws that apply to every state and provide a foundation for protections, regardless of the presence of state-level laws and policies. These protections include the right to form GSA clubs; numerous measures in support of transgender and gender nonconforming (nonbinary, gender-expansive) youth; and the rights of students, faculty, and staff to be *out,* or open, about their sexuality, gender identity, and membership in the LGBTQ community and for these groups to keep their gender identity and sexuality private. Constitutionally, the Equal Protection Clause of the Fourteenth Amendment guarantees every citizen equal protection under the law. This clause is used to protect LGBTQ youth in schools who face unfair or discriminatory school actions. The Civil Rights Act of 1964 prohibits discrimination in public spaces, employment, and education on the basis of race, color, religion, sex (which includes gender identity, expression, and nonconformity), or national origin. Title IV of this act applies to students, and Title VI clarifies that it applies to schools that receive federal funds. Title IX of the Education Amendment of 1972 prohibits schools receiving public funding from discriminating on the basis of sex, which includes actual or perceived sexual orientation and gender identity and expression. The Equal Access Act requires that all students receive equal access to extracurricular clubs: if the school offers one student-led club, it must offer access to space and resources for all clubs, including those in support of LGBTQ identities.

The US Department of Education, primarily through its Office of Civil Rights (OCR), publishes guidance letters ("Dear Colleague" letters) that assist schools in applying federal law. Such letters include guidance on bullying and harassment; protecting transgender and gender-expansive youth under Title IX; and equal access to student groups or clubs, such as those that support LGBTQ students. For example, the US Department of Justice and the US Department of Education's Office of Civil Rights have filed suit against school districts, particularly from 2005 to 2013, for failing to protect LGBTQ students from discrimination and harassment. Results of these lawsuits include assertions that all districts have a duty to address and prevent bullying, harassment, and discrimination, including cyberbullying; regardless of whether such acts take place on or off campus, schools are liable under federal law in every state; non-discrimination protections based on sex include gender identity and expression.

The dignity and safety of LGBTQ people remain at risk as states around the country have recently worked to pass anti-LGBTQ laws in the context of historic and current federal antidiscrimination laws and policies about gender identity and expression, and sexual orientation. For example, in a recent update from the Human Rights Campaign, 201 anti-LGBT bills have been introduced in 34 states, comprising 76% of legislatures in the 2017 session. However, only 3% of the total measures have been enacted. In Kansas, for example, senators encouraged schools and universities to disregard federal Title IX guidance that protects against discrimination based on sexual orientation, gender identity, and gender expression. Other state laws restrict the inclusion of LGBTQ topics in schools. In early 2016, North Carolina passed HB2, which denies trans people the right to use the bathroom aligned with their gender identity.

In a historic 2016 speech, US Attorney General Loretta Lynch spoke on the issue of the US Department of Justice suing North Carolina over anti-LGBTQ law:

> This is a time to summon our national virtues of inclusivity, diversity, compassion and open-mindedness. What we must not do—what we must never do—is turn on our neighbors, our family members, our fellow Americans, for something they cannot control, and deny what makes them human. This is why none of us can stand by when a state enters the business of legislating identity and insists that a person pretend to be something they are not, or invents a problem that doesn't exist as a pretext for discrimination and harassment.

As a reader, you may be in a state that has few to no laws designed specifically to protect LGBTQ students in schools. However, all states in the USA have anti-bullying laws that should be inclusive and enumerate specific vulnerable populations of students who are protected under the law (Stop Bullying, 2016). There may also be state nondiscrimination laws that apply to students and school employees as well as school climate and discipline. There are disparities in discipline policies, such as zero-tolerance suspension policies, that negatively impact particular populations of students. School administration has been found to treat students of color and LGBTQ students more harshly, with an overrepresentation of both student populations in suspension and dropout rates, and the juvenile justice system (Townes, 2014). Regardless of federal laws, OCR guidance letters, and the outcomes of lawsuits, there remain disparities in statewide protections for gender-expansive and transgender students. Specifically, protections related to student rights to bodily privacy and to use school facilities in line with their gender identity, though guaranteed in every state under federal Title IX legislation, remain unevenly upheld across the country.

State laws are most effective when schools, districts, and county offices of education provide professional development and ongoing support to school professionals to ensure their effective implementation. When this does not happen, students remain unevenly protected. As an example, California is a state with many model LGBTQ-inclusive laws and policies that apply to all schools who receive public funds (see "Snapshot of LGBTQ-Inclusive California Laws"); yet there is inconsistent implementation of these laws and policies across the state. These inconsistencies pose particular difficulties for LGBTQ students in more conservative areas of the state as these tend to be less inclined to implement LGBTQ safe school laws, leaving students in these areas at unique risk (Hatzenbuehler, 2011). The Orange County Equality Coalition, an educational advocacy nonprofit organization, settled a lawsuit with the CDE in 2016 for its failure to adequately investigate complaint appeals related to bullying, discrimination, and harassment in Orange County schools. Most recently in the state, the rights of transgender and intersex students, despite clear education codes and laws, have been the subjects of much debate. As a result, many schools in the state do not have plans in place for children and youth who are in the process of gender transition or alignment. Despite the efforts of professional advocacy and nonprofit organizations like the California Safe Schools Coalition and Gender Spectrum, who have identified training tools and school-based resources to support gender-expansive and transgender youth, schools seem unsure of how to comply with the laws. The 2011 passing of the FAIR Education Act has highlighted these disconnects between state laws and codes, the lack of support and enforcement from the California Department of Education (CDE), and the resulting uneven implementation of the law by individual schools and districts across the state.

In light of these disconnects, some educators have turned to organizations like Teaching Tolerance, Rethinking Schools, the National Council for Social Studies, and the University of California, Berkeley Social Science-History Project. These largely nonprofit organizations have expertly attempted to fill the information void left by the CDE by providing curriculum and model policies in line with state and federal laws. However, in the absence of CDE support, oversight, or formal enforcement policies, many educators remain unaware of the many excellent resources that exist. On a more positive note, since

2014, the CDE has worked to revise its Social Studies Framework for grades K-12, seeking public feedback—including input from educational communities knowledgeable in gender and queer studies, ethnic studies and sociology. This public, collaborative approach to LGBTQ curriculum inclusivity development is a positive sign and may indicate a growing willingness on the part of the state to take a leadership role in matters pertaining to LGBTQ student rights. You can investigate the LGBTQ-inclusive policies in your state by visiting the Welcoming Schools and Human Rights Campaign websites. Once you have identified your state's policies on nondiscrimination and anti-bullying, analyze them and begin to investigate how they are being implemented in your community.

SNAPSHOT OF LGBTQ-INCLUSIVE CALIFORNIA LAWS

Senate Bill (SB) 48 (The FAIR Education Act): Adds language to existing education code that prescribes the inclusion of the contributions of various groups in the history of California and the USA—including men and women; Native Americans; African-Americans; Mexican Americans; Asian-Americans; Pacific Islanders; European Americans; lesbian, gay, bisexual, and transgender Americans; persons with disabilities; and members of other ethnic and cultural groups—to the economic, political, and social development of California and the USA (2011).

Assembly Bill (AB) 1156: Encourages the inclusion of policies aimed at the prevention of bullying and cyberbullying in comprehensive school safety plans (2012).

AB 9 (Seth's Law): Strengthens state anti-bullying laws, requiring schools to update their anti-bullying policies and programs, protecting students who are bullied based on their actual or perceived sexual orientation and gender identity/gender expression as well as race, ethnicity, nationality, gender, disability, and religion (2012).

AB 1266: Reinforces existing protections for students under California's nondiscrimination law, ensuring that transgender students have access to facilities and activities with respect to their gender identity (2013).

Comprehensive Sexual Education (AB 329): Outlines that comprehensive sexual health education shall be age-appropriate; medically accurate and objective; available on an equal basis to English language learners; appropriate for use with pupils of all races, genders, sexual orientations, and ethnic and cultural backgrounds; and appropriate for and accessible to pupils with disabilities (2015).

Safe Schools: Safe Place to Learn Act (AB 827): Requires publicizing antidiscrimination, anti-harassment, anti-intimidation, and anti-bullying policies and requires publicizing LGBTQ resources and information to those serving students in grades 7–12 (2016).

Principles Guiding This Book

With these definitions and laws in mind, it is time to begin our work together! In each chapter, you will see four intersecting principles: being an advocate and ally, building an inclusive school environment, transforming curriculum and pedagogy, and engaging with community and family partners. We have elaborated on each principle here.

Principle One: Educators should be advocates and allies to young people in relation to all their intersectional identities and communities.

Educators make daily choices about mentoring and allying with and for LGBTQ youth and families as they navigate their worlds and intersectional identities. Gaffney (2016) suggests that, "Being an ally means recognizing oppression broadly and standing in solidarity with anyone who experiences oppression—whether or not the ally also belongs to a targeted group" (Screen 1). School spaces and peer relationships often challenge the dignity and safety of LGBTQ youth. Going to school for them often takes courage and may be done in isolation from supportive family members or school professionals. We, as educators, can learn to reach out to social workers and community organizations that can help us with resources, such as information about immigration, restorative justice, and counseling. We can prevent and intervene in bias-based bullying on campus. We can examine our own assumptions and privileges, and identify ways in which to transform them. We can articulate to others what it means to be an ally.

Principle Two: School environments should be safe, welcoming, and inclusive of gender-diverse and LGBTQ youth and families.

LGBTQ youth are more likely to be engaged in school if the environment is safe, welcoming, and inclusive. We can examine our campuses systemically through the lens of LGBTQ inclusion: how do our policies and regulations reflect gender and family diversity? What professional development do school professionals and university students in teacher preparation receive? What do our forms and procedures look like? What signage and visual symbols of inclusion do we have on campus? Do we have an inclusive restroom and facility policy? Do we support student groups interested in LGBTQ topics and experiences? Are the school's antidiscrimination and anti-bullying policies up-to-date and publicly posted, and do they enumerate specific communities that are most often targeted by bias?

Principle Three: School-based curriculum and pedagogy should respond to and sustain youth's identities, communities, cultures, and histories.

School curriculum is a contested space in which many stakeholders argue over the importance of some knowledge and ways of learning over others. We believe that the purpose of schooling is in part to support youth in the realization of their own identities and goals for learning in relation to the communities to which they belong and the histories from which they come. To be LGBTQ responsive and sustaining at school, we believe in queering education through curriculum: decentering and examining heteronormativity and gender binaries; addressing intersecting identities at all levels of schooling; positioning counter-narratives as central to the body of knowledge, including contributions and histories of LGBTQ communities; and articulating the ways in which LGBTQ-inclusive curriculum can reach twenty-first-century learning goals (the Common Core, creativity, critical thinking, and collaboration). Queering education through pedagogy includes advocating for LGBTQ youth as part of teaching; including youth action research and political actions as part of schooling; teaching about bias as part of class meetings on peer relationships; including multiple learning modalities; and celebrating students' multiple strengths and differences as resources in the classroom.

Principle Four: Community- and family-based approaches toward being LGBTQ-inclusive can enrich school-based practices.

Schools often work separately rather than in collaboration with families and community organizations. We have witnessed the power of community-based approaches and family-based advocacy in helping LGBTQ youth thrive. We can listen to the stories of families who have successfully and unsuccessfully navigated barriers and challenges with schools. We can attend and volunteer at LGBTQ youth events, such as Pride celebrations and art exhibitions. We can talk to and collaborate with community organizers, social workers, and counselors who have spent decades in the LGBTQ community. We can build partnerships with university teacher education programs to mutually learn how to integrate LGBTQ topics into curriculum and pedagogy as well as how to initiate and sustain LGBTQ advocacy efforts at schools. We can learn from one another about what it means to be an ally and support our ongoing self-reflection as we take actions at school.

The story that follows emphasizes the importance to develop partnerships with families and build gender inclusive school environments. Lori Duron shares her experiences preparing for the school year with her gender expansive son.

The second story illustrates one teacher's efforts to build a gender-expansive classroom.

STORY ONE: "Back to School Blues... and Pinks" by Lori Duron, Raising My Rainbow

Originally published: https://raisingmyrainbow.com/2016/09/12/back-to-school-bluesand-pinks/

All summer, every summer, I can't wait for school to start again. When the kids are in school, there are less "I'm bored" complaints, less money spent, less full layers of sunscreen to apply/reapply, less sand everywhere and there's more time for me to work, write, watch Netflix and Google random things.

But, then, sure as shit, one week before school starts, I start to panic and worry about what the school year holds for gender-nonconforming C.J.

I can clearly remember my worries by grade level – which, as I look back now, are proof that it truly does get better. I'll take my fourth grade worries over my first grade worries any day. (And, I refuse to think about my middle school worries, so don't even bring them up. I know it will get worse.)

Preschool: Will the kids make fun of C.J. for wearing girl clothes? Will he get teased?

Kindergarten: Will the kids make fun of him for drawing himself as a girl and wearing girl socks, jewelry and lip gloss? Will he get teased?

First Grade: Will he be comfortable and safe in the boys' bathroom? Will he get teased?

Second Grade: I hope his teacher will be more accepting and thoughtful than his last. Will he get teased?

Third Grade: He's been at the same school for four years. I hope he has an accepting and supportive friend in his class. Will he get teased?

Fourth Grade: I hope the other kids continue to be cool to him.

This year, the hardest part of going back to school was school supply shopping; it's when I realized how much of his sparkle C.J. tames and edits for school. I know it feels necessary for him, but it feels sad for me.

I want to tell him "You do you! Who cares what other people think! Screw them!," but I don't because he can read the crowd of his peers better than I can. Just like I won't dye my hair purple and let all of my tattoos show at work, C.J. doesn't wear a skirt or carry a purse to school.

We hide our authentic selves sometimes, because it seems like the right or easiest thing to do – but we let just enough of our true selves show so that we don't feel like we've surrendered completely.

C.J. needed to get spiral notebooks for school. He wanted these: (Figure 1.2)

He got these: (Figure 1.3)

He needed a binder. He wanted one of these: (Figure 1.4)

He got this coral one: (not pictured)

He wanted this lunchbox: (Figure 1.5)

He got this one (which Chase told us privately is equally as girly and attention-grabbing): (not pictured)

He was brave enough to go with these highlighters: (not pictured)

As the first day of school got closer, C.J. got more nervous and so did I.

The night before, C.J. asked me to help him make sure his French braid was perfect and to paint one of his fingernails blue. If nobody said

FIGURE 1.2 Back to school supplies: Wanted. Photo by Lori Duron.

FIGURE 1.3 Back to school supplies: Chose. Photo by Lori Duron.

anything about his nail, he'd paint an additional nail each night until he worked up to two, fully manicured hands. Then, he'd go from blue to a more fabulous color.

He's careful and measured in how much of himself he reveals to people at first.

FIGURE 1.4 Back to school supplies: Wanted. Photo by Lori Duron.

FIGURE 1.5 Back to school supplies: Wanted. Photo by Lori Duron.

So far so good for fourth grade. He's worn French braids, ponytails and crimped hair. His nails are polished. The friendship bracelets have started to amass on his wrist.

The anxiety has started to subside as we settle into the comfortable routine of the school year. From here until summer, we stand ready for what could happen, but we are more joyful than fearful.

STORY TWO: "Creating a Gender-Expansive Classroom" by Lisa Richardson

It was the first day of a new school year. The students bustled in and searched for their names on one of the desks. After the usual hustle and bustle of Day One in second grade, the students were seated, awaiting further instructions. They looked around to see who they knew and where their friends were sitting. It wasn't long before one of the students blurted out, "Hey, wait! There are some boys sitting with boys and girls sitting with girls!" "Will we be changing seats later?" I explained that in our classroom community, we will not be separating students based on if they are a boy or a girl. Most students shrugged their shoulders as if to say, "huh!" Some looked confused, and some smiled. It was the first of many unexpected changes to what students had become accustomed to as part of the "normal elementary school classroom experience."

Years prior to this, I had an epiphany. My 16-year-old son had come out to my husband and me, and told us that he was gay. We had the usual parental concerns for his safety, worries about what prejudice and discrimination he might suffer, thoughts about what his life would hold for him and what limitations would be placed upon him as a gay man. We thought the hopes and dreams we, as parents, had for him were somehow going to be unfulfilled, but, in general, we were fine with it. We loved him, and he was the same son we had loved before we knew that he was gay. It took us a few hours to come to terms with those concerns, but we were fine after a bit and just prayed that he would have a happy life.

It wasn't long before I decided to join PFLAG (Parents and Friends of Lesbians and Gays), a national organization that offers support and education to the LGBTQ community and their friends, families, and allies. Although my husband and I were very accepting of our son, I wanted to learn more about the community of which I knew very little in order to better support him. At the meeting, we were reassured that his life could be all that we had hoped it could be. But I was heartbroken as I heard the stories of so many young LGBTQ people and the horrible messages they were getting from their teachers, classmates, and educational community in general. Stories of bullying from teachers as well as classmates, students feeling like they didn't belong and that they were all alone, thoughts of drug and alcohol abuse, cutting, suicide, and attempted suicides dominated the conversations. My thoughts suddenly went beyond supporting my son. I came to the realization that I needed to make some major changes in the way in which I ran my classroom in order to make it more welcoming for all students and to do my part to make sure that none of my students suffered these indignities.

My thinking began to shift. I learned that at the very least, 10% of all people consider themselves members of the LGBTQ community at some point in their lives. This meant that in my class of 32 students, at least 3 or 4 would fall into this category. (Not to mention the number of students who would have someone significant in their lives who would identify as gay, lesbian, bisexual, transgender, or queer.) Continuing with the status quo was no longer an option for me.

I began making small changes at first. I stopped addressing the students as "boys and girls." Instead, I called them "class," "scholars," "second graders," "friends," and so forth. I seated students according to behavioral issues and academic strengths and needs without regard to gender. I started using non-gendered words, such as police officer, firefighter, and mail carrier, and pointing out the misnomers in books. Every time I read a book using a word such as fireman, I would point out that the word was limiting and that, of course, there were many women firefighters as well.

As I began to make these small changes, I became more aware of the incredible amount of literature and educational procedures that bombard our students with messages that reinforce the stereotypical roles of boys and girls. There was a constant influx of implications that falling outside the gender norms was somehow not acceptable. What did this mean for those students who were girls and had a more masculine presentation or preference for "boy's activities" and for boys who preferred more typically female activities or presented in a more feminine way? I began to address these stereotypes in the classroom. As I read books to the children, we discussed the stereotypes that were present in the books. We talked about why there were stereotypes, namely, that these were the most common ways people of a certain gender acted, the most common things many of them enjoyed, and the most common ways in which many of them chose to dress, and many people generalized that all people felt the same way. I also began to purchase books that contained stories and pictures that were more reflective of the diversity in our classroom and in the world around us.

The children began to open their minds to the fact that there are many ways to be a boy and many ways to be a girl, and that there is no "right way" and no "wrong way." That sentiment was repeated frequently as it came up throughout the day in student comments and in curricular materials.

When pairing or partnering students, I used the colors of the cups (our school colors—blue and green) in the caddies in front of them to identify Partner One and Partner Two. Children lined up in number order (assigned by name alphabetically). There was no boys' side or girls' side to the backpack hangers. I posted signs that said, "This is a no bullying zone" and "Standing out from the crowd is a good thing." I made every attempt to create a climate in which gender was unimportant, basically a nonfactor, and a classroom where all kinds of diversity were celebrated!

At the beginning of the school year, the music teacher sent out a letter of introduction via email to the teaching staff and requested that each teacher have their students line up in boy/girl order before coming to music class. I responded and explained that I never have students line up by gender, but I was happy to ensure that students with behavioral problems were separated. I asked her to let me know if she had any problems with my class. She would accept my decision. I told her that I would be happy to discuss my reasons for this with her, but she replied that it was not necessary. I found it interesting, however, that each of the other classes was asked to follow the girl/boy order request.

I taught the traditional curriculum but with a new lens, noting when there were gender stereotypes and when someone broke out of the gender norms. The students soon began to embrace these ideals. One of my favorite experiences was when our class was studying "Famous Americans." The children read books about Albert Einstein, Helen Keller, George Washington, Amelia Earhart, Abraham Lincoln, The Wright Brothers, and others. Each child wrote about their favorite famous American and noted the characteristics that this person exhibited that contributed to their fame and greatness. The culminating activity was to compare the various individuals and identify characteristics that all of these famous Americans had in common. It was determined by the class that bravery was one such characteristic. While discussing the ways in which each Famous American was brave, one of the students said,

> Amelia Earhart was very brave when she decided she would wear overalls instead of dresses and build rollercoasters when she was

young because that was not what was expected of girls in those days. That must have been hard because people laughed at her. Maybe that helped her learn to be brave enough to fly across the ocean.

Throughout the year, I made it clear to my students that there was no such thing as "girl colors" or "boy colors," "girl toys" or "boy toys," that colors were for everyone and toys were for everyone. I reinforced that everyone was free to play with whomever or whatever they wished and that people can dress in whatever makes them feel comfortable. During Black History Month, I read one of the American Girl books, _Meet Addy_, to the students. I told the class that the book was about a young girl who was about their age and who lived in slavery a long time ago. All of the children were fascinated with this historical fiction story. When we finished the book, the students asked if there were more stories like it, and so I introduced them to the collection I had in the classroom library. One of the boys said, "I thought that American Girl books were just for girls. I mean they have the dolls and all. My sister has them." Others agreed. I explained that I had and continue to read stories with boys as the main character and that they had probably read stories about boys and girls too. I reminded them that books are for everyone. It wasn't long before the American Girl books became incredibly popular with the boys as well as the girls in the class, and both boys and girls started comparing books and recommending their favorites to their classmates of both genders.

We also talked about the power of words in my class and how words can be used in a hurtful or a kind way. We also talked about the connotation of words, how "weird" has a negative connotation while "unique" has a positive connotation. This understanding was one of the most critical understandings developed in the classroom. We discussed other words we could use that would say what we mean but not be hurtful. We could say that something was weird, or we could say that it was different. Students could say that they would like to do something different rather than "That idea is lame." (Pointing out that the word "lame" used in that context is a really hurtful way of referring to a disabled person rather than saying that you don't like that idea.)

We had discussions about bullying and the importance of being an "upstander" and not a "bystander," in particular with our classmates as we are a family. The classroom became a celebration of diversity, and a surprising thing began to happen. The children became more accepting of other differences in our classroom. Students with different learning abilities, autistic students, physically disabled students, and students of different ethnicities and cultures were embraced.

When a new student entered the class from an inner-city school, the students noticed that his head was shaved, a look uncommon in Irvine. No one commented to him or to the class, but during group work, I overheard a conversation a group of students was having. One child said, "It's weird that Keshon is bald. I thought only old people were bald." I didn't intervene right away; rather, I listened from a distance to hear how the conversation would unfold. Another student asked, "What do you mean it's weird? Do you mean it's different?" "Yeah, I guess that's what I meant," replied the first child. They both agreed that having no hair was different from what they were used to seeing and that things were probably different where Keshon had come from. They decided he was probably a nice kid.

One of my students had a prosthetic leg, and his mother wrote to me and told me that this was the first year of his school career during which he was invited to his classmates' birthday parties. Another year, a parent told me that this was the first year that her daughter had not been a victim of the "mean girls," even though some of those girls were in our class.

A word of caution. When teaching that gender stereotypes are limiting, it is important to acknowledge that many children do naturally adhere to the heteronormative or stereotypical ways of being a girl or a boy. They may very well love football if they are a boy and love princess dresses and tiaras if they are a girl. When one student raised his hand and asked, "Mrs. R., I'm a boy and I like to play football and basketball a lot. Is that okay?" I had to admit that in my zeal to ensure that all students were free to explore their gender roles, perhaps I had gone a bit overboard in emphasizing that it is okay to break outside of the gender norms. So, from then on, I made sure that all students understood that whatever way they chose to be a boy or a girl was wonderful, regardless of whether their likes and dislikes conformed to the gender norms or not.

It is also critical, in my opinion, to accept and respect the fact that some of the students may come from families that may not agree with some of the social structures we are discussing when reading books, such as those showing same-sex parents or boys wearing dresses. It is, however, very important to stress that it is respect for everyone and their beliefs that we are generating in our classroom. We needn't all agree on everything. However, by showing that respect, there are no "put downs," no name-calling, and no bullying of anyone for any reason. That is the lesson I want my students to learn.

In order to create a truly gender-expansive classroom that was welcoming to all of my students, I searched for lesson resources, and, to my surprise, I found a huge number of free lesson resources online. Human

Rights Campaign (HRC)'s Welcoming Schools provides over 20 lessons, which include videos, arranged by grade level, with the Common Core Standards included. The lesson plans focus on embracing family diversity, avoiding gender stereotyping, and ending bullying and name-calling. I also used GLSEN's Ready, Set, Respect tool kit lesson plans, which are also free to educators. These lessons are designed to be integrated into other lessons or to be used during "Teachable Moments" in the classroom.

Another great resource is Teaching Tolerance, an organization created by the Southern Poverty Law Center. They offer an excellent magazine that is free to educators as well as lesson plans for kindergarten through twelfth-grade classrooms, including videos and posters that are linked to Common Core Standards. This magazine and its lesson plans tend to be more acceptable to those community members who have more conservative viewpoints as they focus not only on LGBTQ issues but also on other forms of biases and discrimination, such as race, religion, poverty, and more. The magazine included a great poster explaining the differences between gender expression, gender identity, and sexual orientation, something that many adults struggle to understand. The magazine also offers great articles for educators, such as articles on examining our own biases and how they affect our students and teaching. (I subscribe to both the online edition and the hard copy of the magazine, both of which are free.)

I chose each of my lessons carefully and tweaked them as needed to ensure that they were grade-level appropriate and as inoffensive as possible to the conservative community in which I taught. Overall, I have to say that since implementing this teaching model, my classes have had fewer behavior problems, more peer camaraderie, and practically no bullying in class or by my students out on the playground. Their astonishment when students from other classes did engage in bullying and their willingness to stand up for others have been heartwarming.

I have been teaching since 1979 and definitely consider myself to be an "old dog." But if this old dog can learn some new tricks, anyone can. And I certainly hope you do, because all students need to feel welcomed in their classrooms. They need to see themselves and their families represented in the books we read in class. They need to know that they have the support of their teacher and their classmates, and they need to feel safe. By supporting students in this way and implementing some of these changes, you might enable a child to look back one day and say that at least one teacher told them they are perfect just the way they are. Who knows? You might even save a life.

LISA'S TIPS FOR GETTING STARTED IN CREATING A GENDER-EXPANSIVE CLASSROOM

Simple steps to creating a safe space for children in an atmosphere of acceptance that supports all students.

1. When making seating assignments, consider behavior, academic strengths and needs, and cultural backgrounds; do not attend to gender.
2. Refer to students as scholars, students, friends, class, and so forth as opposed to boys and girls.
3. Have students line up by student number, rows, table groups, left/right side of the room, and so forth, not boy/girl.
4. When arranging students in a line for an assembly, music class, or other event, have them line up by behavior (well-behaved, challenges with behavior) rather than boy/girl.
5. Divide students to do partner work, and choose a partner by blue cup/ green cup in caddies, desk partners, odd/even student numbers, and so forth.
6. Although some children may enjoy scholarly competition with boys versus girls, it is uncomfortable for some and should be avoided. Instead, students can be divided into teams by side of the room, rows, and so forth.
7. When dividing PE teams, divide the class into teams that fairly represent the range of athletic strengths, not gender.
8. Have books in the classroom library and read books to the class that show children and adults in atypical gender roles: for example, Pinky and Rex—a series about a boy who loves the color pink and a girl who loves dinosaurs—and Amelia Earhart, who chose not to conform to the gender stereotypes of her day. Also include books showing cultural and religious diversity, family diversity, and people with a variety of physical and mental challenges.

Questions for Reflection

1. Return to your early memories of your gender identity or learning about someone who is gay. Talk with a colleague about these memories, how your ideas have changed over time, and how these ideas might inform your current educational practice.
2. What are your own gender biases? We all have them. Where, when, and under what circumstances do you think you were first influenced to embrace them?

3. What are some additional ways/situations in which you can move toward creating a gender-expansive classroom?
4. What will you say to students when you hear things like "That's so gay!" or "That's just for girls"?
5. What is the environment like in your school and community with regard to LGBTQ inclusion and advocacy? What challenges do you see? After reading Lisa's story about teaching second grade, what goals do you have for your educational setting?

References

American Educational Research Association (AERA). (2013). *Prevention of bullying in schools, colleges, and universities: Research report and recommendations.* Washington, DC: American Educational Research Association.

American Educational Research Association. (2017). *LGBTQ issues in education.* Retrieved from www.aera.net/EducationResearch/IssuesandInitiatives/IssuesandInitiatives LGBTQIssuesinEducation/tabid/16010/

Anzaldúa, G. (2012). *Borderlands: La frontera* (4th ed.). San Francisco, CA: Aunt Lute Books.

Atkinson, E., & Depalma, R. (2008). Imagining the homonormative: Performative subversion in education for social justice. *British Journal of Sociology of Education, 29*(1), 25–35.

Au, W. (2014). *Rethinking multicultural education: Teaching for racial and cultural justice* (2nd ed.). Milwaukee, WI: Rethinking Schools, Ltd.

Bell, L. A., & Roberts, R. A. (2010). The storytelling project model: A theoretical framework for critical examination of racism through the arts. *Teachers College Record, 112*(9), 2295–2319.

Bilodeau, B. L., & Renn, K. A. (2005). Analysis of LGBT identity development models and implications for practice. *New Directions for Student Services, 111*(111), 25–39.

Britzman, D. P. (1998). *Lost subjects, contested objects.* Albany, NY: State University of New York Press.

Buckel, D. S. (2000). Legal perspective on ensuring a safe and nondiscriminatory school environment for lesbian, gay, bisexual and transgendered students. *Education and Urban Society, 32*(3), 390–398.

Butler, J. (1993). *Bodies that matter: On the discursive limits of "sex."* New York, NY: Routledge.

Butler, J. (2004). *Undoing gender.* New York, NY: Routledge.

California Safe Schools Coalition. (2016). *Safe schools research brief 8: Multiple forms of bias-related harassment at school.* Retrieved from www.casafeschools.org/CSSC_Research_Brief_8.pdf

Carrera, M. V., Depalma, R., & Lameiras, M. (2012). Sex/gender identity: Moving beyond fixed and 'natural' categories. *Sexualities, 15*(8), 995–1016.

Chappell, D., & Chappell, S. (2015). Stories of resistant play: Narrative construction as a counter-colonial methodology. *Narrative Works, 5*(1) Retrieved from https://journals.lib.unb.ca/index.php/nw/article/view/23782/27554

Clandinin, D. J., & Connelly, F. M. (2000). *Narrative inquiry: Experience and story in qualitative research.* San Francisco, CA: Jossey-Bass Publishers.

Cruz, B. C. (2002). Don Juan and rebels under palm trees: Depictions of Latin Americans in US history textbooks. *Critique of Anthropology: A Journal for the Critical Reconstruction of Anthropology, 22*(3), 323–342.

Curran, G., Chiarolli, S., & Pallotta-Chiarolli, M. (2009). 'The c words': Clitorises, childhood and challenging compulsory heterosexuality discourses with pre-service primary teachers. *Sex Education, 9*(2), 155–168.

Davis, E. C. (2009). Situating "fluidity": (trans) gender identification and the regulation of gender diversity. *GLQ: A Journal of Lesbian and Gay Studies, 15*(1), 97–130.

Davis, D. E., & Kellinger, J. J. (2014). Teacher educators using encounter stories. *Qualitative Report, 19*(5), 1–18. Retrieved from www.nova.edu/ssss/QR/QR19/davis10.pdf

Depalma, R., & Atkinson, E. (2006). The sound of silence: Talking about sexual orientation and schooling. *Sex Education: Sexuality, Society, and Learning, 6*(4), 333–349.

Depalma, R., & Atkinson, E. (2009). 'No outsiders': Moving beyond a discourse of tolerance to challenge heteronormativity in primary schools. *British Educational Research Journal, 35*(6), 837–855.

Espelage, D. L., Aragon, Sr., Birkett, M., & Koenig, B. (2008). Homophobic teasing, psychological outcomes, and sexual orientation among high school students: What influence do parents and schools have? *School Psychology Review, 37*(2), 202–216.

Espelage, D. L., Basile, K. C., & Hamburger, M. E. (2012). Bullying perpetration and subsequent sexual violence perpetration among middle school students. *Journal of Adolescent Health, 50*(1), 60–65.

Flores, G. (2012). Toward a more inclusive multicultural education: Methods for including LGBT themes in K-12 classrooms. *American Journal of Sexuality Education, 7*(3), 187–197.

Flores, G. (2014). Teachers working cooperatively with parents and caregivers when implementing LGBT themes in the elementary classroom. *American Journal of Sexuality Education, 9*(1), 114–120.

Gaffney, C. (2016, Summer). Anatomy of an ally—Be there for kids and colleagues when caring isn't enough. *Teaching Tolerance.* Retrieved from www.tolerance.org/magazine/summer-2016/anatomy-of-an-ally

Geertz, C. (1995). *After the fact: Two countries, four decades, one anthropologist.* Cambridge, MA: Harvard University Press.

Goffman, E. (1974). *Frame analysis: An essay on the organization of experience.* New York, NY: Harper & Row.

Grant, J. M., Mottet, J. D., & Tanis, J. (2011). Injustice at every turn: A report of the national transgender discrimination survey. *National Center for Transgender Equality.* Retrieved from www.transequality.org/sites/default/files/docs/resources/NTDS_Exec_Summary.pdf

Griffin, P., & Ouellett, M. (2003). From silence to safety and beyond: Historical trends in addressing lesbian, gay, bisexual, transgender issues in K-12 schools. *Equity & Excellence in Education, 36*(2), 106–114.

Hatzenbuehler, M. L. (2011). The social environment and suicide attempts in lesbian, gay, and bisexual youth. *Pediatrics, 127*(5), 896–903.

Hermann-Wilmarth, J. (2010). More than book talks: Preservice teacher dialogue after reading gay and lesbian children's literature. *Language Arts, 87*(3) 188–198.

hooks, b. (2013). *Writing beyond race: Living theory and practice.* New York, NY: Routledge.

Jennings, T., & Sherwin, G. (2008). Sexual orientation topics in elementary teacher preparation programs in the USA. *Teaching Education, 19*(4), 261–278.

Kosciw, J. G., Greytak, E. A., & Diaz, E. M. (2009). Who, what, when, where, and why: Demographic and ecological factors contributing to hostile school climate for lesbian, gay, bisexual, and transgender youth. *Journal of Youth and Adolescence 38*, 976–988.

Malmquist, A., Gustavson, M., & Schmitt, I. (2013). Queering school, queers in school: An introduction. *Confero: Essays on Education, Philosophy and Politics, 1*(2), 5–15.

Meyer, E. J. (2009). *Gender, bullying, and harassment: Strategies to end sexism and homophobia in schools.* New York, NY: Teachers College Press.

Miller, sj. (2015). A queer literacy framework promoting (a)gender and (a)sexuality self-determination and justice. *English Journal, 104*(5), 37–44.

Miller, sj. (2016). *Teaching, affirming, and recognizing trans* and gender creative youth: A queer literacy framework.* New York, NY: Palgrave MacMillan.

Monro, S. (2008). Beyond male and female: Poststructuralism and the spectrum of gender. *International Journal of Transgenderism, 8*(1), 3–22.

Naidoo, J. C. (2012). *Rainbow family collections: Selecting and using children's books with lesbian, gay, bisexual, transgender, and queer content.* Santa Barbara, CA: Libraries Unlimited.

PFLAG New York City. (2016). Retrieved from www.pflagnyc.org/safeschools/statistics

Phillips, D. K., & Larson, M. L. (2012). Preservice teachers respond to "and tango makes three": Deconstructing disciplinary power and the heteronormative in teacher education. *Gender and Education, 24*(2), 159–175.

Poteat, V. P., & Espelage, D. L. (2005). Exploring the relation between bullying and homophobic verbal content: The homophobic content agent target (HCAT) scale. *Violence and Victims, 20*(5), 513–528.

Poteat, V. P., & Rivers, I. (2010). The use of homophobic language across bullying roles during adolescence. *Journal of Applied Developmental Psychology, 31*(2), 166–172.

Prevent School Violence Illinois. (2017). *Bias-based bullying survey.* Retrieved from www.psvillinois.org/psvi-s-work/bias-based-bullying.html

A Project by the ACLU of California, My School My Rights. (2017). *Know Your Rights.* Retrieved from www.myschoolmyrights.com

Renn, K. A. (2010). LGBT and queer research in higher education—The state and status of the field. *Educational Researcher, 39*(2), 132–141.

Sanders, J. (1997). Teacher education and gender equity. *ERIC Clearinghouse on Teaching and Teacher Education*, Washington DC. Retrieved from www.ericdigests.org/1998-1/gender.htm

Sears, J. T. (2009). Interrogating the subject: Queering elementary education, 10 years on. *Sex Education: Sexuality, Society and Learning, 9*(2), 193–200.

Skurnik, J. (2016). *Creating gender inclusive schools.* Youth & Gender Media Project. Retrieved at www.newday.com/film/creating-gender-inclusive-schools

Solórzano, D. G., & Yosso, T. J. (2002). Critical race methodology: Counter-storytelling as an analytical framework for education research. *Qualitative Inquiry, 8*(1), 23–44.

Stop Bullying. (2016). *Policies & laws.* Retrieved from www.stopbullying.gov/laws/

Takaki, R. (2008). A different mirror: A history of multicultural America. Backbay Books.

Townes, C. (2014, June 13). The disastrous fallout of suspending LGBT students, students with disabilities & children of color. *Think Progress.* Retrieved from http://think progress.org/justice/2014/06/13/3448718/school-discipline-disproportionate/

Walton, G. (2005). The hidden curriculum in schools: Implications for lesbian, gay, bisexual, transgender, and queer youth. *Alternate Routes: A Journal of Critical Social Research, 21,* 18–39.

Welcoming Schools – A Project of the Human Rights Campaign Foundation, (2016, October). *An overview of laws & policies that support safe and welcoming schools.* Retrieved from http://hrc-assets.s3-website-us-east-1.amazonaws.com//welcoming-schools/documents/WS_Laws_Policies_Safe_Welcoming_Schools.pdf

Welcoming Schools – A Project of the Human Rights Campaign Foundation. (2017). *Laws & policies, research and responding to concerns.* Retrieved from www.welcoming schools.org/research/

PART I
Elementary School

2

ELEMENTARY SCHOOL ENVIRONMENT

Costumes by Sharon Chappell

On a blank paper, I draw:
Myself in a princess dress
My brother with a cape
I don't remember anyone telling us the rules, we just knew
I tried on his fabric, wrapped it around my shoulders
Imagined tall buildings and cavernous holes in the ground
that I could soar over with ease
He never wore my dress
None of the boys tried them: at preschool, during the school play, on
Halloween
No one told us the rules, we just knew

We wriggle in our skin
Some like a softened pair of jeans
Some in pain, wishing for another fabric, color, character

I want to break the rules
Scream out from behind my drawing
  Is everything a costume made by someone else?
  Is everything either/or?
I am too young to have words for these questions.
I am too young to tell you
  Not to call me pretty or sweet or bossy
  Not to notice my hair first
  Not to call me a girl
  Not to scan my body
  Not to force me to hug you

What costume can I wear to protect myself?
To show the real me?

I give up on saving the world—or even myself—
For now.
I roll in the grass, ball up my drawing and toss it as far as I can.
I run my fingers through the mud
And dream of rainbows.

In this chapter, we consider the elementary school environment and how we as educators can ensure that lesbian, gay, bisexual, transgender, and queer (LGBTQ) students, and all students, experience these initial formative years as positive and affirming. Student experiences in elementary school set a foundation for the rest of their lives as learners. Because of this, ensuring that all students feel supported, welcomed, and seen—in all their complexity—is critical. In this chapter, we introduce you to the stories of two very different students: Dannon and Freddy. We also discuss school culture and specific strategies that support classroom diversity in all its forms but particularly in terms of gender diversity. Additionally, we discuss the significance of Title IX in offering guidance as we attempt to respond to, and understand, the increasing gender complexity of our transgender and gender-expansive students. But first, as you can see from the poem beginning this chapter, we must explore the role and significance of gender identity and expression within the traditional elementary school environment.

As cultural understandings of gender identity and gender expression begin to shift, in part due to the prevalence of new models of gender in the media as well as new scientific research, young people are increasingly entering schools with more nuanced experiences of gender and less rigid understandings of their own gender. It is even the case that from family to family, ideas and norms around gender identity, gender expression, and gender roles can, and do, fluctuate, sometimes dramatically. As educators then, we must consider all three of these—school policies, individual student identities, and varying family values—in creating classrooms that support all learners. In addition, we also must consider our obligations under state and federal education codes, laws, and proven best practices. And to make things even more complicated, current understandings of gender are quite different than those that prevailed during the establishment of our educational institutions. This effectively means that the way in which gendered categories and identities work in the minds and on the bodies of our students can be fundamentally at odds with the way these categories have worked within and through our educational institutions in the past. We begin by discussing these different aspects and experiences of gender and how these have functioned historically within the US system of public education.

Pink or Blue Childhoods

Within the US system of education, elementary schools have historically relied most heavily on normative understandings of gender in the socialization of children. Gender might even be thought of as the fundamental underlying organizational system in most elementary school settings, including the organization of classrooms, playgrounds, and ancillary activities. From seating charts to recess lines, elementary schools have traditionally organized students by "boys over here, and girls over there." Indeed, a great deal of childhood experience in the USA generally is structured around normative binary gender categories. From toys to athletics to social activities, girls and boys (the feminine and the masculine) are very often segregated and strictly, if not formally, enforced (Kaiser, 2013).

Photographer JeongMee Yoon makes this point in a strikingly visual way in her "Pink and Blue Project" (2005). Her collection documents the gendered nature of contemporary childhood through photographs of over 60 children. The photos are staged by the artist in each child's bedroom or playroom, surrounded by their gendered clothing and possessions. The photos make their point viscerally as each child pictured within them is rendered nearly invisible, awash in a kind of monotonous sea of pink or blue, the child's own physical presence in the room all but lost within each dizzying array. The series also makes a stark statement about the way in which gendered categories are embedded in cultural practices and, in turn, in identities. The sea of pink in which many (most?) girls are immersed, like the blue of contemporary boyhood, is reinforced throughout many of our social institutions as a normal part of childhood experience, reflective of innocence and fun, even invoking a kind of nostalgic response from the adults who, of course, are its perpetuators—something the manufacturers of children's toys and clothing have certainly harnessed in the interest of profit-making. And, as Yoon notes in her artist's statement about this powerful project, these socially and culturally constructed norms "deeply affect children's gender group identification and social learning" (Yoon, 2005).

Children are not born with a natural liking for blue or pink depending on their gender; there is no biological or "natural" affinity for color. This, like many aspects of gender expression, is culturally constructed. We can use two questions to determine just how *"natural"* some of our gendered assumptions really are. *Question 1: Does this aspect of gender change across history (time)? Question 2: Does this aspect of gender change across cultures (space)?* If either of these questions can be answered yes, then we have positively identified the workings of culture. Characteristics that are solely biological will remain constant across time/history and space/culture. One need only apply the first of our gender litmus test questions to the phenomenon of pink and blue to get a decidedly clear understanding of its origins: does the gendered meaning of pink and blue change across time, in other words, across history? The answer is telling.

Pre-twentieth-century, pink, in fact, was thought to be a color best suited for boys. And for girls? Blue. Even as recently as 1918, one popular baby clothing magazine, *Ladies Home Journal*, wrote,

> There has been a great diversity of opinion on this subject, but the generally accepted rule is pink for the boy and blue for the girl. The reason is that pink being a more decided and stronger color, is more suitable for the boy; while blue, which is more delicate and dainty is prettier for the girl.
>
> *(Kaiser, 2013; Paoletti, 1997)*

In addition to gendered colors, when we apply our litmus test to many other aspects of gender expression, we find that a great deal of "*doing gender*" is more about conforming to current cultural norms than it is about expressing some innate, biological inner truth of self (Butler, 2004, 2006). Dresses, as one easy example, in contemporary Western cultures and institutions—including public schools—seem appropriate only for girls and women, and yet wearing a dress is, and has been, understood as a sign of dominant *masculinity* in different historic and cultural contexts (see Figures 2.1–2.3).

FIGURE 2.1 Pink and Blue Project, 2005. By JeongMee Yoon.

FIGURE 2.2 Pink and Blue Project, 2005. By JeongMee Yoon.

FIGURE 2.3 The Ambassadors" by Hans Holbein the Younger, c. 1533. In the collection of the National Gallery, London. Public Domain.

Likewise, gendered norms around dress and behavior relate to the feminine change, depending on historical period and cultural context. Given the shifting nature of these culturally constructed norms we understand as *gender*, what are we reinforcing when we invoke, patrol, and insist upon normative, binary-based gender identities and expressions in our schools and classrooms? From dress codes to the unconscious gender biases many of us unknowingly enact, how and why has this unstable identity category—gender—come to structure so much of childhood, including elementary school traditions, practices, and policies? Let's turn once more to the history of gender in the USA for some ideas on this (Figures 2.4 and 2.5).

FIGURE 2.4 3rd Duke of Fife, "Allan Warren" 2015, Wikimedia Commons.

FIGURE 2.5 Franklin Delano-Roosevelt-1884. Wikimedia Commons.

The Gendering of Culture and Society

Along with the early twentieth-century invention of a new consumer culture, whose marketing efforts cemented blue as masculine and pink as feminine, this period saw a number of other large-scale cultural and economic changes that made their own contribution to the consolidation and naturalization of what we now think of as "traditional" gender roles and expressions. New models of work life and home life, brought on by nineteenth-century industrialization, influenced the cultural construction and consolidation of the rigid gender norms that still operate unevenly across the USA today (Greenwald, 1989). Up until this period, the US economy had largely been an agrarian economy. It revolved around family farming and family-owned businesses that participated in small, locally based economies. The nineteenth-century home was frequently the workplace, and family members toiled side by side, regardless of gender or often even age.

The advent of the industrial revolution changed these practices. Mass migration to urban centers, a nascent middle class with new purchasing power, a formalized gendered division of labor through maintenance of new public and the private spheres, an ensconcing of the heteronormative nuclear family, and the emergence of gendered patterns of consumer consumption (men work, women shop) came together in a formalized social system that offered critical support to the new "Industrial Age" (Greenwald, 1989). This economic and social system with its division of labor codified and consolidated rigid ideas about gender (Fausto-Sterling, 2012; Greenwald, 1989).

Further, the concept of a "family wage" was put to new use in this period. It helped solve the problem of men, women, and children all vying for factory jobs (there were no child labor laws at the time). Based on the ideal of a male breadwinner—wherein men's labor financially supports the family and women's otherwise unpaid labor takes care of the home and children—well-paying factory jobs went first to married men.

The idea of a family wage was also steeped in a newly developing moralistic economic doctrine. Financial need alone, according to its tenets, should determine who had a *legitimate* moral claim to the new wage work of factories (Greenwald, 1989). These divisions between the public sphere—where men worked and negotiated professional lives—and the private sphere—where women worked and raised children—gave rise to a whole host of other kinds of gendered divisions, practices, representations, and institutions. Enacting institutionalized gender norms, for example, through one's dress and behavior came to signify participation in modernity and the exciting possibilities of a new industrialized economy.

With its very strict gender norms, roles, and divisions of labor, the heterosexual nuclear family of the industrial age quickly replaced the extended family of the agrarian age as the ideal model, uniquely *fit* for the new economy and a new national future. Within the cultural imaginary of the time, this highly gendered system also came to signify coveted middle-class status and quickly was idealized and enshrined as "normal." Such hyperbolically gendered conceptions of *normal* flourished throughout the first half of the twentieth century. Even as late as the 1950s and 1960s, when models of racialized (white) middle-class economic stability were beamed into living rooms by way of the Golden Age of Television's prime-time programming (think *Leave It to Beaver* and *Ozzie and Harriett*), rigid gendered norms (and whiteness) were the hallmark of a successful family and a modern society. It wasn't until the social tumult of the 1960s that these gender norms began to loosen their hold on US culture. The civil rights movements of the 1960s and 1970s, particularly the feminist movement, made it their goal to challenge the "natural," inevitable, and newly developing biological conceptions of rigid binary gender socialization—a project that arguably continues today.

Gendering in Public Education

A critical component of a gendered, industrialized economy came in the form of socialization through the institutionalized, mandated, and free public education for all children beginning in the 1850s (up until this point, education was a luxury afforded only by the rich). Schools became the institution to train and discipline a certain kind of worker, which, along with the training of typically female teachers, organized the socialization of gender as a principle of labor (Rothermel, 2003). The moniker assigned to these early twentieth-century teacher training institutions, *normal schools*, tells us a great deal about the explicit nature of their goals and aims. These new professional/vocational schools sought to instruct teachers on how to *norm* their students: creating a citizenry and workforce that could be reliably and uniformly reproduced, generation after generation, so that, as workers aged out of the economy, new ones would be available to fill factory floors and universities (men) and maintain family structures and household duties, and complete secretarial and caretaking work like nursing and teaching (women) (Fitzgerald, 2001; Madigan, 2009). Through schooling, students would learn a predetermined set of roles, skills, and behaviors in the form of an *official curriculum* (Apple, 2004), which was established to ensure that at the end of the educational process, out would come the worker/citizen with reliable skills. At the same time, schools taught the *hidden curriculum*, disciplining the "right" value and ideas—including an affective desire to participate in the new middle class and its requisite gender norms (Apple, 2004).

The organizational principles of our schools today still largely assume, and even insist upon, the same gendered organizational norms so popular in the period of their founding. In a UNESCO cross-national report, Stromquist (2007) identified five dimensions through which the gendered socialization process occurs:

1. Teacher-based dynamics, such as teacher attitudes and expectations, and their interactions with students in the classroom evince different patterns toward boys and girls, generally to the disadvantage of girls.
2. Within the formal curriculum, sex education continues to miss important aspects of sexuality affecting adolescent students, despite changes in social mores.
3. The school environment contains aspects of gendered violence that are slowly being recognized as contributing to polarized conceptions of femininity and masculinity.
4. Peer influences play a significant but not easily visible gate-keeping role in reproducing gender ideologies.
5. Teachers—key actors in the everyday life of schools—do not have access to training in gender issues and, consequently, tend not to foster gender equity in their classrooms (p. 2).

Today's more flexible and expansive understandings and lived experiences of gender are incompatible with the historical gendered formation of our educational system. While students now bring increasingly complex gender identities—including nonbinary forms of gender, sexual orientation, and masculine/feminine—as well as rich understandings of their rights as students to enact those identities, our educational institutions remain steeped in policies and ideologies based on outdated binary gender norms—norms perhaps very well-suited for a previous economy and culture but less so for a new twentieth-century creative, technology-based, and innovation-heavy economy.

Questions of Gender and Identity

How can we as teachers create safe, welcoming, and inclusive spaces that respond to young people's increasingly complex gender identities—including nonbinary forms of gender, sexual orientation, and masculine/feminine? We must start with learning and reflecting on a few key concepts that will help inform our decisions as we reflect on our practice to become more aware and inclusive. As illustrated in Chapter 1 in the Gender Unicorn Diagram, an individual's gender is experienced around two distinct but variously related axes: gender *identity* and gender *expression*. Gender *identity* refers to an individual's psychological relationship to the symbols, tropes, and behavioral patterns associated with masculinity and femininity. Fausto-Sterling (2012) articulates that our gender identity and expression are constructed and performed throughout our lives by way of a confluence of biology, socialization, and culture.

In trying to understand gender identity, it is also helpful to consider what it is not. Gender identity unfolds as part of the workings of the mind, and thus gender identity is not necessarily visible. Gender identity is not the same as biological sex. Biological sex refers to the multifaceted measurable, physical characteristics associated with being male, female, or intersex. There are four markers of biological sex: chromosomal sex, gonadal sex, hormonal sex, and genital sex (Alexander & Hines, 2002; Fausto-Sterling, 2012; Jadva, Hines, & Golombok, 2010; Lamminmaki et al., 2012). These distinct measures of biological sex can vary within a single individual, who falls outside of the binary biological sex categories of male or female and is referred to as intersex. An estimated 2 in 100 people have some form of intersex biology (Fausto-Sterling, 2012). Gender identity is likewise not sexuality, nor does it tell us what an individual's sexual orientation might be in the present or in the future.

Finally, gender identity is also not the same as gender expression. Gender expression refers to the visible signs, symbols, and tropes we read, through a culturally and historically specific lens, as feminine and masculine or neither. From hairstyle to temperament to voice quality and how one moves in the physical world, gender expression appears, is perceptible, and perhaps because of this, it is often mistakenly misread as a reflection of some inner truth of who we are as individuals—particularly in terms of sexuality. In other words, gender expression that is nonconforming, or gender-expansive, is sometimes misread as a sign that an individual either is, or will be, gay. To develop these ideas further, let's turn now to the story of one gender-nonconforming student, Freddy, and how his teacher, a gay man who himself struggled with the stereotypes of gender expression as a student, created a more supportive learning environment for his student.

STORY ONE: "Freddy's Story" by Salvador González-Padilla

"Mr. González, are you afraid of anything?"

The question caught me by surprise. Unaffected and curious, it floated softly from Freddy's mouth as I walked the group of 20 second graders to the front gates of our elementary school at dismissal time. Freddy was the line leader for the week. He followed close behind me.

I stopped our march forward and turned to face him. "What a terrific question, Freddy."

Freddy was one of the smallest of my students. He had vitreous, watery eyes that always gave the impression that he had just awakened from a long, restful, slumber or had spent time crying. They were set in copper-colored flesh, with cheeks that easily turned red when he was too warm. He was inquisitive and upbeat. "What made you ask it?"

"Just wondering." He smiled. Unfeigned. Serene.

I smiled back, one of those smiles that bubbles up naturally from the delightful sort of satisfaction a teacher feels when a student surprises with the contemplative caliber of a question or insight. "Yes, I fear many, many, things."

"Really??" The inflection in his voice conceded surprise, if not skepticism. "Like what?"

Matters of concern from the absurdly quotidian to the more existential darted through my mind, but one worry in particular ambled and froze front and center at that moment. We reached the dismissal gate.

"Your mom is waiting, Freddy. I'll tell you about some of those things tomorrow."

Back alone in my classroom, I thought about Freddy's sense of humor and his ability to disarm me with his often very sophisticated observations. I thought about how much I enjoyed what his presence brought to my class. I thought about his question. And about my own fears.

I feared that one day, Freddy would find that simply being himself would be painful. I worried that soon spending recess playing Chinese jump rope with the girls instead of soccer with the boys would be frowned upon, that loving to pick flowers, being soft-spoken and gentle, and wearing fairy wings would result in bullying. I feared that one day, the very act of being authentically himself would wilt his spirit and force him to pretend or to hide and, almost certainly, to hurt.

A day earlier, I had read about yet another cyberbullying incident of an LGBTQ student by school peers. The student had attempted suicide.

Reflecting on that occurrence and Freddy's question that afternoon, I thought about my own childhood experiences with sexuality and gender. I was curious about all types of toys but, even at that young age, was acutely aware of the culturally defined delineations between male and female interests. So, I tended to play with toys that would not bring undue and hostile attention from the adults (or other children) around me. I never felt trapped in the wrong body as with those who identify as transgender; but, like Freddy, I felt more at ease around girls than boys and was always intrigued by and drawn to those things generally associated with the feminine.

When I was old enough to understand the complexities of sexuality, I would come to identify as a gay, cisgender male. My gender identity corresponds with my biological sex. That is to say, I have male body parts, view myself as male—and am attracted to other males. I would also come to identify the source of so much of my alienation and social unease growing up. I would come to recognize the cultural construction of a heterosexual/homosexual binary that renders non-heterosexual ways of being as unnatural and perverse, and the stunting way this binary dictates gendered norms for boys and men. A binary whose pernicious effects are nowhere more damaging than in the school setting.

During my own upper elementary years, as I entered puberty and began truly experiencing romantic attraction, the heterosexual/homosexual binary's prescribed "rules" collided head-on with my sense of self, eliciting a dispiriting incongruence that marked the beginning of my social detachment throughout my schooling. The nature of my heart's quickening, according to the heteronormative ideals, was at odds with… nature, itself?

The older I turned, the more I isolated myself. In high school, while my friends spoke feverishly of girls and girl parts, I quietly and gradually receded into the background and eventually into myself. And, although I believed that I lacked the overt manifestations that are often thought of as signaling same-sex orientation for men and boys (in other words, I did not express myself in overtly feminine ways), there were those peers along the way that figured it out and made me the object of ridicule. My social anxieties deepened, as did my rupture from people and social events.

As a grave angst prevented me from confiding in anyone about my sexuality, I told no one about my hardships; not my mother, nor my siblings, nor my teachers, nor my friends. (Did I have any anymore?) I was alone with my fears. According to what I heard all around me, I was abnormal and perverse, an offensive anomaly. How could I tell anyone about what I felt?

I did not know then (nor do I now) what path of sexual identification/expression Freddy would eventually find. A gay man? (This was my suspicion.) A transgender woman? Some other position along the nuanced, intersecting, multidimensional array of possibilities that is the gender spectrum? Whatever his ultimate identification, having watched him interact with his classmates throughout that year, I saw myself in him. Certainly, I had been more shy at his age, but there were undeniable similarities in our sensitive temperaments, our interest in activities generally, closely associated with the feminine.

If in my own schooling experience, one, if just ONE teacher had openly spoken of the need for acceptance and respect with regards to LGBTQ people; if just one teacher had had the courage to honestly address the LGBTQ experience, its members' contributions, achievements, and struggles; if just one teacher had stood up for LGBTQ rights, just ONE...What a difference it would have made for me and, I imagine, for others like me who felt just as frightened and alone as I did in those classrooms.

Today, it is still often difficult for LGBTQ students to find solace and support. Despite progressive policies enacted here in California to promote LGBTQ inclusion and safeguard the safety of these students at school, research indicates that for a number of reasons, including lack of support from administration, lack of curricular materials, and teachers' fears of parental backlash, LGBT topics and themes are still notably absent in classrooms, and educators are not building inclusive climates that support LGBTQ students in their classroom and school environment.

I feared, thus, that Freddy, as in my own experience and in the many whose stories I have known, would one day be the target of ostracism, harassment, and even assault at the hands of ignorant and cruel peers. I feared that Freddy, like myself, would decide to disconnect to protect himself, only to find hurt and angst in the isolation itself.

LGBTQ inclusion in the classroom must continue to be a high priority in this country. High levels of harassment; verbal and physical assault; and discrimination that lead to higher levels of school suspensions and expulsions, increased dropout rates, anxiety, depression, and disproportionate suicide rates all call attention to the exigent need for relevant genuine inclusion of LGBTQ curricular content and experiences in the school environment. Moreover, this inclusion needs to be introduced in early childhood education if we are to foster positive and lasting changes in the academic, affective, and social lives of LGBTQ students, all the while advocating for authentic change to the heteronormative hierarchy. The safety and well-being of LGBTQ youth and the pursuit of a just, inclusive, and equitable education for every student depend on the agency of our effort in this regard. LGBTQ inclusion in the elementary school curriculum is a social justice issue that cannot continue to languish in society's heteronormative, misguided unease.

The day after Freddy asked me his question, I approached him at his desk to work on a writing assignment. I took a moment to answer.

"Freddy, remember the question you asked yesterday? You asked me if I was afraid of anything?"

"Oh, yea." He looked at me with watery eyes. His cheeks were red.

"Well, like I said yesterday, I fear many, many things. I fear snakes, for instance, and the creatures of the deep ocean. And rodents."

"Rodents?" Again, he was surprised. "I didn't think you'd be scared of mouses."

"Why wouldn't I be?"

"Because you're big and a man and mouses are little!"

Freddy rolled a small colorful eraser in the shape of a diamond ring in his left hand.

"Yea. And, you know, some big men would be shy about admitting that, but I'm not shy about telling you. And you know why?"

Freddy gently let the eraser fall next to his pencil and the lined piece of paper with barely one sentence on it. "Why?" he queried.

"Because I discovered that no matter what I look like on the outside, there are things that are inside of me, that make me, me. Being afraid of rodents is a part of what makes me, me... As you grow up and become a big man yourself, you're going to discover many new and interesting things about yourself. And some of those things, you may be shy about. But you always remember, Freddy, that you're special and wonderful just the way you are. Like I'm still special and wonderful even if I am scared of rodents... Be proud of the things you discover about you, because they make you, you! Those things make you Freddy. They make you special. They make you awesome!... Don't ever, ever, believe anyone that tells you that you're not awesome! Got it?!"

I held up my right hand, palm outward.

"Got it!"

He slapped my hand with his own and smiled. A smile unfeigned and serene.

The Effects of Gender-Rigid Norms in Schools

Having himself experienced the stunting effects of gender-rigid norms when he was a young student, Mr. González has an advantage when it comes to understanding the unique challenges faced by Freddy and other students who do not easily enact the stereotypes of dominant forms of gender expression. Likewise, Mr. González also understands, and in fact has experienced, the lifelong emotional pain that can be a result of gender stigma—a stigma that often begins in these early elementary school years. As Mr. González relates, to be a boy who doesn't find a way to authentically express his identity through dominant forms of masculinity, means to leave oneself open to bullying and discrimination at the hands of peers and sometimes even at the hands of teachers and administrators. Starting as early as preschool, boys learn that any sign of femininity can put them at risk of discrimination and bullying (Friedman, Koeske, Silvestre, Korr, & Sites, 2006). When gender norms are rigid, boys are given a very clear message that to be sensitive, quiet, gentle, or caring; to love the arts, music, dance; to be more passive or thoughtful, as opposed to being more active, assertive, or aggressive, can set them up as a potential target. Boys learn to associate feminine traits with shame and devaluation. For boys in these environments, being gentle, kind, caring, thoughtful, or vulnerable comes with great risks, while aggression and dominance can come with rewards.

By way of this, campuses and classrooms can become places where boys are compelled to adopt the most hyperbolic and aggressive forms of masculinity, potentially creating campus and classroom cultures where heightened aggression among boys is the norm (Phoenix, Frosh, & Pattman, 2003; Reigeluth & Addis, 2016). Importantly, Freddy's story tells us very little about who Freddy might be as he eventually matures into his sexuality and later gender identity or expression. Problematically, many still read someone's gender *expression* as a projection of their inner sense of self and as reflective of some inner *truth* of who they are, including, and in some sense particularly, their sexual orientation. Yet gender *identity* and gender *expression* are not necessarily related in any way to sexual orientation.

Regardless of whether rigid gender norms are enforced formally, through written school policies and classroom procedures, or informally, through teasing, bullying, and/or ostracism, the systemic results are the same: *rigid gender norms create learning environments that ultimately do not feel safe for many students* (Friedman et al., 2006). Likewise, school campus environments often do not feel safe for faculty and staff who are gender-nonconforming, LGBTQ, or have someone in their family or friend circle who identifies within LGBTQ communities. And while it may go without saying, learning is compromised when students (and teachers) don't feel safe.

Creating Gender-Expansive School Environments

Within the context of elementary schools, teachers can and should identify and respond to assumptions based on normative gender *expression* in order to create campus and classroom environments that support all students. This is also critical for LGBTQ students, and all students who may experience their gender expression differently, so they may thrive. Further, teacher prevention and intervention of bias-based bullying will ensure that schools are in compliance with relevant state and important federal education codes and laws, including Title IX. As Mr. Gonzalez points out in Freddy's Story, LGBTQ students and adults have significantly higher levels of suicidal ideation and lower mental health measures as compared to their peers (The Trevor Project, 2016).

A safe, welcoming, and affirming school can make a vital difference for student well-being. When we honor and see our students in all their individuality—their unique ways of thinking, their singular talents, and their inimitable forms of self-expression—including their distinctive gender expression—we are also setting a firm and positive foundation for their future education and for their experiences into adulthood. When we create campuses and classrooms where gender is not relied upon and thereby reinforced as a reductive and ultimately artificial and limiting binary, all members in our learning community benefit. Let's look a bit more closely now at federal Title IX law and consider what guidance it offers to educators as we respond to growing gender diversity in our classrooms.

Title IX, one of the Education Amendments signed into federal law in 1972, prohibits sex discrimination in any federally funded education program or activity (American Bar Association, 2016). Within this law, sex is defined as inclusive of *gender*. Title IX, being a federal legal mandate, applies to all schools regardless of extant state laws, codes, or regulations. Title IX is perhaps most often thought of in terms of athletics, where it guarantees equal funding for sports teams regardless of gender. Yet the amendment has also becoming increasingly well known for the role it plays in ensuring equitable treatment for transgender and gender nonconforming students in publicly funded schools and programs.

"KNOW YOUR RIGHTS IN SCHOOL" FROM THE NATIONAL CENTER FOR TRANSGENDER EQUALITY

The Rights of Transgender and Gender Nonconforming Students Under Federal Title IX Law

Transgender and gender nonconforming students in schools and school programs that receive public funds have the right to be treated according to the gender they identify with. Schools cannot require these students to provide legal or medical evidence in order to have their gender respected.

- You have the right to be called by the name and pronouns consistent with your gender identity.
- You have the right not to be bullied or harassed because you are transgender or gender nonconforming. If school administrators become aware of bullying or harassment, they must take action to end it.
- You have the right to equal educational opportunities regardless of your gender, including your gender identity or expression, or your race, nationality, or disability. This includes not being punished or excluded from school activities or events because you are transgender or gender nonconforming.
- You have the right to dress and present yourself in a way that is consistent with your gender identity, so long as you follow rules for how to dress that apply to all students. This includes how you dress at school every day as well as for dances, graduation, and other school events.
- You have the right to use restrooms, locker rooms, and other facilities that are consistent with your gender identity and can't be forced to use separate facilities.
- You have the right to privacy concerning your transgender status and gender transition. Any such information kept in school records must be kept private and not shared without your permission unless the school has a legitimate reason that is not based on gender bias.
- You have the right not to be harassed or discriminated against based gender stereotypes, including stereotypes about sexual orientation.
- You have the right to join or start a Gay–Straight Alliance or Pride Alliance and to have your group treated like other student groups.

—From the National Center for Transgender Equality

While some of the rights covered in Title IX are more relevant in middle school and high school, a student's right to be recognized by, and use facilities in accordance with, their gender identity applies in all grades. There is no question that as educators, you will have gender nonconforming students, intersex students, and transgender students in your classrooms. These folks have existed throughout history and in every culture (Driskill, Justice, Miranda, & Tatonetti, 2011).

The following story illustrates what Title IX looks like in action and how a school should respond to the needs of gender nonconforming students, transgender students, and students whose biology might mean they do not neatly fit into binary identity categories. Dannon's story gives us a glimpse into how one elementary school supported the needs and rights of a transgender student through compliance with Title IX. As you read, take note of the model provided in the story to create schools that are gender-expansive.

STORY TWO: "Dannon's Story" by Sarah Tyler

My hands shook as I dialed the number; I had a script ready that I had rehearsed numerous times. Yet, when the perky female voice answered, my throat constricted, and my chest tightened.

"Hi, this is Mrs. S, district psychologist."

The words started tumbling out: "This is Sarah Tyler, my daughter will be starting school at Forest View elementary school and…and she is transgender."

"Ok, wonderful (without a beat)" Mrs. S responded. "How can I help you?"

"Do you know what that means?" I asked in disbelief.

"Yes, your daughter was born male and identifies as a female, correct?"

"Yes, um, is that going to be ok?" I asked. Nothing in my script had prepared me for her reaction to my words. I had written out answers to several scenarios in which I would be met with resistance or, worse, disdain. But she continued, answering my question with "of course, she will be our first elementary transgender student, but let me get some more information so we can do everything possible to support her and set her up for success."

I burst into tears, so grateful that the kind voice on the phone was going to help me and my daughter. This was not going to be another enormous hurdle in my daughter's young life. Finally, something was going right.

When my daughter D, then my son, was two years old and started speaking, he always referred to himself as a girl, not that he wanted to be a girl, but that he was a girl. He loved anything pink, and when he started daycare, he would always play with girls and dress up in princess costumes. At home, he would go through the laundry basket, grab my tights, and place them on his head declaring, "look at my long hair, Mommy!"

At first my husband and I didn't think much of D's behavior, but, as time went on, D became more adamant about being a girl. We consulted his pediatrician, who believed it was "Just a phase." The phase didn't end, and I started to believe I just had a gay son, which was fine with me. I dreamed of the days we could watch *Project Runway* together, and he could help me with my lack of style.

But my husband, a police officer in a gang unit, started to feel disturbed. And my gay male friends explained, for themselves, that although they had been interested in typically female-associated toys and clothes, they never felt like they were girls. One afternoon, when I was picking D up from daycare, the daycare provider was very concerned because a little girl was having her diaper changed and D was distraught, wondering what had happened to the little girl's "pee-pee." The nice older lady had tried to explain the difference between boys and girls (boys have a pee-pee, girls do not, you are a boy). The Sunday after the incident, I was getting D and his brother ready for church. D resisted getting dressed, looked at me with his big brown eyes, and said, "I don't want to go to church, God isn't that great. He made a mistake when he made me." Shortly thereafter I caught D in the playroom, trying to cut off his penis with a pair of craft scissors.

The pediatrician referred us to a child psychologist. The psychologist felt that I had returned to work too soon after D was born, and this was a cry for attention. I quit my corporate job to stay home with my son and be a stronger influence. Nothing changed.

When D started kindergarten, he and his brother attended a private Lutheran school, not because we were Lutheran but because our older son had negative experiences in the public school system. Kindergarten was easy for D; he enjoyed the multitude of arts and crafts, and was adored by the older kids at school for his "quirky" ways in the after-school program (the school was K-8, and D entertained everyone with his performance of Disney songs blended with *Phantom of the Opera*). At home, tensions were rising, despite a new psychologist encouraging us to buy female gender-oriented toys and not restrict D in exploring his "sensitive" side.

A week before first grade started, we went shopping for school supplies; D was obsessed with having a Cinderella backpack. My husband refused, but I didn't think it was a problem and argued that if it made D happy, who cares? The second day of school, we received a letter from the principal of the school stating that D's "princess backpack was confusing and upsetting the other children" and including a list of "Christian psychiatrists to get our child 'fixed.'" We changed the backpack to a generic plaid, and from then on, every morning became a battle to get D to school.

By second grade, my child was miserable as the leniency of first grade (sans backpack) where D could stand in the girl's line and do female-biased crafts disappeared. His teacher had D's brother the year before and adored him. She had nothing adorable to say about D, however. She punished him constantly for going into the girl's line or choosing pink paper over blue. I watched as my son slipped into a deep depression. We consulted yet another psychologist who was the first person to say the word transgender to me.

I had never heard the word before, and upon going on the internet, I could only find information on transsexuals and cross-dressers. By this time, it comforted D to wear bracelets and necklaces under his shirts and long sleeves. We visited our special place, Disneyland, where he could proudly sport his Ariel sweatshirt and princess crown. My husband was bewildered, and I just wanted to see my little boy happy again.

Halloween came around. My one son wanted to be a pirate, but D demanded to be a southern belle. We had always allowed D to be a gender-neutral character (vampire witch, witch), but I had to call halt on the southern belle because I knew my husband would have a massive melt-down and refuse. D had the meltdown first, however, and I had to carry him out of the costume store kicking and screaming. The drive home was a nightmare. D tried to break the windows of the car and attacked his brother and myself. I did a scan of which hospital I should take him. I was terrified and didn't know what to do as he screamed that he wanted to die. Once home, I opened his car door, and he pushed past me and ran into traffic on our busy street. D was nearly hit by a car. The poor man got out of his car to make sure D was alright, and D stood in the middle of the street screaming "Why didn't you hit me? I just want to die!"

We met with an endocrinologist, psychiatrist, and psychologist at Children's Hospital of Orange County (CHOC). The diagnosis: trans-gender. We were referred to a wonderful psychologist who encouraged us to allow D to immediately begin life as a girl. We were hesitant, but the psychologist looked us in the eyes and said "Your child is six. If you don't allow her to be who she is, she will be dead by ten."

We submitted a letter from the team of doctors to the principal and teacher, explaining that D was transgender and requesting that, though she would not present as a girl for the remainder of the school year, to please understand and be sensitive. Her teacher took that to mean *You're failing as parents, and I will be even more strict with your child. Your child does not dictate who they are. You tell them who they are.* The teacher started treat-ing D as a pariah, her classmates followed suit, and D came home with scrapes and bruises from being pushed around. Her principal denied any knowledge of the abuse, and her teacher claimed, "Well, you can't watch the kids all the time." We pulled her out of the school, and she finished second grade at the Montessori school where her babysitter worked. She attended as a girl.

I separated from my husband the summer before D was starting third grade. We moved to Orange County. I was very nervous about public school and how my new daughter would fit in. I had been warned that the school district and the school itself would most likely restrict my daughter to using the nurse's bathroom instead of the girl's restroom and that there would be issues with her being classified as a male on the attendance sheet.

My concerns were for naught. I talked extensively with the school district psychologist and met with her and D's new principal and teacher prior to school starting. The principal was thrilled for the opportunity to have a transgender child amongst her students. D was free to use the girl's restroom. The school also changed her gender on all her records moving forward and, since D has a gender-neutral name, that was the only change that needed to happen.

On the first day of school, the principal went to D's classroom and scanned the room, looking for what she thought a transgender child might look like. Each time she would approach a child, the teacher, Mrs. L, would shake her head (they both shared this with me laughingly). Finally, Mrs. L indicated where D was, and the principal was stunned: "she's such a little girl!" she exclaimed, and I responded, "I know, I just wish I had known sooner."

D went on to have a great school year. Her grades were the best she had ever received, and she and her teacher had a very special bond. D made many friends. Moving on to fourth and fifth grades went very smoothly. During that time our family participated in a documentary called *Trans the Movie*. Upon its release, we were asked to be on several talk shows. During the airing of these shows, the principal of her school put the campus on lockdown in the event there may be any adverse reactions if D were recognized. Nothing occurred and, after receiving my permission, the principal required all the teachers to not only watch the movie but the related programming as well. She felt it was mandatory education to support D.

I want to mention that not only was the public school system supportive of my daughter, but they also were very aware of what my son, her older brother, might be going through. The school provided counseling to both children. My son's teachers were extremely attentive to him, and I could not be more grateful.

I know that I am one of the lucky parents and that not all children are treated as fairly or supported as my child has been and still is. Teachers, next to parents and caregivers, are the most influential people in a child's life. The more they can have an open heart and mind, the more change can happen in a peaceful and successful way.

Dannon's final elementary school in Orange County was ready for her. The school psychologist and principal clearly understood what it means to be a "transgirl." (Her biology at birth was identified as "male," but her gender identity is female; thus, we always name in accordance with *identity*.) The school was educated on the importance of ensuring that all of Dannon's records reflected her actual gender identity, as female, and that her rights to use the restroom in accordance with her gender—as clearly outlined in federal Title IX legislation—would be respected. Dannon's teacher also understood the importance of both honoring Dannon's identity and maintaining confidentiality.

Dannon's story is unique—as is the story of each of us! Whether child or adult, no two individual's gender identities play out in the same way. Some students, like Dannon, experience their gender identities with great clarity and urgency, and, for these students, the call to enact their gender identity through their gender expression—thereby being recognized accurately—is persistent and overwhelming. Students like this, who identify strongly in direct opposition to their sex assigned at birth, are frequently referred to as transgender—though they may also be considered on the gender-nonconforming spectrum. Medical research institutions, such as Los Angeles Children's Hospital, have developed sophisticated psychological measures to gauge these various forms of gender and body dysphoric. Going as far as injuring one's self as a response to the drive to be recognized in accordance with gender identity (the gender of your mind), as described here in Dannon's story, is not uncommon among these children and youth (Olson-Kennedy, 2016; Olson-Kennedy, Cohen-Kettenis, Kreukels, Meyer-Bahlburg, Garofalo, Meyer, & Rosenthal, 2016).

Gender-nonconforming students are not always transgender. Gender-nonconformity is a spectrum of traits and characteristics and ultimately no two students will be alike. As educators, our role then is one of support and affirmation: when our students tell us, or show us, who they are, our job is quite simply to believe them. We follow their lead, all the while observing and questioning whether our classroom and campus is doing all it can to minimize normative gender roles and thus to honor and enable the complexity of all our students, gender nonconforming, trans, intersex, and otherwise.

With the excellent support provided for educators from organizations like Welcoming Schools (www.welcomingschools.org) and Gender Spectrum (www.genderspectrum.org), to name but a few organizations doing this good work, teachers have state-of-the art information literally sitting on their desks in the form of their computers. Within each of us, even those of us that understand ourselves as cisgender, lives a whole host of complicated and conflicting relationships to the matrix of gender. If you unproblematically define yourself through femininity, but are also physically strong, or even sometimes outspoken, we might say you too are gender nonconforming. Likewise, if you unproblematically define yourself through masculinity, but have ever found yourself in tears, you might be consider yourself to be somewhere on the gender-nonconforming spectrum according to the artificial restrictions of dominant Western gender norms. A gender-expansive environment gives permission for all of us to access the vast and varied spectrum of emotions, ideas, and behaviors that enrich the experience of being human.

Questions for Reflection

Take a moment now to reflect on your own elementary school years. When did you become aware of the expectations and limitations put onto you by gender norms? Were you discouraged from pursuing some activity or way of being, or appearing, because of these gender norms? How did gender affect your interactions with peers? How did it affect the way that your teachers and other adults interacted with you? And now, just for a moment, try to imagine yourself as being understood through some differently gendered label.

Cultural theorist, Roland Barthes, calls this kind of exercise a *"commutation test,"* as it requires that we commute, or switch, opposing ideas, and in this case identity stereotypes, in our imaginations to see what effects this might have. The results are often illuminating. Commutation tests can tell us a great deal about how particular labels work to encourage certain ideas, expectations, and ways of being in the world and discourage, or drastically delimit, others (Barthes & Heath, 1977). Commuting these meanings can also demonstrate the psychological violence that culturally constructed norms can inflict on individuals who naturally fall outside of their strictures.

Take a moment and consider:

- Had you been gendered differently and been allowed to freely express any gender ideas and behaviors, had you been in an educational environment where gender expression and norms were understood as faulty culturally constructed stereotypes to be avoided, how would your school experiences have changed?
- How would this safe, inclusive, and expansive space have changed who you are today?

References

Alexander, G. M., & Hines, M. (2002). Sex differences in response to children's toys in nonhuman primates (cercopithecus aethiops sabaeus). *Evolution and Human Behavior, 23*(6), 467–479.

American Bar Association. (2016). *The application of Title IX to LGBT students.* Retrieved from www.americanbar.org/content/dam/aba/administrative/crsj/programmaterials titleixandlgbtstudents.authcheckdam.pdf

Apple, M. (2004). *Ideology and curriculum* (3rd ed.). New York, NY: Routledge.

Barthes, R., & Heath, S. (1977). *Image, music, text.* New York, NY: Hill and Wang.

Butler, J. (2004). *Gender trouble: Feminism and the subversion of identity.* New York, NY: Routledge.

Butler, J. (2006). *Undoing gender.* New York, NY: Routledge.

Driskill, Q., Justice, D., Miranda, D., & Tatonetti, L. (2011). *Sovereign erotics: A collection of two-spirit literature.* Tucson: University of Arizona Press.

Fausto-Sterling, A. (2012). *Sex/gender: Biology in a social world.* New York, NY: Routledge.

Fitzgerald, K. (2001). A rediscovered tradition: European pedagogy and composition in nineteenth-century midwestern normal schools. *College Composition and Communication, 53*(2), 224–250.

Friedman, M. S., Koeske, G. F., Silvestre, A. J., Korr, W. S., & Sites, E. W. (2006). The impact of gender-role nonconforming behavior, bullying, and social support on suicidality among gay male youth. *Journal of Adolescent Health, 38*(5), 621–623.

Greenwald, M. W. (1989). Working-class feminism and the family wage ideal: The Seattle debate on married women's right to work, 1914–1920. *The Journal of American History, 76*(1), 118–149.

Jadva, V., Hines, M., & Golombok, S. (2010). Infants' preferences for toys, colors and shapes: Sex differences and similarities. *Archives of Sexual Behavior, 39*(6), 1261–1273.

Kaiser, S. B. (2013). *Fashion and cultural studies.* New York, NY: Bloomsbury Academic.

Lamminmaki, A., Hines, M., Kuiri-Hanninen, T., Kilpelainen, L., Dunkel, L., & Sankilampi, U. (2012). Testosterone measured in infancy predicts subsequent sex-typed behavior in girls and in boys. *Hormones and Behavior, 61*(4), 611–616.

Madigan, J. C. (2009). The education of women and girls in the United States: A historical perspective. *Advances in Gender and Education, 1,* 11–13.

National Center for Transgender Equality. (n.d.). *Know your rights: Schools.* Retrieved from www.transequality.org/sites/default/files/docs/kyr/KYR-school-June17.pdf

Olson-Kennedy, J. (2016). Mental health disparities among transgender youth: Rethinking the role of professionals. *Journal of the American Medical Association Pediatrics, 170*(5), 423–424.

Olson-Kennedy, J., Cohen-Kettenis, P. T., Kreukels, B. P., Meyer-Bahlburg, H. F., Garofalo R., Meyer, W., Rosenthal, S.M. (2016). Research priorities for gender nonconforming/transgender youth: Gender identity development and biopsychosocial outcomes. *Current Opinions on Endocrinology, Diabetes and Obesity, 23*(2), 172–179.

Paoletti, J. B. (1997). The gendering of infants' and toddlers' clothing in America. In K. Martinez & K. Ames (Eds.), *The material culture of gender/the gender of material culture* (pp. 27–35). Winterthur, DE: The Henry Francis du Pont Winterthur Museum.

Phoenix, A., Frosh, S., & Pattman, R. (2003). Producing contradictory masculine subject positions: Narratives of threat, homophobia and bullying in 11–14 year old boys. *Journal of Social Issues, 59*(1), 179–195.

Reigeluth, C. S., & Addis, M. E. (2016). Adolescent boys' experiences with policing of masculinity: Forms, functions, and consequences. *Psychology of Men & Masculinity, 17*(1), 74–83.

Rothermel, B. A. (2003). A sphere of noble action: Gender, rhetoric, and influence at a nineteenth-century Massachusetts state normal school. *Rhetoric Society Quarterly, 33*(1), 35–64.

Stromquist, N. P. (2007). *The gender socialization process in schools: A cross-national comparison.* Education for All: Global Monitoring Report, UNESCO. Retrieved from http://unesdoc.unesco.org/images/0015/001555/155587e.pdf

The Trevor Project. (2016). Facts about suicide. Retrieved from www.thetrevorproject.org/resources/preventing-suicide/facts-about-suicide/

Yoon, J. (2005). *The pink and blue project.* Retrieved from www.jeongmeeyoon.com/aw_pinkblue.htm

3

ELEMENTARY SCHOOL CURRICULUM

You are preparing your classroom for the new school year. The door is open, and you are airing everything out. This summer, you read Unbound *by Ann E. Burg, a historical fiction novel in verse about a child named Grace and her family escaping enslavement and living as one of the maroons in the Great Dismal Swamp of Virginia and North Carolina. You had never heard this history before: that many African–American people built a community from vines and reeds to live in freedom. Grace was strong, and her brothers were tender. Defying rigid gender norms, defying institutional racism.* What else do I not know? *you wonder.*

The district gave you a small stipend to refresh your literature library, and your grade level is learning to teach new standards in social studies and math, and to continue readers and writers' workshops for the second year. You will meet with your grade level team in a few days, and you have agreed to review the standards and curriculum, and discuss new ideas.

Summer was definitely a time of learning: you subscribed to Teaching Tolerance *and began reading broadly about activist kids, like Marly Dias, creator of #1000BlackGirl-Books, who "wanted to read more books where black girls are characters." You had never really thought about seeing your library through Marlene's eyes or including books like* Unbound (Grass Roots Community Foundation, 2017).

Yesterday, while online, you stumbled upon ways to review children's books for bias, which inspired you to unpack your literature and make a mental list of the characters, time periods, and problems that your library includes (National Association for the Education of Young Children, 2010). *You wonder about who makes decisions, who has influence, who speaks and takes action. You wonder about who doesn't and what stories you are certain have been left out, but you have no idea because now you are wondering what parts of history you never knew existed.*

You think about the media coverage of transgender kids that flashed through your news feed and inspired you to read more, to learn more. Earlier this summer, you read

Gracefully Grayson, which is about a transgender girl who comes out while playing a girl's part in the school play. Because you teach in California, you have heard that the new social studies standards include elements from the Fair, Accurate, Inclusive and Respectful (FAIR) Education Act, such as changing family roles, gender expectations, and the overlapping fights for civil rights across diverse communities. How are you going to learn enough to be current? You have made assumptions about whose stories and perspectives are central to the curriculum. How will you discuss all these new questions you have with your grade level team? What impact will your new thinking have on your curriculum?

This chapter focuses on the role of curriculum in elementary schools. Ensuring LGBTQ and gender diversity inclusion means that our curriculum must contain both windows and mirrors: stories that provide windows into the lives of others and stories that are mirrors reflecting our own experiences (Bishop, 1990). Windows and mirrors are strongly tied to students' self-worth and connect to social emotional learning. With diversity at the center of the curriculum, we will ask students to take perspectives, exercise their empathy muscles, and make connections. Because humans are complex, we must teach from a curriculum that connects our overlapping and changing identities across race/ethnicities, socioeconomic classes, genders, sexual orientations, (dis)abilities, languages, nationalities, immigration statuses, and family structures. Further, because of oppression and abuses of power, we must examine how our curriculum tells stories: whose voices are present and absent, and who benefits or is limited by the current ways in which our curriculum engages community histories. In this book, we ask you to adopt a critical stance toward the curriculum, both toward those texts adopted by your district and state, and toward new texts that you select in order to reform or enhance your curriculum. We ask you to focus on the representation of multiple, diverse perspectives in classroom libraries and lesson plans.

In this chapter, you will learn the current legislative context for LGBTQ-focused curricular reform in elementary schools. Then you will encounter several frameworks that you can use to analyze, evaluate, and enhance your curriculum to build a safer, more welcoming and inclusive learning experience. We will describe each framework and then discuss their similarities and differences, and provide examples of how to examine your curriculum utilizing those frameworks. Finally, you will read and reflect on two stories of practice in relation to the frameworks addressed in this chapter.

Policies Impacting LGBTQ and Gender Diversity Curriculum in Schools

At least eight states in the USA have "no promo homo" anti-LGBT laws prohibiting schools from utilizing inclusive school curricula (Lambda Legal – Making the Case for Equality, n.d.). Some states, like Alabama and Texas, have legislated that the curriculum should teach that being LGBT is unacceptable.

California, however, has become the first state to adopt curricula recognizing LGBTQ histories and contributions to public life. Other states, like New York, are working to make schools more welcoming for LGBT families (Bishop & Atlas, 2013). Further, in states with anti-LGBT curriculum laws, students have resisted these laws, creating Gay–Straight Alliances (GSAs); teachers are speaking out; and legislators are writing new bills (Segal, 2017, January 29). The struggle over knowledge—what is officially taught versus what is possible—is exemplified in this teacher's story:

> Kimberlee Irvine, an 8th-grade English teacher at South Ogden Junior High, said the Utah law reflects the fact that many parents want to be in charge of "the teaching of morals and sexuality." But it can also hinder her from doing her job, she said.
>
> In 2013, her class was discussing a passage in which a character has two dads. A student raised his hand to ask if the reference to two dads was a "typo." When something like that happens, "I lose teaching moments," she said. "I had to skirt around the issue and not talk about it. ... I thought, if I could just answer this, it would create understanding."
>
> (Segal, 2017, January 29)

Organizations like the Human Rights Campaign, Lambda Legal, and the National Center for Lesbian Rights are engaged in ongoing legal battles to ensure that the silencing of the range of human experiences will not continue in schools. Anti-LGBT laws, as eighth-grade teacher Kimberlee Irvine articulates, prevent teachable moments through which we can help students develop comfort and joy in human diversity and accurate language to describe similarities and differences.

As allies of LGBTQ communities, and advocates for the youth in our classrooms, we ask you to examine the purpose of curriculum and, more broadly, of schooling in general. While schools used to exist as preparation for factory work and tools for the Americanization of a largely immigrant population in the 1800s, today, schools have a humanizing potential toward supporting children's self-determination (Spring, 2013). Through an inclusive teaching disposition and an application of the principles and frameworks we outline here, you can help empower children to be seen and heard, and to fulfill their potential.

NAEYC Antibias Framework

With the support of the National Association for the Education of Young Children (NAEYC), Louise Derman-Sparks and Julie Olsen Edwards developed a framework to enhance children's self-worth in the classroom. This antibias approach suggests that children's self-worth depends in large part on understanding of others: children cannot feel good about themselves if they are receiving negative messages during the school day. These messages can take the shape of microaggressions; erasure from curricula; or explicit shame or violence against the child and/or their family, community, or history. Working preventatively is key to addressing bias-based bullying and discrimination. Derman-Sparks and Olsen Edwards (2010) outline four principles of an antibias framework to support teachers in creating safer, more welcoming, and inclusive school spaces.

NAEYC ANTIBIAS PRINCIPLES:

1. Each child will demonstrate self-awareness, confidence, family pride, and positive social identities
2. Each child will express comfort and joy with human diversity; accurate language for human differences; and deep, caring human connections
3. Each child will increasingly recognize unfairness, have language to describe unfairness, and understand that unfairness hurts
4. Each child will demonstrate empowerment and the skills to act, with others or alone, against prejudice and/or discriminatory actions.

Let's apply these antibias principles to the context of LGBTQ and gender diversity inclusion. As teachers, we make choices about what our students read, what they investigate, and what they create. Our students will make choices about the types of toys they play with, the roles they enact, the clothing they wear, and the colors they paint with. They share diverse family structures and histories. Some of our students will be gender creative and trans. Through Principle One, we can create and use curricula that honors each child's identity and family. Through Principle Two, we can teach children about gender identities, gender expressions, and family structures different from their own through a lens of appreciation and celebration. We can tell stories about connectedness and inclusion. Through Principle Three, we can have discussions about unfairness, both in the classroom and in society. We can look at the ways in which unfairness is exercised in policies and practices like rigid gender-based norms of behavior, segregation of toys and play by gender, and bias-based bullying related to assumptions about gender. Through Principle Four, we can practice ways in which to address unfairness, prejudice, and discrimination. We can teach upstanding behaviors and praise inclusive actions and words that our students use in school spaces. We can practice think-alouds in which we reflect on our own moments of bias and assumption, our struggles to intervene, and our goals for ourselves as inclusive people.

This approach helps children move from self to other through building awareness about unfairness, prejudice, and discrimination, and through taking action as a classroom community. For example, Welcoming Schools (www.welcomingschools.org) has created K-5 lesson plans to help children recognize similarities and differences across human experience, examine gender stereotypes, identify safe and unsafe spaces at school, and practice upstanding behaviors when they see name-calling and other forms of bullying. See the text box for another antibias curriculum example.

SAMPLE IWEEK SCHEDULE

iWeek: Celebrating Diversity

Monday: iWeek "Selfie"

What does another person see when they look at your selfie? Does it tell them all about who you are? Can they tell your hobbies? Your cultural background(s)? Your musical interests?

Activity: Create selfies with a tech tool. Then build a selfie wall in the classroom.

Books: *Looking Like Me, My Name is Yoon, Looking after Louis, All the Colors of the Earth*

Resource: www.tolerance.org/lesson/discovering-my-identity

Tuesday: Me and My Family

"Our Family": What is a family? How many different ways are there to be a family?

Activity: Interview your family on Monday evening. Write a family "I am from" poem. Create a class anthology.

Books: *And Tango Makes Three, Big Book of Families, Families, Cuadras de mi Familia*

Event: Family viewing night for "Our Family." Join us and view a film in which various kids talk about their own family. There are sections on mixed families (in terms of ethnicity, religion, language, and race), adoption, divorce, lesbian and gay parents, single parents, grandparents, and guardians. https://vimeo.com/135679243, Password: family

Wednesday: A Global Village

How do you say friend in another language? How do you give a compliment? Sois gentil! ¡Sé amable!

Activity: Create a classroom door decoration of world languages.

Books: *If the World Were a Village, Whoever You Are, Passport to the World*

Thursday: Dreams for Our School

In honor of Dr. Martin Luther King Jr.'s message and famous speech, what are your dreams for our school?

Activity: "I have a dream..." poems. Write individual or class poems and combine into a school slideshow.

Books: *A Little Peace, The Peace Book, What Does Peace Feel Like, My Heart Will Not Sit Down, Biographies of dreamers like Martin Luther King Jr., Cesar Chavez, Sitting Bull, Malala Yousefzi, Harvey Milk, Helen Keller*

Friday: Love is the Answer

Giving kindness is the key to a happy heart.

Activity: Create a Valentine's Day card for seniors at different care facilities. Collect as a class or school and deliver to senior centers.

Books: *Wilfred Gordon McDonald Partridge; Nana Upstairs, Nana Downstairs; The Bee Tree; Our Grandparents; Grandfather's Journey*

This week of activities prompts students to reflect about their own families and then celebrating elders in the larger community.

Multicultural Curricular Reform Framework

The aforementioned antibias framework is informed by James Banks's (1989) writing on multicultural curricular reform. In this seminal work, Banks identifies four approaches used in schools to include diverse communities in the curriculum (Banks, 1989).

The contributions approach: Curriculum features heroes, holidays, and discrete cultural elements of diverse communities.

The additive approach: Content, concepts, themes, and perspectives are added to the curriculum without changing its structure.

The transformation approach: The structure of the curriculum is changed to enable students to view concepts, issues, and events from the perspectives of diverse cultural groups.

The social action approach: Students make decisions on important social issues and take actions to help solve them as part of the curriculum and in relation to what they have learned about diverse perspectives and inequities impacting diverse communities.

The first two approaches (contributions and additions) do not change the current curricular structure, delivery, or content used in schools. Instead, cultural elements are added to the corpus. The limitation of an additive or "heroes and holidays" approach is that we are adding to a problematic curriculum, which has misrepresented or erased minoritized communities from the literature, study of society, and history. These misrepresentations must be addressed as they occur in the curriculum and replaced with more accurate depictions of communities and community members. Adding a single contribution or cultural element of a community will not redress harmful representations or narrative erasure.

For example, Cruz (2002) analyzed history textbooks and found an overwhelming portrayal of Latino people as "alternately violent, passive, lazy and unwilling to assimilate into mainstream US society – when they are included at all" (p. 323). The recent advocacy for an ethnic studies K-12 curriculum demonstrates a need to shift toward transformation and social action approaches to curriculum (Tintiangco-Cubales et al., 2015). From an indigenous perspective, the curriculum must be revised toward cultural and community responsiveness, with sensitivity toward diverse cultural ways of knowing the world in concert with teachers' critical identity development. We must examine how we construct knowledge with students, what we assume, how we communicate, and what knowledge we value. We cannot undertake this process with isolated additions of multicultural contributions to the current curriculum.

This includes reforming the curriculum, policies, and practices of schools toward gender inclusivity. For example, Gender Spectrum (www.gender spectrum.org) identifies a list of 12 things you can do as an educator. These social actions recognize that a curriculum includes all texts that children encounter at school, such as school signage and posters. When texts implicitly instruct but are not explicitly discussed, this is called the hidden curriculum (Apple, 2004). As educators, we can become reflective and critical of both the official and hidden curriculum in our school, inspecting it for the messages we communicate about gender and family diversity. Here are some items from Gender Spectrum's "12 Things" list:

- Seek out and use the name and pronoun a student uses, regardless of what is written on their birth certificate
- Invite all students to share the name and/or pronoun they use (especially early in the year)
- Post pictures depicting gender-expansive individuals or cultures in which gender is expressed differently than typically represented by traditional binary norms (two-spirit individuals found in many First Nations communities, the Hijra of India, Arabic men holding hands)
- Display examples of people doing things not traditionally expected of their gender (male nurses, childcare providers, dancers; female auto mechanics, scientists, athletes)
- Don't divide kids into boy and girl groups or use boy and girl language
- Use language that is not all or nothing and use gender-expansive terms (students, friends, class, and third graders).

Equity Literacy Framework

As we adopt antibias goals and multicultural curricular reform, we can further utilize an equity literacy framework. This framework helps us understand why it is important to think systematically when addressing social change in the classroom. Gorski (2014) identified a series of reflective stances that teachers can utilize in the classroom when undertaking curricular reform, which he calls building equity literacy. These stances help us understand the implications for us as teacher advocates and allies. Being an advocate means placing importance on the needs and rights of our students and families as well as on the needs and rights of voices that have been traditionally marginalized or erased from school. Being an ally means recognizing oppression in all its forms and working from our positions in education to stand against abuses of power and exclusions of all kinds in our learning spaces. Gorski discusses teachers' strategic positioning with regard to developing cultural competence, cultural proficiency, and equity literacy about social identities and histories. In the text box, we have applied his framework to LGBTQ and gender diversity inclusion.

MOVING TOWARD EQUITY LITERACY

Cultural competence: I learn about gender diversity so that I can communicate with my gender-expansive and trans students and their families.
Cultural proficiency: Acknowledging the tremendous diversity among people's gender identities and expressions, including those of my students, I learn about the many cultures, identities, and stories of LGBTQ people.
Equity literacy: I engage students in conversations about the absence of gender-expansive and gender-creative voices in literature and social studies textbooks, and fight to ensure that students are able to express their gender authentically.

A shift toward equity literacy requires teachers to learn how to identify and redress inequities that we have observed or might anticipate based on strong data, such as LGBTQ students' being bullied or pushed out of school, or gay families' being excluded from gender-based events or school policies and procedures. Inequities include utilizing classroom practices and curricula that assume and reproduce rigid gender norms and heteronormative relationships. These assumptions will be detailed through the application of a critical queer literacy framework.

Critical/Queer Literacy Framework

As we analyze our curriculum, utilizing a critical literacy framework will clarify the positionalities we take about what it means to be inclusive of LGBTQ and gender diversity in classroom learning. Critical literacy views learners as active meaning-makers in their own learning (Souto-Manning, 2009). Children are not "blank slates" or "empty vessels" who receive information deposited by adults. Learners position themselves in relation to one another and to texts, based on their subjectivities, identities, experiences, and histories. Simultaneously, texts position readers. Texts make assumptions about who is reading as well as the assumed norms and important aspects of knowledge within the text. In this way, teachers working from a critical literacy perspective will explicitly teach about the power embedded in and conferred by texts as well as the active critical stances that readers can take toward texts. We can question and resist assumptions, values, beliefs, and knowledge in texts based on our personal experiences, stories, and histories. We can deconstruct the values and beliefs in texts and in doing so construct greater critical understandings about ourselves and the world.

A critical, _queer_ literacy framework is necessary when applying an active stance toward texts to support LGBTQ equity and inclusion in schools. Miller (2015) suggests that examining texts from a queer, critical perspective means understanding how:

- Gender is socially constructed and affected by multiple, intersecting factors (social, historical, cultural, economic, religious, etc.)
- Masculinity and femininity are assigned gender norms and are regularly (re)performed
- Gender and sexuality are more fluid than rigid gender norms assume
- Society perpetuates prejudice, discrimination, and violence of LGBTQ people, identities and expressions, and social histories through heteronormative assumptions and LGBTQ erasures, misrepresentations, and biases
- Gender and sexual identities intersect with many other identities that inform our learning and being in school.

From these understandings, we can begin to deconstruct and dismantle rigid gender norms and heteronormative assumptions in our own thinking, in policies and practices of school, and at work in the curriculum.

For example, Miller (2015) identifies five specific actions teachers can take as critical advocates:

- Refrain from possible presumptions that students are heterosexual or ascribe to an assumed gender
- Open up spaces for students to self-define with chosen (a)genders, (a)sexuality, (a)pronouns, or names
- Engage in ongoing critique of how gender norms are reinforced in literature, media, technology, art, history, science, math, and so forth

- Advocate for equity across all categories of (a)gender and (a)sexual orientation
- Ensure that students who identify on a continuum of gender and sexual minorities (GSM) will learn in environments free of bullying and harassment.

We can approach these actions through higher-order critical thinking discussions and deliberations, project-based learning, community research, and the arts. We can model gender-neutral practices, such as by asking for a few "really strong students" to carry some books to the office and selecting both girls and boys to be the "helpers." We can ask our students to make text-to-self, text-to-text, and text-to-world connections as they encounter texts. We can ask them to be "textbook detectives" (Bigelow, 2007) as they work to decenter gendered expectations and think more expansively about relationships, identities, and expressions of self.

For example, *Teaching Tolerance* suggests having a "Gender-Neutral Day" to help all school participants examine how gender-based assumptions impact our everyday lives, thinking, and actions. Once you have implemented a day like this, it is important to follow up through regular reflection, curricular intervention and innovation, and supporting students in their own social action to disrupt rigid gender roles and heteronormative assumptions. One lesson plan example is "Using Role Play to Understand How Gender Stereotypes Affect Our Lives," in which students dramatize and discuss common school scenarios, such as calling names on the playground for being a "tomboy" or a "sissy" (Teaching Tolerance, n.d.). By engaging students in thinking critically about the texts they read and exploring methods for making connections to the communities and world in which students live, we are empowering students to become compassionate and empathetic individuals who respect and celebrate all people.

Integrating Critical Curricular Reform Frameworks

Engaging in curricular reform means supporting students' self-worth, determination, and identities while at the same time supporting a developing appreciation of their peers and a celebration of differences. Further, curricular reform means examining missing stories and histories, and misrepresentations and bias in school texts as well as identifying new texts and new ways to organize and present these texts that are more equitable and inclusive. Finally, reform requires that we position critical thinking, examinations of power and oppression, and social action as integral to the curriculum we teach.

California is the first state to require curriculum about LGBTQ contributions, communities, and histories. Table 3.1 shows an example of recent revisions to the History Social Studies Framework (California Department of Education, 2016).

TABLE 3.1 California History Social Studies Framework Revisions with LGBTQ and Gender Diversity Inclusions

History/Social Studies Framework Topic	Example of Curricular Content
Citizenship	"We want [students] to develop a keen sense of ethics and citizenship. We want them to develop respect for all persons as equals regardless of ethnicity, nationality, gender identity, sexual orientation, and beliefs. And we want them to care deeply about the quality of life in their community, the nation, and their world" (Introduction, p. 20).
Ethics	"To bring California's history, geography, diverse society, and economy to life for students and to promote respect and understanding, teachers emphasize its people in all their ethnic, racial, gender, and cultural diversity" (Grade 4, p. 87).
Family diversity	"Students start their study of people who make a difference by studying the families and people they know. Through studying the stories of diverse families in the past, including immigrant families, lesbian and gay parents and their children, families of color, step– and blended families, families headed by single parents, extended families, families with disabled members, and adoptive families, students can both locate themselves and their own families in history and learn about the lives and historical struggles of their peers" (Grade 2, p. 62).
Civil rights	"Students can also study … the emergence of the nation's first gay rights organizations in the 1950s. In the 1970s, California gay rights groups fought for the right of gay men and women to teach, and, in the 2000s, for their right to get married, culminating in the 2013 and 2015 U.S. Supreme Court decisions Hollingsworth v. Perry and Obergefell v. Hodges" (Grade 4, p. 116).
Electoral politics	"They learn about the contributions of immigrants to California from across the country and globe, such as Dalip Singh Saund, an Indian Sikh immigrant from the Punjab region of South Asia who in 1957 became the first Asian American to serve in the United States Congress, Civil Rights activists Cesar Chavez and Dolores Huerta, Tech titans Sergey Brin (Google), and Jerry Yang (Yahoo), and Harvey Milk, a New Yorker who was elected to the San Francisco Board of Supervisors in 1977 as California's first openly gay public official" (Grade 4, p. 117).
Gender roles in history	"Led by William Bradford, the Pilgrims settled Plymouth in 1620. In keeping with the times, they did not ask women to sign. This is a powerful opportunity to discuss the meaning of self-government, gender norms within society and religion, and to reflect on the importance of political rights" (Grade 5, p. 139).

The California History Social Studies Framework (2017) is a starting point from which schools and teachers across the USA can identify how to integrate the contributions of LGBT individuals, examine changing gender roles and gender biases, and depict LGBTQ family structures and identities in curricular content and student citizenship.

Now, you will read about one teacher's efforts to create an inclusive and welcoming classroom by creating curriculum that reflects gender-fluid roles and inclusion of diverse family structures. You will then read the experiences of a family with two moms and their participation in both a school with heteronormative expectations of families and a school that is welcoming to the family diversity that exists in our communities.

STORY ONE: "Creating and Implementing Inclusive Curriculum" by Emily Maeda

As a wide-eyed and determined child development major, I didn't know what to do. My fellow peers in the Cal State Fullerton Honors Program quickly narrowed their list of ideas for their senior honors projects. I wanted to do something that would be interesting and impactful, something that would stimulate critical thinking and thoughtful discussions, and something of which I would be very proud. However, I just couldn't seem to pinpoint that one topic.

I carried around my list almost everywhere I went. Random everyday moments would make me think of new ideas. Maybe I could do a project on the growth mind-set? How about the benefits of hands-on learning? Most of my ideas could have grown into projects that would have met the senior honors project criteria, but none of them really sang to me. As a future teacher, I wanted my honors project to build my experiences as a multiculturally competent educator.

I ultimately decided to create and implement inclusive curriculum, which focused on gender stereotypes and family diversity in a transitional kindergarten (TK) classroom. Teaching about family diversity in the early grades allowed me to start with the familiarity of family. When teachers fail to acknowledge the diverse family structures within their communities, schools, and classrooms, we are neglecting the needs of all of our students. Students from "nontraditional" families hope to see their particular family structure reflected in the classroom and can become discouraged when their family structure isn't shown in books or discussed. Without instruction on the diversity of American families, students from "traditional" family structures will continue to incorrectly believe that the stereotypical father, mother, and children family is the only "true" family. Since bullying often arises from misconceptions and biases, both students who do and those who do not come from these family structures are negatively impacted from silence around family diversity.

As I discussed my project with my honors program peers and with my friends, I was met with countless questions and concerns. Some of my peers worried about young children learning about same-sex parents. They held a misconception that teaching about same-sex parents would mean teaching about sex. Others commented that they didn't think that I could even talk about same-sex parents in elementary school. Some of my friends asked why I even wanted to do a project on such a "controversial" subject.

I wasn't discouraged. I have seen the negative societal impacts that occur when we neglect to create a welcoming and inclusive environment for all of our students and families. I've seen peers, students, and teachers bully students for not fitting into rigid gender norms. For example, one of my past students came to school with his nails painted. The teacher commented to another teacher, "Why would parents allow their son to paint his nails?" Some curious students questioned him about why he painted his nails. He responded that his sister painted her nails, so he wanted to do it too. The little boy was obviously very troubled with all of the questions because the next day, he no longer had painted nails.

With my project, I wanted to focus on teaching students about gender stereotypes, family diversity, and bullying. I wanted my students to understand that we should celebrate differences and embrace our individuality. As I created my inclusive curriculum, I wanted to include literature that would portray a variety of characters with different family structures and personal characteristics. I built my lessons around five children's books and created whole class discussions that provoked critical thinking and promoted student communication skills. Along with the reading of the book and a discussion, I created three center time activities for each book, between which the students would rotate. I created activities that included hands-on exploratory activities, such as creating unique play dough families and building a nest for a baby bird with materials they found on the playground.

Each lesson expanded on the new knowledge that students had learned the previous day. I assessed what they already knew about gender. We discussed gender stereotypes and what types of clothes, activities, and toys are associated with each gender. I utilized the book *William's*

Doll as the focus for this day's lesson. After reading and discussing the gender stereotypes that were described in the book, students engaged in three centers that allowed them to express what they learned. The first center was an art center. At this center, students were asked to decorate a doll outline and write what they would do with their doll. The second center was held in the drama area of the classroom. Students worked together to take care of the baby dolls. The last center was a writing center where students illustrated and wrote three things that all children should be able to do, regardless of their gender.

The next day, we continued to talk about gender stereotypes, but focused more on individual characteristics of each gender. For example, we talked about which gender is typically considered strong, smart, creative, caring, and other defining characteristics. We talked about jobs that are typically associated with men and women. I explained how anyone can do any job as long as they work hard and have the personal characteristics needed to do the job successfully. We read and discussed two books for this day to demonstrate how children can challenge gender stereotypes. We read *Rosie Revere Engineer* by Andrea Beaty and *Ballerino Nate* by Kimberly Brubaker Bradley. Students engaged in a building center, where they used pretzels and marshmallows to build their own gadget. The second center was in the blocks area of the classroom. Students were given the task of creating a shelter for different kinds of animals. They had to keep the animal's needs and characteristics in mind. For the last center, students illustrated and wrote about an invention they could make that would help people in need.

The following day, we discussed the people who make up families. The literature connection for this day was Todd Parr's book *The Family Book*. This was an introduction to the next day's topic of same-sex parents. Our centers consisted of a play dough center, a drawing center, and a math center. The play dough center required students to think of and create a family that was different from their own. For the drawing center, students drew their own family doing a fun activity. By completing this activity, many students realized that they enjoyed doing some of the same types of activities as other students' families. Lastly, for the math center, students had to count and connect the images of families to the correct number of family members. The images of families included diverse family structures to help students understand that families come in all kinds of different shapes and sizes!

On the fourth day, we focused on same-sex parents. The lesson on same-sex parents focused on the personal characteristics that make people "good parents." I decided to pair gender stereotypes and family diversity together into one unit because of society's rigid perceptions about what roles a certain gender is supposed to play in a family unit. When the family unit differs from the "traditional" male and female couple, some people start to question the ability of same-sex couples to effectively care for a child. The literature connection for this day was *And Tango Makes Three* by Justin Richardson and Peter Parnell. The writing center asked students to compare and contrast something that Tango's parents did to take care of her to something that their parents do to take care of them. Our art center for this day required students to go outside to find materials to build a bird's nest. After finding these materials, students created their nests and orally presented their nests to the rest of their group. The last center was a painting center where students used watercolors to paint their favorite part of the story.

Finally, on the last day, students learned about bullying and how the stereotypes portrayed in the past lessons can cause students to be bullied. We finished up the family diversity unit with ways that students can stand up for others and how they can be advocates for people who need help. To discuss this topic, we read the book, *One*, by Kathryn Otoshi. The "everyone counts" math center asked students to trace numbers and words. They then drew the correct number of items for each number. For the art center, they traced their hands and drew images within their hands about how they could make the world a better place. Students also wrote a sentence to describe what they drew. Lastly, for the drama center, students acted out parts of the book and other possible bullying situations that they may encounter in their everyday lives (Table 3.2).

After writing the lesson plans, I implemented this unit in a transitional kindergarten classroom. I was pleasantly surprised to see that the group of students both shifted their way of thinking and had fun exploring new concepts and perspectives. I was also intrigued to learn about the perceptions that the group of four-year-olds had about gender stereotypes and family diversity. For the most part, they were very accepting about the concepts of same-sex parents and how individual children can express their gender in unique ways.

However, the one concept that some of them had a difficult time grasping was the concept of certain jobs for a particular gender. More specifically, my students couldn't wrap their mind around the fact that firefighters and doctors could be female. When I asked them why they had this perception, they responded that they simply haven't ever seen

TABLE 3.2 Gender and LGBTQ Activities and Literature in Transitional Kindergarten

Day	Concept	Activities	Literature
1	Gender and gender stereotypes	Doll art Role play caring for doll Writing about what all kids should be able to do	*William's Doll*
2	Gender, jobs, and gender stereotypes	Build a gadget Create a shelter for animals Design an invention to help others	*Rosie Revere, Engineer* *Ballerino Nate*
3	Diverse families	Sculpt a family different from your own Draw your own family doing a favorite activity Count the members of diverse families	*The Family Book*
4	Same-sex parents and caregiving	Build a bird's nest Talk about how birds care for their babies Paint a scene from the book	*And Tango Makes Three*
5	Bullying and caring for others	Everyone counts math Hand drawings about making the world better Role-playing scenes from the book	*One*

women firefighters or doctors. No one in the class had ever seen a female firefighter. On the other hand, some did disagree with the concept of doctors only being male and responded that their doctors were actually female. My students who had never seen a female doctor before were amazed by this revelation and stated that women doctors must exist! This friendly back and forth discussion helped some of my students change their initial perceptions. I was fascinated to learn that students at this age, at least in this specific classroom, weren't necessarily permanently biased by society's rigid gender norms but that their thinking was much more malleable.

Overall, this experience has been truly eye-opening. I am very aware of the need to create inclusive curriculum. I want to create welcoming classrooms where my students can be themselves and still flourish and connect with other diverse individuals. It is crucial for teachers to create inclusive curriculum for students of all ages, especially for young children. As we get older, it can become increasingly challenging to overcome misconceptions and biases. Teachers shouldn't be afraid to educate their students about controversial subjects because bullying often arises from the misconceptions and biases that we form when we lack the knowledge about those very subjects. As the great Nelson Mandela once said, "Education is the most powerful weapon which you can use to change the world."

STORY TWO: "Queer Moms and Schools" by Mollie Blackburn and Mindi Rhoades

We are teacher educators and community advocates, but here we are writing from the point of view as queer moms. We raise two children together. One of them is in middle school and the other is in elementary. The older one has two fathers, one biological and the other his partner at the time of her conception. They both live far from where we are raising our children, but the fathers are invested in their lives. Both of our children have two god fathers, who also live far from us but are invested in the lives of our children. We say all of this to convey that our family structure can be understood as complicated. It doesn't feel like it in the day-to-day, where it's really just two parents raising two kids, which, of course, has plenty of its own complications.

When our older child went to preschool, we carefully selected a place where our family would be respected, and it was, for the most part. The school was diverse in terms of race and class, and our family, which is white and middle class, was not the only one with same-sex parents. There was one other, and the child in that family and our child were placed in the same class. When our younger child went to the same preschool, there wasn't another kid in her class with same-sex parents, but one of her teachers was an out lesbian. The administrators and faculty made deliberate efforts to acknowledge and embrace our family not just in theory, but as part of their philosophy, practice, and community. They provided positive recognition and reception of our family as one of the many kinds of different families represented within the preschool and the larger community. As parents of preschoolers, we wanted our children to feel welcomed, included, recognized, and valued in their educational experiences and contexts. We wanted an environment that was intellectually and socially stimulating, where our kids would be excited about learning while feeling happy and secure in who they were.

In the preschool, we saw books like *And Tango Makes Three* on the shelves. We saw a lesson in which a teacher taught students to create bar graphs beginning with "How many sisters do you have? How many brothers do you have? How many moms do you have? How many dads do you have?" While we recognize this approach creates problems for people whose family members identify beyond the gender binary, it was a beginning at acknowledging family diversity. It invited but did not require students to participate. So, our child could say she has two moms and two dads; there was space for that. But she didn't have to say anything. She could choose not to participate. She could choose to say she had a mom and a dad. She had options. And the stakes weren't high.

But we also saw a struggle to be respectful of the diverse families at the school. Some parents, for example, didn't want their children to engage in creative gender play. They worried that their children would be more vulnerable to abuse in their neighborhood if they learned that gender creativity was acceptable. The teachers didn't know the answers to such questions and concerns, but they honored the families in their classroom and worked together to serve their children well. We admired the struggle.

When our older child went to kindergarten, we were very nervous. The school was in a neighborhood, our neighborhood, with a lot of same-sex households, particularly those of white women. But many of our neighborhood families sent their kids to a lottery school to which our child had not been admitted. On the first day, we made the strategic decision for Mollie alone to walk our child to school. With only one of us, it was not immediately evident that our child had same-sex parents. Plus, Mollie is more normatively cisgender in terms of expression and presentation than Mindi. Arriving at the classroom, Mollie was relieved to see another parent who she read as queer. When Mollie came for pickup at the end of the day, the queer-presenting mom was several people in front of her in line. When this parent got to the front of the line, the teacher called out our child's name as if to send our child home with the other lesbian mom.

In retrospect, we get it. How could the teacher be expected to know her students and their parents after a single day? And people make these kinds of mistakes. We too make these kinds of mistakes. We get it. Really. But in the moment, Mollie hated it, hated the conflation of one lesbian for another. Still, this was not the teacher's fault. What was, though, is how that teacher averted eye contact with Mindi when we attended parent-teacher conferences together, how she refused to engage her as a parent. When our child was asked to represent her family as a part of her turn as "Star of the Week," instead of drawing herself with two moms, she drew her cats, omitting the visual reminder to her teacher and class-mates of our difference. And when we explained to the principal that we would be leaving her school for the aforementioned lottery school because we did not experience the school as respectful of our family, the principal stated defensively that there were many same-sex headed families in the school. The problem was not only in her defensiveness but also in her misconception that the mere visible presence of queer families signifies respect for queer families.

Just before our older child started the following year at the lottery school, there was an orientation. When we arrived at the classroom, the teacher and her partner, both women, were putting up the bulletin board together. We never had to look for eye contact, it was automat-ically there. We never had to wonder. We could see ourselves repre-sented here, fitting naturally within the fabric of the school community already.

Years later, though, in the same school, in a class that had at least four queer families, a teacher compiled a collection of student work in a book that she had published and asked parents and guardians to purchase. The book was dedicated generically to "mom and dad." It was distributed around parent-teacher conference time. Mollie prepared for how to ad-dress the concerns, but when it was her turn to meet with the teacher, in the last time slot of the evening of a very long day, the teacher looked exhausted, on edge. Mollie worried the teacher was going to cry, and identifying so closely with her as a teacher, Mollie conceded this op-portunity for direct confrontation. Instead, Mollie vented to family and friends. She tore out the dedication page. (Later she spoke with another one of the queer parents who also taught at the school. This parent and teacher spoke with our child's teacher about the concern, and, indeed, the teacher cried.)

Now the older child is in middle school, and many things have changed. At her new school, during a day of elective workshops for students, Mollie provided a well-attended session on LGBTQ litera-ture. This school community intentionally and explicitly recognizes our family as a family, without any hesitations or reservations, and seeks to include and support us and our children, and families like ours. It is not perfect. The annual Father/Daughter Dance clearly re-veals there is work to do here too. But their actions indicated their ac-tive commitment to creating a more inclusive community and culture: like participating as a school group in the Pride Parade; convening

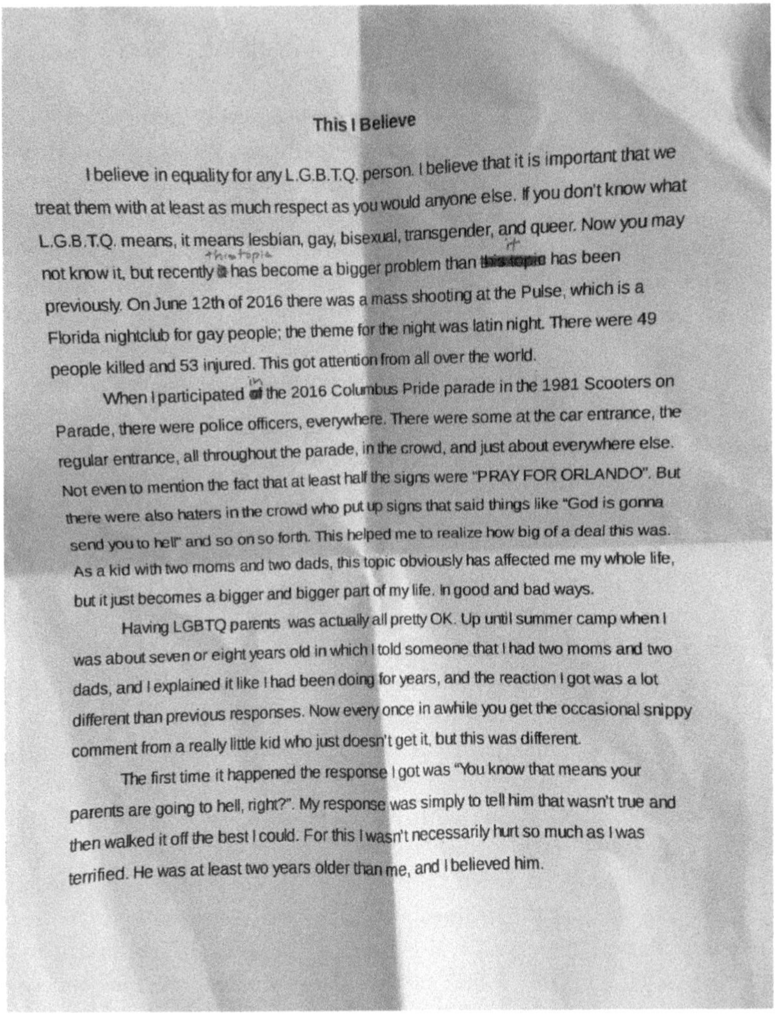

This I Believe

I believe in equality for any L.G.B.T.Q. person. I believe that it is important that we treat them with at least as much respect as you would anyone else. If you don't know what L.G.B.T.Q. means, it means lesbian, gay, bisexual, transgender, and queer. Now you may not know it, but recently it has become a bigger problem than this topic has been previously. On June 12th of 2016 there was a mass shooting at the Pulse, which is a Florida nightclub for gay people; the theme for the night was latin night. There were 49 people killed and 53 injured. This got attention from all over the world.

When I participated in the 2016 Columbus Pride parade in the 1981 Scooters on Parade, there were police officers, everywhere. There were some at the car entrance, the regular entrance, all throughout the parade, in the crowd, and just about everywhere else. Not even to mention the fact that at least half the signs were "PRAY FOR ORLANDO". But there were also haters in the crowd who put up signs that said things like "God is gonna send you to hell" and so on so forth. This helped me to realize how big of a deal this was. As a kid with two moms and two dads, this topic obviously has affected me my whole life, but it just becomes a bigger and bigger part of my life, in good and bad ways.

Having LGBTQ parents was actually all pretty OK. Up until summer camp when I was about seven or eight years old in which I told someone that I had two moms and two dads, and I explained it like I had been doing for years, and the reaction I got was a lot different than previous responses. Now every once in awhile you get the occasional snippy comment from a really little kid who just doesn't get it, but this was different.

The first time it happened the response I got was "You know that means your parents are going to hell, right?". My response was simply to tell him that wasn't true and then walked it off the best I could. For this I wasn't necessarily hurt so much as I was terrified. He was at least two years older than me, and I believed him.

FIGURE 3.1 This I Believe Essay, prepared for presentation. Photo by Mollie Blackburn.

school-initiated groups of parents, faculty, and administrative staff to work LGBTQ diversity and support; including LGBTQ families in the promotional materials; and advertising the school in LGBTQ-specific media.

At the very start of this school year, our older child was required to write and present an essay entitled, "This I Believe." (Figures 3.1 and 3.2). She began with, "I believe in equality for any LGBT person. I believe

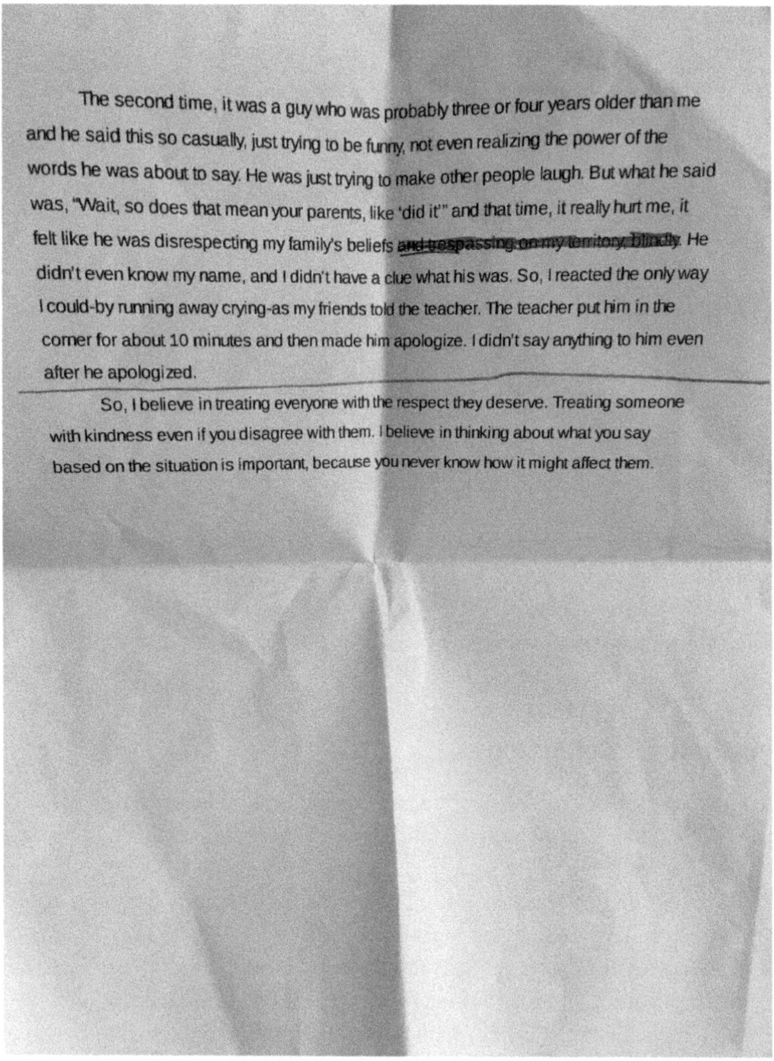

The second time, it was a guy who was probably three or four years older than me and he said this so casually, just trying to be funny, not even realizing the power of the words he was about to say. He was just trying to make other people laugh. But what he said was, "Wait, so does that mean your parents, like 'did it'" and that time, it really hurt me, it felt like he was disrespecting my family's beliefs ~~and trespassing on my territory blindly~~. He didn't even know my name, and I didn't have a clue what his was. So, I reacted the only way I could–by running away crying–as my friends told the teacher. The teacher put him in the corner for about 10 minutes and then made him apologize. I didn't say anything to him even after he apologized.

So, I believe in treating everyone with the respect they deserve. Treating someone with kindness even if you disagree with them. I believe in thinking about what you say based on the situation is important, because you never know how it might affect them.

FIGURE 3.2   This I Believe Essay, prepared for presentation. Photo by Mollie Blackburn.

that it is important that we treat them with as much respect as you would anyone else." She talked about the Pride Parade and about seeing people holding signs supporting the massacre of LGBTQ people at the Orlando nightclub Pulse, signs equating LGBTQ people and sin. She talked about having to explain her family to other kids, about one person telling her that her parents were going to hell, about how she had believed them; about how another person asked her crass questions about sex and her conception. And still, she concluded with,

> I believe in treating everyone with the respect they deserve. Treating someone with kindness even if you disagree with them. I believe it is important to think about what we say to others because you never know how it might affect them.

She received praise from her teacher and some of her peers, telling her she was strong and brave. With her permission, we sent her essay to her dads and her godfathers. They were proud of her. We were proud of her. She had come a long way since she represented her family as cats, in part despite her schools and teachers, in part because of them.

These two stories illustrate the inclusion of the NAEYC Antibias Principles. Students' social identities are validated, and an environment has been created that enables them to express their comfort and joy with human diversity. The teacher demonstrates cultural proficiency by recognizing and embracing the diversity among her students.

Questions for Reflection

1. How do you define the purpose of curriculum, education in general?
2. Which perspectives or representations are missing from your classroom library?
3. How will you select and obtain books to add to your curriculum ensuring that it is inclusive of all students and cultures?
4. Which texts will you remove from your curriculum or classroom library due to harmful representations of marginalized communities?
5. Which posters or examples will you choose to display to ensure that gender roles are not displayed only as binary or stereotypical?
6. How will the thoughts or ideas that came to mind as you read these stories influence your future classroom practices, curriculum, and interactions with parents and the community?
7. In what ways will you use the frameworks described in this chapter to ensure that your curriculum and classroom practices help build a safer and more inclusive learning experience?
8. How will you transform or eliminate classroom practices to be respectful of gender and cultural differences in your students?

9. Which content resources, that is Teaching Tolerance lessons, HRC's Welcoming Schools lesson plans, or others, will you begin to use in order to build a safer, more inclusive classroom environment and curriculum?

Selected Children's Literature Titles

Atkinson, C. J., & Pike, O. (2017). *Can I tell you about gender diversity?* Philadelphia, PA: Jessica Kingsley Publishers.

Ewert, M. (2008). *10,000 dresses.* New York, NY: Triangle Square.

Hall, M. (2015). *Red: A crayon's story.* New York, NY: Greenwillow Books.

Herthel, J., & Jennings, J. (2014). *I am Jazz.* New York, NY: TransKids Purple Rainbow Foundation and Penguin Group.

Hoffman, S., & Hoffman, I. (2014). *Jacob's new dress.* Chicago, IL: Albert Whitman and Company.

Kilodavis, C. (2010). *My princess boy.* New York, NY: Aladdin.

Kuklin, S. (2006). *Families.* New York, NY: Hyperion Books for Children.

Leaf, M. (1936). *The story of Ferdinand.* New York, NY: Viking Press.

Newman, L. (2000). *Heather has two mommies.* New York, NY: Alyson Books.

Otoshi, K. (2008). *One.* Novato, CA: KO Kids Books.

Richardson, J., & Parnell, P. (2005). *And Tango makes three.* New York, NY: Simon & Schuster.

Ronter, S. (2015). *Families.* New York, NY: Holiday House.

For more, see bibliographies from Welcoming Schools: www.welcomingschools.org/resources/

For a full list of resources, see Gender Spectrum: www.genderspectrum.org/resources/education-2/#more-424

References

Banks, J. A. (1989). Approaches to multicultural curriculum reform. *Trotter Review, 3*(3). Retrieved from http://scholarworks.umb.edu/trotter_review/vol3/iss3/5

Bigelow, B. (2007). Students as textbook detectives. *Rethinking our classrooms* (vol. 1). Seattle, Washington: Rethinking Schools.

Bishop, R. S. (1990). Mirrors, windows, and sliding glass doors. *Perspectives, 6*(3), ix–xi.

Bishop, C. M., & Atlas, J. G. (2013). School curriculum, policies, and practices regarding lesbian, gay, bisexual, and transgender families. *Education and Urban Society, 47*(7), 766–784.

California Department of Education. (2016, July). 2016 history-social science framework. Retrieved from www.cde.ca.gov/ci/hs/cf/sbedrafthssfw.asp

Cruz, B. C. (2002). Don Juan and rebels under palm trees: Depictions of Latin Americans in US history textbooks. *Critique of Anthropology, 22*, 323–342.

Derman-Sparks, L., & Edwards, J. O. (2010). *Anti-bias education for young children and ourselves.* Washington, D.C.: National Association for the Education of Young Children.

Gender Spectrum. (2017). Things anyone can do tomorrow. Retrieved from www.genderspectrum.org/resources/

Gorski, P. (2014). Imagining equity literacy. Retrieved from www.tolerance.org/magazine/imagining-equity-literacy

Grass Roots Community Foundation. (2017). *One-thousand black girl books resource guide.* Retrieved from http://grassrootscommunityfoundation.org/1000-black-girl-books-resource-guide/#1458589376556-1fa71d56-6d86

Lambda Legal – Making the Case for Equality. (n.d.). *#Donteraseus: FAQ about anti-LGBT curriculum laws.* Retrieved from www.lambdalegal.org/dont-erase-us/faq

Miller, sj. (2015). A queer literacy framework promoting (a)gender and (a)sexuality self-determination and justice. *English Journal, 104*(5), 37–44.

National Association for the Education of Young Children. (2010). *Ten steps for reviewing children's books.* Retrieved from www.naeyc.org/files/naeyc/file/Publications/Ten%20Steps.pdf

Segal, C. (2017, January 29). Eight states censor LGBTQ topics in school. Now, a lawsuit is challenging that. *PBS Newshour.* Retrieved from www.pbs.org/newshour/updates/lgbtq-issues-class-lawsuit-utah/

Souto-Manning, M. (2009). Acting out and talking back: Negotiating discourses in American early educational settings. *Early Child Development and Care, 179*(8), 1083–1094.

Spring, J. (2013). *The American school, a global context: From the Puritans to the Obama administration* (9th ed.). New York: HSSL Publishers.

Teaching Tolerance. (2013, Summer). Toolkit for "gender spectrum." *Teaching Tolerance.* Retrieved from www.tolerance.org/magazine/summer-2013/toolkit-for-gender-spectrum

Teaching Tolerance. (n.d.). Role plays to reduce gender stereotypes. *Teaching Tolerance.* Retrieved from www.tolerance.org/lesson/what-happens-if-using-role-plays-understand-how-gender-stere

Tintiangco-Cubales, A., Kohli, R., Sacramento, J., Henning, N., Agarwal-Rangnath, R., & Sleeter, C. (2015). Toward an ethnic studies pedagogy: Implications for K-12 schools from the research. *The Urban Review, 47*(1), 104–125.

4

ELEMENTARY SCHOOL PEDAGOGY

You are a second-year teacher in a district that has been in the news recently for a homophobic event at another elementary school campus. A child called another child "f#@&t" and pushed him to the ground. The targeted child twisted his ankle and needed medical attention. The school did not discipline the child perpetrating the violence, and now, the family of the injured child is suing the district. You are in this school's district and are hoping that something happens that will impact all district schools toward being more inclusive and addressing bias-based bullying. You too have noticed gender- and LGBTQ-based name-calling and have tried to intervene on your school campus. But other teachers hear these same student interactions and ignore them. You wonder what good you can do as a single person.

You also realize that inclusive peer relationships need to be cultivated in the classroom through the strategic use of pedagogy. You had learned in your teaching credential program about interactive approaches like cooperative learning, inquiry- and project-based learning, and using the arts for creative expression. You wonder how these approaches might help you toward your goal of inclusive classroom interactions and building your students' awareness, respect, and appreciation of gender-expansive identities and family diversity. You are eager to apply your training in your third-grade classroom this year.

When you approach another teacher on your grade level team about your ideas, relaying your concern about the bullying incident at the other school, your colleague warns you. She says that if you mention the word gay *when you teach, you will hear from parents. Some will be upset. "Be ready for that," she warns, shaking her head. "I just don't bother. It's not worth making waves." You sit silently through the rest of the meeting. Back in your classroom, you sigh and rest your head on your desk. How can you possibly build an inclusive classroom when it feels like you are all alone, still so new at teaching, and without many tools in your toolbox? How can you connect with families and learn from and with them? All you have is a little bravery and your commitment to protecting and preparing your students to be active, engaged, and caring citizens in a richly, culturally diverse world. What will this year look like?*

In this chapter, we will explore pedagogies utilized in elementary schools that are caring, supportive, and inclusive. We will work on questioning typical ways of teaching in order to build justice- and equity-oriented classrooms. We begin the chapter by examining our roles as teacher allies and advocates, like the teacher in the previous vignette, focusing on how to apply a lens of intersectionality to dismantle privileges and how to build expansive classroom norms. Then we will explore several humanizing pedagogical approaches and apply these approaches to an analysis of two practitioner stories. Let's begin with a poem that explores teaching and learning about privilege:

Blowing and Bursting Bubbles by Sharon Chappell

Adapted from the original poem, published in the *Journal of Language and Literacy Education* Vol. 11, Issue 1—Spring 2015

Created from a child's breath
Blown from a wand of any shape
A perfect sphere
Surface tension holds strong as it
Spins alongside the others
Reflecting iridescent colors in sunlight

To catch them,
my daughter reaches through
her whole body
Fingertips almost touching
their strong yet fragile whole
Personal space is a bubble
Built from invisible energy

I burst the bubble once when I was four,
prancing around another child at preschool
chanting his name,
foreign on my tongue
While he cried under the blanket
we wrapped him in
Pop

I watch the school burst bubbles—
One so delicately and intentionally blown
through the coos of parent to baby,
her name in whispers—
pale pink, golden yellow, cerulean blue swirls—

the many *I love yous*
heard in languages
unspoken at school
Those words kept her bubble whole
Until one day in kindergarten
It bobbed onto a pencil tip that
wrote a new name for her.
Her American name.
Pop

I wonder about
The blowing and bursting of bubbles
Who gets to dip into the sticky substance
of life's self worth?
To hold the wand and blow?
Who gets to burst?
And what follows—
      a squeal of excitement
      a tear of loss
      Some other quiet rupture?

How can I be a mother now
based on what I wished I had known as a girl,
About the fragile sureness of belonging?
About differences held in stark relief against a cookie cutter body
a news anchor accent
Kid characters on TV, written to fit in—
(In assumed ways)
Girls with cute tops, boys with sideways baseball caps
Boys and girls with crushes on each other, holding hands.
What if that's not me? My daughter asks.

How can I attend to those who feel
the sticky bursts of bubbles everyday
From the not-saying and not-hearing,
From being on the outside
      of norms, assumptions and privilege.
What if I cannot work in the school to do it?
What if those four walls box the bubbles in?
What if everyone in charge says there is no time or space at school
To start a new bubble blowing project.

I am too old to be young, too young to forget
And my daughter is just the right age
when it comes to the joy of bubbles.

Our bodies stretch to the open sky
She shows me what is possible
We have bubbles to burst,
and so many new ones to blow.

Teachers as Allies and Advocates

In the poem "Blowing and Bursting Bubbles," Chappell moves between memories of her own childhood participation in bias-based bullying and her adult observations of rigid cultural norms that impact children's lives, including her daughter's. As an elementary and middle school teacher, Chappell learned the importance of being an advocate and an ally for the marginalized and oppressed communities she worked with, which led her to focus on social justice as a teacher educator and a parent.

Being an advocate means prioritizing the needs and rights of our students and families as well as the needs and rights of voices that have been traditionally marginalized or erased from school. Being an ally means recognizing oppression in all its forms and working from our positions in education to stand against abuses of power and exclusions of all kinds in our learning spaces (Boucher, 2016; Gaffney, 2016; Smith, 2015). Being an advocate and ally means specifically working through three facets of inclusion-oriented pedagogy: teaching through intersectionality, dismantling privileges, and expanding norms. Intersectionality is the study of how our identity communities intersect, overlap, and even contradict one another examined in the context of power and oppression historically and today. Dismantling privileges requires us to examine oppressive ways of thinking, behaving, and structuring our institutions (Katz, 2017). Expanding norms means that we examine the ways in which privilege and power have constituted an assumed normative way of being, knowing, and relating in the world, and then we create spaces to engage multiple perspectives and position the margins at the center. This occurs through engaging in intersectional identity development, making daily commitments, and participating in pluralist community-building in and out of the classroom as well as through critical self-reflection (Crowley, 2009; PBS LearningMedia California, 2018).

Tarah Fleming, Education Director of Our Family Coalition, works with pK-12 schools and districts on LGBTQ inclusion in Northern California. In an interview for this book, Fleming reflected on her identity and work as a fierce ally. In 2017, we asked her what it means to be an ally; what role(s) allies should play in educational spaces and during discussions about oppression and resistance; and what pedagogies does she utilize while working in intersectional LGBTQ and gender diverse spaces at schools. Fleming articulated the act of being "fierce" as a dynamic pedagogical stance in which she models speaking about anti-racist work and building solidarity for change in a way that is hypervigilant. This vigilance means noticing and being aware of privilege and where it is playing out in different educational situations.

For example, Fleming talked about when she is in an educational space with multiple racial identities present. She is hyperaware of her white-identifying presence, how much she talks, how much space she takes up, how often she raises her hand, and how often the facilitator gives her eye contact. She works to notice when inequities occur and then behaves differently, such as by talking less or speaking up and saying, "Maybe we should hear from other people." This anti-racist alliedship runs parallel to what we are asking of teachers in this book as we build our LGBTQ ally and advocacy skills at schools.

This is what it means to be a super ally, as the children in Madison, WI, illustrate here. To learn more about the work of their art teacher, and about being a super ally, see Michele Hatchell's story at the end of this chapter (Figures 4.1–4.4).

FIGURE 4.1 Super Hero Ally Project. Photo by Michele Hatchell.

FIGURE 4.2 Super Hero Ally Project. Photo by Michele Hatchell.

FIGURE 4.3 Super Hero Ally Project. Photo by Michele Hatchell.

FIGURE 4.4 Super Hero Ally Project. Photo by Michele Hatchell.

Asset-Based Pedagogies

Being inclusive of LGBTQ and gender diversity at school requires us to examine the pedagogical approaches we use for instruction. In this chapter, we discuss instructional dispositions and strategies that embrace and utilize the assets and resources of our students, families, and communities (Moll, Amanti, Neff, & Gonzalez, 1992). Asset-based pedagogies acknowledge that those who struggle for recognition and inclusion offer unique and valuable perspectives about society and history that enrich the classroom in addition to those perspectives typically valued and acknowledged in schooling policies, practices, and texts (Yosso, 2005).

Teaching from an asset-based perspective means demonstrating that we see our students, families, and communities in all their rich complexity, as explored and represented through inclusive curriculum and pedagogies (Bingham, 2001). The educational application of the term "inclusion" began in the field of special education as the Individuals with Disabilities Act required schools to place students with special needs in the least restrictive environment (Leal, Smith, Shank, Turnbull, & Turnbull, 2002). Inclusive pedagogies ensure that students in "mainstream" environments with typically developing peers will be included in meaningful ways rather than through assumed and limited interactions based on deterministic expectations for students with special needs. Multicultural education researchers have applied the concept of "inclusive pedagogies" toward practices that safeguard the social inclusion of the students or student communities most vulnerable to exclusion from the school or classroom (Chappell, & Chappell, 2015).

The following is Florian and Black-Hawkins's (2011) framework for participation, which we apply to the inclusion of LGBTQ and gender-diverse students
and families (p. 817).

1. Participation and access: being there
   - Joining the class
   - Staying in the class
   - Access to spaces and places in the class
   - Access to the curriculum.
   ~ Who is given access and by whom? Who is denied access and by whom?
   ~ What are the teaching strategies and practices that promote access? What
   are the teaching strategies and practices that reinforce barriers to access?
   ~ Why, within the culture (values and beliefs) of the class, is greater access
   afforded to some individuals/groups? And why is access withheld from
   some individuals/groups?

2. Participation and collaboration: learning together
   - Children learning together in the class
   - Members of staff learning together in the class
   - Members of staff learning with others from beyond the class.
   ~ Who learns together? Who does not learn together?
   ~ What are the teaching strategies and practices that promote collabora-
   tion? What are the teaching strategies and practices that reinforce barriers
   to collaboration?
   ~ Why, within the culture (values and beliefs) of the class, do some individu-
   als/groups learn together? And why are there barriers to some individuals/
   groups learning together?

3. Participation and achievement: inclusive pedagogy
   - Members of staff using ("doing") inclusive pedagogy
   - Members of staff knowing about inclusive pedagogy
   - Members of staff believing in inclusive pedagogy.
   ~ Who achieves? Who does not achieve?
   ~ What are the teaching strategies/practices that promote achievement for
   all? What are the teaching strategies/practices that reinforce barriers to
   achievement?
   ~ Why, within the culture (values and beliefs) of the class, do some individ-
   uals/groups achieve? And why are there barriers to the achievement of
   some individuals/groups?

4. Participation and diversity: recognition and acceptance
   - Recognition and acceptance of children by staff
   - Recognition and acceptance of staff by staff
   - Recognition and acceptance of children by children.

~ Who is recognized and accepted as a person and by whom? Who is not recognized and accepted as a person and by whom?

~ What are the teaching strategies and practices that promote recognition and acceptance? What are the teaching strategies and practices that form barriers to recognition and acceptance?

~ Why, within the culture (values and beliefs) of the class, are some individuals/groups recognized and accepted? And why are there barriers to the recognition and acceptance of some individuals/groups?

This framework asks us to reflect on participation structures, processes of recognition and acceptance, and access to curriculum and classroom community for specific students and identity communities. Reflection asks us to consider how we ask students "to be" in the classroom.

For example, we can work to prevent misrecognition or malrecognition caused by rigid gender norms, expectations, and assumptions at work in many school spaces (Bingham, 2001). We can do this by analyzing how rigid gender norms prevent us from recognizing and embracing all the assets that our students bring into the classroom. (If we work from inside a predetermined "gender box," what happens when our students have other ideas, values, beliefs, expressions, and interests outside a gender binary that we can't see from inside the box?) We can teach about gender stereotyping, notice bias-based bullying, and educate our students, so they may become gender-expansive in their thinking and interactions. When a peer group challenges gender norms together, they "generate social momentum to eliminate the perpetuation of inequality and discrimination related to gender stereotypes and segregation" (Mulvey, & Killen, 2015, p. 681). With teacher facilitation and scaffolding, students can recognize one another's assets and not be limited by gendered expectations about their play and social and academic activities (Mulvey, & Killen, 2015).

Humanizing Pedagogies

Inclusive classrooms need pedagogies that recognize the ways in which traditional schooling policies and practices too often have required students of color, students in poverty, and LGBTQ and gender-fluid students to divest themselves of their cultures, languages, identities and expressions, families, and communities while at school (Del Carmen Salazar, 2013). Harm includes social and school-based bullying and discrimination, such as disciplining against the use of home languages, gender-nonconforming behaviors and interests, and same sex or queer relationships and families. Divestment means that in order for minoritized students to be successful at school, they must enact the values, beliefs, behaviors, roles, interests, and relationships that have been traditionally normatized at school, regardless of the need to be their authentic selves. For example, a fifth-grade boy decides he should not gesture with his hands as he talks, or he might be seen as gay and become a target of ridicule. At the core of rigid, intolerant classrooms is the notion that there is a single valued way to be in the world, one that views other ways of being as deficient and in need of implicit, if not explicit, disciplinary regulation. A deficit-oriented approach to teaching views children with scripted detachment from their human diversity and tends to utilize an uncritical behavioral method of teaching and learning (Del Carmen Salazar, 2013).

By contrast, humanizing pedagogies work from Paulo Freire's vision of education as a process of becoming more human. Freire (2004) describes his vision for critical pedagogy as one that "ceases to be an instrument by which teachers can manipulate students, but rather expresses the consciousness of the students themselves" (p. 51). This pedagogy focuses on the roles of instructional disposition and intention, rather than technical strategies. These strategies engage students and access the curriculum in the service of a humanizing purpose for education. Del Carmen Salazar (2013) identifies five principles of humanizing pedagogy:

FIVE PRINCIPLES OF HUMANIZING PEDAGOGY

1. The full development of the person is essential for humanization.
2. To deny someone else's humanization is also to deny one's own.
3. The journey for humanization is an individual and collective endeavor toward critical consciousness.
4. Critical reflection and action can transform structures that impede our own and others' humanness, thus facilitating liberation for all.
5. Educators are responsible for promoting a more fully human world through their pedagogical principles and practices (Del Carmen Salazar, 2013, p. 128).

Humanizing education means being culturally and linguistically responsive, and viewing families and communities as learning partners and producers of knowledge, with assets integral to students' identities and learning in the classroom. This approach is also known as a pedagogy of care or cariño, and its advocates suggest that relationships, respect, and love must be at education's core and paired with a commitment to social justice (Bartolomé, 2008). In this sense, it is inadequate to interpersonally care about children and families. Rather, teachers should pair this care with allied commitment to critically examine and change how those social systems oppressively impact minoritized communities we work with.

Humanizing education also positions social-emotional learning at the center of the classroom community and relationships. Social-emotional learning includes building self-awareness, self-management, relationship skills, social awareness, and responsible decision-making (CASEL, 2017). We must examine and connect with the full development of our students with equal importance as to the rigorous academic expectations and standards we teach. While our care as teachers has traditionally been focused on building relationships through learning exercises, a humanizing pedagogy focuses on values of empathy, community, and social change (Bartolomé, 2008; Noddings, 1992; Valenzuela, 1999). Such an approach is necessary to ensure that our most vulnerable populations of students, such as gender-diverse and queer youth, experience school as a safe, welcoming, and inclusive place.

Multimodal Pedagogies

Another way to think about inclusive pedagogies is to teach through multiple modalities. We express ourselves, our thinking, and ways of being in and learning about the world in many different ways through many different means. Asset-based, humanizing pedagogies should not depend on a single mode of expression, but instead utilize multiple means in order to ensure that all students have access to learning. One useful model is the Universal Design for Learning (UDL), which derives from special education's focus on instructional and curricular accessibility and inclusion of students with special needs. The UDL can be applied in any classroom setting to assist teachers in examining structures of engagement (the *why* of learning), representation (the *what* of learning), and action and expression (the *how* of learning) (National Center on Universal Design for Learning, 2017).

The Center for Applied Special Technology (CAST) (2011) makes the following suggestions for implementation of a universal design for learning:

- *Multiple means of engagement*: Provide options for generating interest, options for sustaining effort and persistence, and options for self-regulation
- *Multiple means of representation*: Provide options for perception and comprehension; for conveying meaning through diverse languages and symbols
- *Multiple means of action and expression*: Provide options for physical action, options for expression and communication, options for executive functioning.

Degner (2016) suggests that using the UDL approach complements goals to build culturally competent classrooms, in particular around building new ideas about collaboration and community. We can ask students to co-construct lessons, activities, and assessment tools. We can provide opportunities for students to tell personal stories. We can provide spaces and opportunities for students to make authentic connections to the curriculum and to one another. The following table identifies pedagogical strategies complementary to the UDL approach. Note the classroom examples of LGBTQ and gender diversity inclusion for each strategy included within the table (Table 4.1).

TABLE 4.1 Inclusive Pedagogical Approaches

Approach	Description	Classroom Example with LGBTQ Inclusion
Cooperative learning	Strategies that use cooperation or collaboration to make meaning of curriculum. Cooperative learning works best when all students have roles and responsibilities within the group.	In literature circle groups, students discuss the book *Gracefully Grayson*, about a trans girl in a play at school. Student literature jobs include finding text evidence for languages of the discipline, details, patterns, unanswered questions, rules, trends, ethics, big ideas, paradoxes, parallels, changes over time, convergence, and contributions. Students use journals to record quotes and drawings related to their findings. They discuss the text evidence in their groups.
Project-based learning	An approach that supports student learning through projects with goals that can be co-identified by teacher and student. The means of accomplishing those goals can also be co-constructed. Project-based learning usually culminates with sharing the project with peers.	Students identify immigrant US leaders and create multimedia reports about their contributions. Leaders include Dalip Singh Saund, an Indian Sikh immigrant from the Punjab region of South Asia, who, in 1957, became the first Asian-American to serve in the US Congress; Civil Rights activists Cesar Chavez and Dolores Huerta; Tech titans Sergey Brin (Google); Jerry Yang (Yahoo); and Harvey Milk, a New Yorker who was elected to the San Francisco Board of Supervisors in 1977 as California's first openly gay public official.
Inquiry-based learning	An approach that starts with a teacher- or student-generated question. The students investigate the question through an inquiry cycle, using different methods and means to convey findings. Inquiry-based learning usually culminates with sharing the inquiry with peers.	Students ask questions about how we can break the habit of prejudice in society. They read *Rad American Women A to Z* and investigate the efforts of allies during periods of oppression and civil rights, such as historical white anti-racist activist Julia Morgan and current senator Elizabeth Warren. Students portray their findings through comic book stories about ally superheroes.
Service learning	An approach that engages students with their communities. The students identify concerns about the world (in school, community, or larger society). The teacher facilitates student creation and implementation of an action plan to address those social concerns and research questions. Ongoing reflection is a key component of any service-learning project. Service learning usually culminates with sharing reflections and findings with peers.	Students identify activist groups in their community whose goals align with their own interests and concerns. One group chooses to help #BlackLivesMatter and designs a service project to increase awareness for young people about the impact of racism, sexism, and homophobia. They interview #BlackLivesMatter leaders and create a public service announcement video, which they share at a family diversity event at school.

Arts-integrated learning	An approach that centers creative expression as both curricular content and the means of expression about student learning. The arts include visual art, music, theater, and dance. Each arts discipline has its own state standards and can be integrated with other subject areas. The arts are particularly effective at engaging multiple perspectives, perspective taking, and building empathy.	Students participate in a story dramatization of *And Tango Makes Three*, the story of two male penguins raising a chick. The children take the roles of the penguins, the zookeeper, and some children observing at the zoo. At the end of the lesson, they reflect on their perspective-taking process using sentence frames like "I wondered…," "I worried…," and "I will…"
Technology-integrated learning	An approach that utilizes technology as a tool for learning about content and expressing that learning. The use of technology should complement and extend, rather than supplant, other modes of action and expression.	Students use iPads or iPhones to take pictures in the world, "catching" gender stereotypes at work. Once they document the stereotype, they use a video app to display the image and reflect on the message and impact of the stereotype. They share their videos and use a forum to compare and contrast their findings.
Social-emotional learning	An approach that focuses on the affective and relational learning of students. Social emotional learning is a component of all classroom engagement and requires planning around teaching self-awareness and relationship-building skills.	Students participate in a weekly community circle, which offers a time to share joys and concerns. One student confides that his feelings were hurt when his classmates made fun of his short stature while playing basketball at recess. After the circle, the teacher conducts a lesson on examining the impact of gendered expectations for boys and girls.
Socio-cultural learning	An approach that focuses on the social and cultural contexts of learners' lives, community assets and histories, and the broader social contexts for living both in curricular representation and a means of action and expression.	Students interview family and community members about their early memories of gender, when they knew they were their gender. The students write and record these stories, creating a class anthology and video. They design discussion questions for readers and viewers to think about gender in society. (For more on this process, see "My Gender Journey" on the Gender Spectrum website).

In the following practitioner stories, we will see how teachers can utilize multiple pedagogies to build critical, inclusive and expansive thinking about gender and family diversity.

STORY ONE: "From Bystander to Ally: Nico's Gender Journey" by Michele Hatchell

I have been a public school art teacher for the last 23 years in Chicago and Madison, WI. I currently work on staff with the HRC Foundation's Welcoming Schools program. I have the privilege of working with educators all over the USA to create Welcoming Schools for all families, to create gender-and LGBTQ-inclusive school environments, to prevent bias-based bullying, and to support transgender and nonbinary students. I wanted to share a story about one of my students that highlights the impact of gender-inclusive school practices to cultivate empathy and ally behavior. Gender-based bullying and harassment around gender identity and expression, activities, and interests are among the most ignored behaviors in elementary school settings. Gender-inclusive schools benefit all students in academic achievement and social-emotional learning in addition to general safety and well-being. By doing so, they protect some of our most vulnerable children—transgender and nonbinary students.

We know that 75 percent of trans students do not feel safe going to school (GLSEN, 2015 School Climate Survey). It is important to know that transgender and nonbinary students continue to be protected under federal laws, such as Title IX and the Family Educational Rights and Privacy Act (FERPA). It is critical for school districts to write and implement supportive policies and practices that directly support the needs of trans and nonbinary students. Additionally, school staff need training on how to create gender-inclusive schools and specific practices that directly support transgender and nonbinary students. A critical piece of this cultural shift is to raise a generation of children who recognize when they are engaging in bystander behavior and give them the direct skills to grow and become empathetic allies around many areas of bias, including gender. The students in my school know that ally is a verb: it is an action. They know that it takes daily mindfulness and awareness. Nico is a former student who I hold in my heart when I encourage other teachers to create gender-inclusive classrooms that benefit ALL children. His story is one of many I could share about the power of this work in schools to develop empathic allies and give students critical thinking skills that empower them to be changemakers.

Nico was a student who moved to our school in second grade. He was a kid whom I liked immediately, and I also knew that he was going to challenge me and make me a better teacher. Nico was very bright; fluent in three languages; and, if not engaged in the task at hand, would find other ways to occupy himself and distract classmates. I affectionately called him one of my frequent flyers, because when other teachers had reached the end of their patience, Nico would be sent to my room to "take a break." This offered Nico and I a chance to get to know each other quite well over the four years I was blessed to be his art teacher.

During Nico's third-grade year, I developed a lesson plan called Design A Welcoming Toy Store. This lesson is now available on the Welcoming Schools website along with many other resources. I was passionate about creating a classroom that expanded gender and created a space where every child could express themselves free of gender stereotypes and norms. At that time, I was honestly on an experimental journey with my students as there were few resources for educators who wanted to do this work with young children. Welcoming Schools, Gender Spectrum, and GLSEN had some materials, and I built upon what they offered at the time. The assignment for the Welcoming Toy Store was for each student to draw a favorite toy on a Post-it and write the name of the toy at the top. My classroom was a place of peace, and I reminded the children that the toys they chose needed to be nonviolent. I often reminded children that the way they play is how they practice their way of being in our world—and that they needed to practice peace and including others because their generation would have to work together to bring cooperative peace and sustainability to our planet.

All of the kids put their Post-its at the front of the room and enthusiastically shared favorite toys with each other. We then watched a <u>video</u> of a four-year-old named Riley whose rant about toy marketing had gone viral. The video was an excellent conversation starter for my students to get them talking about toys that they liked and toys they felt they could not play with because they were for "boys" or "girls."

The class then talked about creating a toy store that included everyone's toys in the class. The children were tasked with working in teams to sort all the toys without using gender. I decided to let the students choose their own groups. We also talked about adding in all-gender family restrooms and possibly a coffee shop, so the adults would be inclined to stay longer at the toy store.

After about 15 minutes, I moved around the room and listened to the important conversations students were having about toys. One group had decided to add a clothing section to their store, but two of the students were unsure if dresses could be put in an all-gender clothing section. Another group was having a passionate conversation about whether dolls, action figures, and stuffed animals could be put together in the same section.

I approached Nico's table to find that he had formed a group with three other cisgender boys. When I looked on their artwork, I saw that their toy store was filled with incredibly detailed guns and had "Boys Only" written at the top of the paper. I made a teacherly pause and then pointed out to Nico's group that if they were pitching their toy store to the local mall, they would have lost half their customers by making it boys only, and, furthermore, they did not include all of the toys on the Post-its from their classmates. My goal as a teacher was to get students to become critical thinkers and form their own authentic points of view, not to tell them what to think.

The next week in art, Nico's group started on a new toy store. His teammates had persuaded him to begin again and create a nonviolent toy store that included all the toys from their class. This change partly evolved because of the other groups' enthusiasm for their toy stores with names like Enchanted Eides and Global Expressions.

During fourth grade, Nico was part of a project that gained national attention for our school. My students decided to look at all Lego sets (over 600) and gather data on whether the sets were marketed to boys or girls and if they had animals or robots. They also examined the Lego sets for cultural representations and stereotypes. One of our fourth-grade students suggested that we replicate the 1987 Lego ad that said "What It Is Is Beautiful"—a time when Lego was including girls in their advertising for all set of Legos. We took pictures of the children in our school holding the same Lego set just like the ad with the little girl wearing overalls. The children at our school spoke 33 different languages, and the makeup of our classes frequently looked like a tiny trip around the world. The children knew that taking pictures of themselves would instantly send a message of visual inclusion around culture, race, gender expression, and religion. Those photos scroll across the top of a student-created website, www.whatitisisbeautiful.com. This project was entirely student-led and took on a life of its own. The students also designed proposed Lego sets that were inclusive of all kids—all genders, all cultures, with mini-figures that had a wide variety of skin tones and hairstyles.

Once the data were gathered, the students decided to write letters to Lego to report their findings and give some suggestions for improvement. I honestly did not expect Lego to respond to my students, but they did. We received a letter from the company, thanking the students and letting them know that a women scientists Lego set was about to be released. They also received a letter from Cornell University's College of Engineering, thanking them for pushing the Lego Group to be more inclusive of people from all backgrounds. My students were becoming seasoned changemakers. They sent thank you letters to Lego, but also reminded Lego that people are not yellow and that they still strongly recommended making mini-figures in all skin tones free of stereotypes. This was a fabulous end to the school year, and we were all ready for summer break.

In October of the following year, Nico rolled into my class in the morning to say hello. He looked a little uncertain, and I asked him if he was okay. He looked at me and showed me a pen he had brought to school—it was pink. I remarked that it was a nice pen and asked if Nico was going to use it that day. He replied that he wasn't sure. I knew that if Nico used a pink pen, it was not going to be a problem—we had done so much inclusion work in our building, and I often heard children intervene in response to gender-based bullying. I suggested that Nico stop by my room at the end of the day and let me know how the pen experiment went.

By the end of a busy day, I had almost forgotten our conversation when Nico appeared at my door to check in with me. I asked how his day had gone and if he had used the pen. He said yes, he had used the pen, and it was fine. Then Nico paused and looked me in the eye. He said, "Ms. Hatchell, I would never choose to wear a skirt, but I would stick up for a boy who did. I think that would be a brave and very hard thing to do."

STORY TWO: "*And Then Came Tango*: The Play That 'Couldn't Tour'" by Emily Freeman

It is early morning on November 15th, 2012. Second and third grade students from a local charter school sit on the floor of a large room. Students and faculty from University of Texas at Austin's Department of Theatre and Dance are here to perform an original play.

AND THEN CAME TANGO tells the story of Roy and Silo, two male penguins who form a pair bond, build a nest, incubate a rock, and successfully raise an orphaned egg. Lily, a young visitor to the zoo forms an attachment to the penguins and supports Roy and Silo's desire to have a baby chick of their own.

When the public discovers the news, activists collect outside the penguin exhibit in opposition to and support of the male penguins' bond.

We are at one of my favorite moments of the play. Actor/Facilitators from the cast start to engage young audience members in a discussion about the activists and their signs. Next, Lily enters with her own sign. She sits with the young audience on the floor, ready to share what she believes — but she struggles with what to say. She asks them to help her. Sitting on the floor with the audience, I hear youth voices offer suggestions like: "Stay together," "Gay is okay," "Everybody should have their rights," "Everybody should have a family," and "Everybody should be able to love!" As Lily takes a moment to decide which response she will write on her sign, the young audience begins to sit up on their knees and crane their necks in an effort to see what she will choose. Although the brainstorming moment right before was chaotic and loud, this moment is still, tense, and silent. Quivering, engaged, and focused bodies wait eagerly to see what Lily will decide... (Freeman Field Notes, 2012).

I wrote a play called *And Then Came Tango*. A play inspired by true events. A play about penguins, love, family, and youth activism. A play that seeks to expand and deepen representation in theater for youth. A play for LGBTQ justice. A play for young people raised by queer parents, single parents, grandparents, straight parents, the community, or themselves. A play that some told me is not queer enough. A play that some told me couldn't or shouldn't tour. A play that some said a straight woman shouldn't write. A play that invites young people to question and participate. A play that galvanized support, love, and activism. A play that ruffled a lot of feathers.

And Then Came Tango is inspired by the true story of Roy and Silo, two male penguins living at the Central Park Zoo who formed a pair bond, built a nest, and were so determined to be parents that they incubated a rock. When given an orphaned egg, the pair successfully raised a baby fledgling. The play takes audiences on a journey to the penguin exhibit where Lily, a young visitor to the zoo, learns to understand the consequences of doing what she believes is right when faced with a public outcry about Roy and Silo's pair bond. This original work for young audiences weaves movement and storytelling through a narrative that celebrates families of all shapes and sizes. *And Tango Makes Three*, an original children's book, tells Roy and Silo's story through beautiful images and text. The play is not an adaptation of the book and instead introduces fictional characters as well as the conflict and backlash the penguins experienced in real life. Unfortunately, both the play and book received their own backlash. In fact, *And Tango Makes*

Three remains one of the American Library Association's top banned books to this day.

And Then Came Tango, the play, was featured in the Department of Theatre and Dance's 2012–2013 Season at The University of Texas at Austin (UT) while I was a graduate student.

The play was poised to tour to elementary schools and specifically for second- and third-grade audiences. When the production was announced, I felt excited but anxious about the community's reception. Austin is often considered a liberal haven in a conservative state, and yet I still worried that a play about a family that didn't match heteronormative representations might raise some concerns from teachers and parents. To my surprise, things fell into place as we built relationships and alliances with members of the school district and school principals. After pitching the play and sharing the script with the public school arts coordinator, I held additional meetings with the principals. These meetings resulted in scheduling 10 public elementary school performances around Central Austin. Additionally, each school was provided with a teacher packet, which included a welcome letter, show description, and student study guide materials that aligned with Texas State Standards for second and third graders. These materials were developed by graduate students and other students who participated in the UT Austin tour. As a part of my thesis research, I developed an in-depth post-show drama workshop, which was optional for participating classroom teachers. All of the materials and optional post-show workshops focused on themes in the play such as family, penguins, Antarctica, zookeepers, and standing up for yourself and others.

Our nervous and excited cast traveled to the first public elementary school stop on our tour on October 16. Students filed into the small gym that we transformed with live music, a beautiful set, and 16 eager cast members. The show began, and immediately, the audience was engaged. When the male actors playing Roy and Silo began their pair bond dance, a beautiful, wordless movement sequence inspired by authentic chinstrap penguin behavior, my eyes instinctively moved to where the teachers and principal stood. Immediately, it was clear we had a problem. The principal left the gym before the end of the show. She was visibly upset. My heart sunk. The next day the tour was put on hold by the district due to concerns about whether or not the play was appropriate for second- and third-grade students. Not ready to give up, we worked with the district to try and keep the tour afloat. We invited them to see a performance at UT in the hopes of changing their minds.

It's October 23rd and the tension in the air is thick. Principals, district administrators, and university faculty, staff, and administrators sit in the back of the room. A small group of young people from a private school sit close to the stage. After hearing about the potential cancellation, the students, teachers, and administrators agreed to be a test audience for the public school district administrators and principals. Will their presence and reception of the play impact the public school administrators' opinions?

The artistic team is at their places. I face the stage and take a deep breath. The show begins and the young people are immediately engaged. When the final interactive moment arrives, Lily, the young character in the play, asks the students for suggestions for her sign. She needs help standing up for what she believes. One of the students loudly shouts: "It's fine!" There is a moment of silence and finally the actress playing Lily stands holding her sign with the student's message clearly printed in bold letters and chants, "It's fine! It's fine! It's fine!"

It's perfect. I couldn't have asked for a clearer message for the gatekeepers sitting in the room. As the last scene of the play unfolds, I am struck by how clearly art is mimicking life, including the struggle in which we are currently engaged around this play and its content. Lily looks to Walter and asks, "What happens next?" Walter replies, "I don't know." Lily: "They can't take her, can they?" Walter: "I don't know. If you believe in something enough, you'll do anything to make it happen." Lily: "That's how I feel." Walter: "Me too."

After Walter's line, I turn for the first time to brave a look at the group of people responsible for deciding the outcome of the tour. I am struck when I see one principal in tears. It is this moment I am reminded that the artistic team and I are not the only ones engaged in the struggle. These principals and the teachers at their schools are challenged every day—to achieve high test scores, appease parents, balance budgets, balance student and parent needs, and make their classrooms and schools better places. I wonder how many of the principals feel that their own identities, and those of their students, are not welcome in public schools. If they support the play, could their decision jeopardize their jobs? Their students? Their own families? Will their decisions be considered politically driven? What happens next? (Freeman Field Notes, 2012).

In the end, the district canceled the tour. Greg Goodman, the fine arts director from the district, released a statement saying, "The subject matter communicated in the play is a topic that the district believes should be examined by parents/guardians who will discuss with their elementary school age children at a time deemed appropriate by the parents/guardians." Faced with this enormous conflict, I questioned my alliance-building efforts and became obsessed with what people had to say about the state of the tour. I heard a mix of opinions: "This is why I don't work in schools." "This is why we have to work in schools."

"The district is clearly homophobic!" "We have to respect the district's decision." "Many want the show, but are scared." "Is this worth it?" "Who cares?" "Don't comment." "Be patient."

As an ally and activist, I must stand by my decision to create art that not everyone agrees with as much as that tugs at my people-pleasing tendencies. Although many of us who were intimately engaged in the production were deeply angry, disappointed, and hurt, we moved forward. Why? The most important outcome was for young people to see the play and to hear the story. In order to make that possible, we had to continue to build alliances with different school districts as well as public and charter schools in the area. As hard as it is to enter political spaces like schools, it is even harder not to. The struggle we encountered pales in comparison to discrimination LGBTQ individuals and families face in and out of schools.

In many ways, the first tour's cancellation created the momentum we needed for this little play that "couldn't tour." That fall, we performed for extremely receptive private and charter school audiences throughout Austin and experienced capacity crowds at our public performances at UT. Parents and community members galvanized to hold the district accountable to their nondiscrimination policies and bring more inclusive and LGBTQ positive programming to their schools. They held meetings with district administrators and fought for anti-bullying training that specifically included LGBTQ issues. The year 2012 feels like a very long time ago. Since then, *And Then Came Tango* has had over 12 productions, including at 3 churches and 3 universities. The play has been celebrated, challenged, and even cancelled again. *And Then Came Tango* premiered at The Growing Stage in 2015, the same year the Supreme Court ruled in favor of same-sex marriage nationwide. Although this was and still is a significant victory, in our current political climate we are reminded that we can't afford to be passive. We must be vigilant about protecting the rights of LGBTQ young people and families in schools. We must advocate for school programs that honor diversity and inclusion. We can't be patient and we can't be silent.

It's Friday night, November 30th, and I am sitting in the audience during the main stage performance of And Then Came Tango at UT Austin. Our revised tour schedule is over and we have returned to perform our final shows for community audiences, UT students, faculty, and staff. Every seat is taken. Families, young people, and adults from the community are here to participate and experience the play. The play reaches the final moment of interactivity in which Lily needs help from the audience to stand up for Roy and Silo. She asks, "What do I want to say?" After hearing a series of suggestions from young people in the audience, the actress playing Lily makes a decision. She stands with her sign and begins to chant: "Let them love! Let them love! Let them love!" Suddenly, the entire audience, families, young people, and community members start to chant with her. People begin clapping their hands and stomping their feet. I feel the ground and walls around me shake. "Let them love!" As Gloria Anzaldúa said, "May the roaring force of our collective creativity heal the wounds of hate, ignorance, indifference, dissolve the divisions creating chasms between us, open our throats so we who fear speaking out raise our voices" (Anzaldúa & Keating, 2002). May our voices be heard. (Freeman Field Notes, 2012)

Illustrated in these stories of practice, we are entrusted as educators to create safe, inclusive environments for our students so that they can learn and reach their full potential. Teaching and learning about gender can help prevent bullying behaviors, which are often based on gender stereotypes, whether they come from home, school, or the community. Teaching practices that help to create these safe environments also foster the development of a sense of compassion and respect for people who express their gender in ways that differ from the traditional binary of masculine and feminine and the stereotypes they represent. In so doing, educators can help to foster a climate of respect and a celebration of one another regardless of our differences.

Questions for Reflection

1. Whose identities, stories, and histories are the privileged (provided the most space and representation) in your classroom? What are the assumed normative ways of being? Whose identities, stories, and histories are omitted or marginalized?
2. Reflecting on those who are privileged and those who are marginalized in the curriculum, where are your identities positioned: as one of privileged or one of the others? How might you begin to learn about the perspectives of those who find themselves in other, more marginalized communities?
3. In what ways does the current curriculum promote oppressive, biased, and/or exclusionary ways of thinking?
4. How might you create a space within that curriculum to engage multiple perspectives?
5. How might you expand the norms that are portrayed within the curriculum to be more inclusive?
6. How would you talk to your school administration to advocate for the inclusion of more LGBTQ inclusive stories and curriculum?

References

Anzaldúa, G., & Keating, A. L. (Eds.) (2002). *This bridge we call home: Radical visions for transformation.* New York: Routledge.

Bartolomé, L. (2008). Authentic cariño and respect in minority education: The political and ideological dimensions of love. *International Journal of Critical Pedagogy, 1*(1), 1–17.

Bingham, C. W. (2001). *Schools of recognition: Identity politics and classroom practices.* Lanham, MD: Rowman & Littlefield.

Boucher, M. L. (2016). More than an ally: A successful white teacher who builds solidarity with his African American students. *Urban Education, 51*(1), 82–107.

CASEL. (2017). *Core competencies.* Retrieved from www.casel.org/core-competencies/

Center for Applied Special Technology. (2011). *UDL Guidelines –Educator Checklist Version 2.* Retrieved from www.udlcenter.org/sites/udlcenter.org/files/Guidelines_2.0_Educator_Checklist%20(1)_0.pdf

Chappell, S. V., & Chappell, D. (2015). Building social inclusion through critical arts-based pedagogies in university classroom communities. *International Journal of Inclusive Education, 20*(3), 292–308.

Crowley, K. (2009). Pedagogical intersections of gender, race, and identity. In A. R. Regan Gurung & L. R. Prieto (Eds.), *Getting culture; Incorporating diversity across the curriculum* (pp. 137–150). Sterling, VA: Stylus Publishing.

Degner, J. (2016, November 15). How universal design for learning creates culturally accessible classrooms. *Education Week Teacher.* Retrieved from www.edweek.org/tm/articles/2016/11/14/udl-creates-cultural-competency-in-classroom.html

Del Carmen Salazar, M. (2013). A humanizing pedagogy. *Review of Research in Education, 37*(1), 121–148.

Florian, L., & Black-Hawkins, K. (2011). Exploring inclusive pedagogy. *British Educational Research Journal, 35*(5), 813–828.

Freire, P. (2004). *Pedagogy of the oppressed* (30th ed.). New York: Bloomsbury Publishing.

Gaffney, C. (2016). Anatomy of an ally. *Teaching Tolerance, 53.* Retrieved from www.tolerance.org/magazine/number-53-summer-2016/feature/anatomy-ally

GLSEN. (2015). *National School Climate Survey.* Retrieved at www.glsen.org/article/2015-national-school-climate-survey

Katz, M. (2017). This video breaks down the ABC's of intersectionality. *Smithsonian Magazine.* Retrieved at www.smithsonianmag.com/smart-news/what-intersectionality-video-breaks-down-basics-180964665/

Leal, D., Smith, S., Shank, M., Turnbull, A., & Turnbull, R. (2002). *Exceptional lives: Special education in today's schools* (3rd ed.). Upper Saddle River, NJ: Pearson Education, Inc.

Moll, L. C., Amanti, C., Neff, D., & Gonzalez, N. (1992). Funds of knowledge for teaching: Using a qualitative approach to connect homes and classrooms. *Theory into Practice, 31*(2), 132–141.

National Center on Universal Design for Learning. (2017). *Universal Design for Learning Guidelines.* Retrieved from www.udlcenter.org/aboutudl/udlguidelines_theorypractice

Noddings, N. (1992). *The challenge to care in schools: An alternative approach to education.* New York: Teachers College Press.

PBS LearningMedia California. (2018). How to be an Ally. Retrieved at www.pbslearningmedia.org/resource/fp17.lgbtq.nala.ally/how-to-be-an-ally/#.WVZfrxRg5FM

Smith, M. J. (2015). It's a balancing act: The good teacher and ally identity. *Educational Studies, 51*(3), 223–243.

Valenzuela, A. (1999). *Subtractive schooling: U.S.-Mexican youth and the politics of caring.* Albany, NY: State University of New York Press.

Yosso, T. J. (2005). Whose culture has capital? A critical race theory discussion of community cultural wealth. *Race, Ethnicity and Education, 8*(1), 69–91.

PART II
Middle School

5

MIDDLE SCHOOL ENVIRONMENT

"Coming Out through Spoken Word" by Annmarie Noonan, Middle School Principal (originally published by Burrill (2017) in the Huffington Post)

I am purple. It's what makes me different. It's significant.

I am purple.

I finally accepted it at twenty-one, feared being shunned. Stunned parents. Embarrassed. Could I carry this around? Profound confusion. Disillusioned. Would I drown? If my loved ones found me out? Doubts. And even though at times I wanted to shout it out,

I decided instead to lie and hide from the eyes of others that I was, in fact, purple. It wasn't hard. Dark. I parked in the shadows; the hint of my purplish tint hidden by the status quo. To know, you'd have to squint, and even so, you'd simply catch a glint.

It didn't show and you didn't know that I had a purple glow inside...I was born purple. I didn't know it at the time. No eyes, not mine, nor those of my folks could surmise the purplish guise. It wasn't a crime that no one recognized the true color I was inside, deep down inside...I've cried so many tears for the years I've lived in a lie, hiding who I was from everyone I loved, because, well, being purple means being different.

Ignorance.

But consider this: I was raised in a world where talk of purple people was unthinkable. Impermissible. Purple people like me were invisible. Fictional. How was I supposed to know I was purple when I didn't know anyone else that was purple too? Blue. The color of trying to figure this out. Without any purple people on my TV screen. Scenes that could have helped me figure out what my feelings were about. Blacked out in doubt, I never saw ordinary purple folks walking down the street, no purple peers sitting next to me in class. Alas, it came to pass, that I understood with clarity the conspiracy—that our society did not want transparency when it concerned the minority, the impurity of purple people like me.

As long as the culture of silence persisted, I was restricted from simply recognizing my existence. But it was distance, college, both social and academic knowledge that eventually helped me demolish the taboo of my purplish hue. Newly born. Sworn to acceptance of who I was. Because, if you love me, you will accept me for who I am. Demanding equality. Yet not even my own mother could see what it meant to me. A tragedy. The day I told her I was purple in my heart she fell apart; started to impart her disdain regarding my purplish claim. Blamed herself. Framed the shame within the context of stereotypes as she proclaimed:

"I don't understand. Did I raise you wrong?"

"Don't you want a normal life. A life free of strife?"

"Why don't you want the American dream?"

Streaming tears.

"How could you do this to me?" she said.

Dead. Silence from my end. But in my head? Do this to you? How could I do this to you? Being purple isn't something you do. It's you. It's who you are. Who I am, will always be. Please. Mom. Just love me. Love me for me regardless of the color you want to see, to believe, I am. I am me.

See.

Pause.

And just breathe.

Because you will see that underneath it all, love is love—it's enough—to lose the shame. I will not blame myself for being purple. You see, I am a purple person. For better or for worse. Cursed to forever fear that being clear about who I am is something that should be kept quiet. Silent. Compliant no more. Defiant by revealing who you are. Scars of identity no longer an obscenity as a new era of empathy holds out its hand.

So here I stand for everyone that has ever been made to feel that being who you are is something you should hide. Deny it no longer. Being purple, different, can make you stronger. You belong here. Wronged to be scorned or torn apart. So let's open our hearts to all of the abstract art in this colorful world. Swirls of blue, black, orange, red, yellow, green and all that's in-between, even those that are purple like me.

You see, I am purple.

Unquestionably.

Indefinitely.

Unintentionally.

Exceptionally.

And oh so delicately purple.

A middle school principal wrote this moving spoken word poem to share with her students. She reflects on her own schooling, still acutely recalling and carrying the sting and delicacy of feeling different. Young adolescence is marked by several complex developmental changes. Students in these middle school years are engaged in an active and ongoing search for self, and with the complicated process of integrating their many intersectional identities. Herein lies the challenge and reward of working with middle school students. Their highly personal search, as detailed in Noonan's poem, brings a more nuanced understanding of their identities in terms of gender, ethnic and cultural identities, socioeconomic identities, racial identities, and identities coalescing around sexual orientation or desires.

In our interviews with lesbian, gay, bisexual, transgender and queer (LGBTQ) adults, we consistently hear that the middle school years pose the greatest challenge for students who experience their identity as somehow different from peers—particularly for those who develop a clearer understanding of their gender identity and their sexual orientation as somehow different. Middle school LGBTQ students are more likely than high school students to experience derogatory remarks and harassment, as well as physical assault, based on perceived and/or actual sexual orientation or gender expression (GLSEN, 2007). Middle school students are also more likely to report this harassment, but middle school staff often fail to intervene in such bias-based bullying. As a result, many middle school students feel isolated and may choose to miss class or not attend school altogether.

As an example of the normative lack of responsiveness that schools often communicate to LGBTQ students and families, HuffPost author Amelia (2016) conveys a typical exchange with school staff when she began looking for a supportive middle school for her out, gay son:

ME: *"What are your policies about bullying?"*
SCHOOL PERSON: *"We are 100 percent against bullying in all forms."*
ME: *"Great! What are your processes for students dealing with homophobia and hate speech?"*
SCHOOL PERSON: *"Processes?"*
ME: *"It's important to us because our kid has been out for awhile."*
SCHOOL PERSON: *"If your child is going to be out you have to expect problems."*

In this chapter, we discuss the importance of building a safe, welcoming, and inclusive middle school environment as young adolescents are in a deep search for self-integral part to the middle school years. We will discuss the role of creating students' sense of self and belonging as a vital component of a safe, welcoming, and inclusive school environment. We will provide strategies for creating spaces in which middle schoolers see their identity represented both within the school curriculum and in the larger social systems of schools and culture. We will also discuss what we are calling *excavation and extension*, the critical dual processes through which identity in these crucial in-between years begins to coalesce.

The Adolescent Search for "Self": *Excavation* and *Extension*

As the National Middle School Association affirms in their white paper *This We Believe: Keys to Educating Young Adolescents,*

> Middle level education is the crucial link in the pre-K–16 continuum. During these transitional years, students change significantly—physically, intellectually, morally, psychologically, and social-emotionally. The academic growth and personal development experienced during these important years significantly impact their futures.
>
> *(Swaim, Lounsbury, & Brazee, 2003, p. 1)*

Adolescence is a time when middle school students become focused on exploring the unique aspects of who they are and begin to ask questions about where they fit into the world around them—both the larger social and cultural world, and the daily world of peers and school. As educators, we play a critical role in shaping the day-to-day experiences of our middle school students and the kinds of information they receive about who they are and whether they are valued and indeed safe in our classrooms and on campus. Remaining mindful of the physical, intellectual, moral, psychological, and social-emotional growth that takes place during middle school years, and creating positive learning opportunities that facilitate this growth and fulfilling grade-level competencies, can feel daunting. However, it is possible to harness the curiosity and growing individualism of these years in the interest of academic excellence and to create learning environments where students support each other as they grow into their many identities. For us, as adults, it can be difficult to remember the conflicting emotions, physical changes, and new social awareness that comprise early adolescence. A good metaphor can bridge this for us. We propose thinking about this adolescent search for self as unfolding through two related kinds of gestures: excavation and extension.

Excavation refers to the internal, revelatory mining that is critical to growing identity formation in the middle school years. Adolescents search their newly emerging and evolving internal sense and experience of self, their own internal shifting affective landscapes of feelings, and their growing awareness of their individual qualities and characteristics for clues as to who they are at a fundamental level. Excavation is a process of self-discovery, and it takes on particular significance during these years of intense physical changes brought by the onset of puberty (Caskey, & Anfara, 2007). Through the excavation process, the young adolescent becomes aware of the most fundamental and intimate aspects of their identity; their internal emotional lives; and their character, innate talents, unique dispositions, and sensibilities.

This critical process of self-actualization continues, in more or less meaningful forms, throughout students' young adult lives. Through the highly personal excavation process, we discover our identities and capacities as humans.

Temperament, personality, intellectual strengths, and challenges all come more clearly into view during this time of both intense social and physical changes. We come to know our selves. For example, students' first awareness of their sexuality may, if it has not already been experienced, either come into awareness or become more insistent during these middle school years by way of the excavation process (Caskey, & Anfara, 2007).

To fully understand the complexity and profound significance of this developmental period, we must also pay attention to excavation's parallel process: *extension*. Through extension, adolescents assign meaning to their emotional, affective personal landscape, and they begin to sense their potential place in the newly significant social world. In contrast to excavation's inward focus, extension is an outward-focused process, a gathering of information about the environment in which one lives. Through the process of extension, young adolescents attune themselves to the contexts of community, school, and family as they look out to the world for information about their burgeoning sense of self. The perceptions gathered through extension are what students use to interpret the information about themselves that they have gathered through excavation. Extension provides the cultural contexts through which the experiences of our intimate selves gain meaning (Lee, 2001).

Through the combined processes of excavation and extension, young adolescents ask and answer questions like *where do I see myself reflected in the world* and *what does this tell me about who I am? What kinds of cultural meanings are assigned to the feelings, sensibilities, and innate emotional landscapes I have come to recognize as my self through the excavation process? What information about my value and acceptance do I receive from these social and cultural reflections? And will my world, my community, my school, my peers, and my family accept me as I truly am?* When the answer to this final question is "no," or even a provisional "maybe" or "sometimes," the result can be experienced as stigma and shame that lasts a lifetime (Meyer, 2003).

In the case of students for whom the source of this potential stigma is their sexual orientation or their gender identity, the results can be damaging and may even be deadly. As noted by the Trevor Project (2016), the rate of suicide attempts among LGBTQ students is four times greater than that of their straight peers. Rates of suicide attempts are two times greater among youth who are questioning their sexual orientation. Among transgender youth, 30 percent report a history of at least one suicide attempt, and nearly 42 percent report a history of self-injury, such as cutting (Peterson, Matthews, Copps-Smith, & Conard, 2017). There are also other negative effects for LGBTQ students in schools where they do not feel safe, including increased absences and poor academic performance.

In developing his minority stress model as experienced by LGBTQ individuals, psychologist Ilan Meyer highlights two psychological phenomena similar to the concepts of excavation and extension. Meyer (2003) identifies "proximal stress" and "distal stress" to highlight the psychologically damaging negative effects of perceptions that an aspect of the self is stigmatized within the environment. Distal stress is about the contexts of immediate thought, feeling, and action in relation to that perceived or real stigma. Proximal stress connects those immediate feelings to the social experiences of a person's life. By way of excavation and extension, we can understand the negative impact of stigma-induced stress as well as the positive ways in which these dual processes can result in affirming identities, bolstering a sense of belonging, and making a positive contribution to academic achievement.

It is critical that we as educators take an active approach to ensure that our campus and classroom environments include positive representations of all potential student identities, including LGBTQ people and communities, history, and contributions in our classroom curriculum. In addition to curricular support, the creation and visibility of LGBTQ student groups has a significant positive effect on students. The results of the GLSEN's 2015 National School Climate Survey, a subset of which is included in the following text box, make this quite clear.

FINDINGS FROM GLSEN'S 2015 NATIONAL SCHOOL CLIMATE SURVEY

LGBTQ students in schools with an LGBT-inclusive curriculum:

- Were less likely to hear "gay" used in a negative way often or frequently (49.7 percent vs. 72.6 percent)
- Were less likely to hear homophobic remarks such as "fag" or "dyke" often or frequently (40.6 percent vs. 64.1 percent)
- Were less likely to hear negative remarks about gender expression and transgender people often or frequently (gender expression: 50.7 percent vs. 66.6 percent; transgender people: 26.8 percent vs. 44.5 percent)
- Were less likely to feel unsafe because of their sexual orientation (40.4 percent vs. 62.6 percent)
- Were less likely to miss school in the past month (18.6 percent of students with an inclusive curriculum missed school in past month because they felt unsafe or uncomfortable compared to 35.6 percent of other students)
- Were less likely to say they might not graduate high school (1.4 percent vs. 4.1 percent) and less likely to not plan on pursuing post-secondary education (5.1 percent vs. 7.0 percent)
- Were more likely to report that their classmates were somewhat or very accepting of LGBTQ people than other students (75.8 percent vs. 41.6 percent)
- Felt more connected to their school community than other students.

Harnessing the Power of Representation

An inclusive curriculum is not a neutral one. Educators may feel that by remaining neutral, such as not allowing any negative words or images regarding
LGBTQ people in school or class, they are also creating inclusive campus and
classroom spaces. As GLSEN and others make clear, an inclusive school is one
where LGBTQ ideas, people, and histories are both visible and positively represented. This is a critical distinction. Guy DeBord (1967) makes the power of
representation clear: what appears in the systems of representation around us
(stories, texts, images, music, films) matters a great deal, but what matters even
more is what does not appear. An inclusive curriculum has such a powerful
effect on LGBTQ students: when students see themselves reflected in the systems of representation around them, they are validated at the most fundamental
level—the level of excavation.

The opposite is also true. When students consistently do not see their identities reflected in the world around them, they are sent a powerful negative message about who they are. De Bord (1967) suggests, "All that appears is good, all
that is good appears." In the formative years of middle school, young LGBTQ
adolescents need to see themselves as good; they are explicitly trying to understand their sexuality, gender identity, and expression through the excavation
and extension process.

How do we harness the power of representation and use it to create safe and
welcoming schools? We make sure that all student identities appear in all aspects
of the school day, from school clubs, to curriculum (addressed in Chapter 6),
to displaying a "Safe Space" sticker prominently on your classroom door. The
smallest visual display or verbal mention can make the greatest difference. When
students see themselves reflected positively in all the systems of representation
at school, they receive a simple and profound message: they know that they are
"good"—accepted and seen, belonging within the school community.

Social psychologist Dr. Kristin Beals studies the effects of stigma, particularly as related to LGBTQ identities. She tells a powerful story of how a simple
sticker on a teacher's door affected her. As a young gay woman, Dr. Beals, who
was not yet openly acknowledging her identity, was acutely attuned to those
around her, looking for any signs of potential rejection or acceptance from her
peers and from the systems of representation at school. In other words, she was
deeply involved in the excavation and extension process, trying to find where
she fit into her school community. She remembers quite vividly hearing stories
about a teacher who was an advocate for LGBT students on campus, even spon-
soring the school's Gay–Straight Alliance (GSA). One afternoon, while walking through a less familiar area of campus, Kris noticed a classroom door with a
small rainbow sticker on it. The sticker was emboldened with the words, "Safe
Space." She looked at the name on the door and recognized it as the teacher she
had heard so much about.

From that day forward, knowing that the sticker was visible on the door, Kris felt different about her school community and herself in it. The sticker was prominently displayed on a classroom door where everyone in the school could see it, which sent the message that the school accepted LGBTQ students. An important thing to note is that the young Dr. Beals never actually met this teacher nor did she ever attend a GSA meeting. Yet seeing this sticker made all the difference in the world in terms of her feeling accepted at school and knowing that she was in a safe space to learn. As Dr. Beals now tells the story, she would on occasion walk past this door, just to make sure the sticker was still there. The symbolism of the sticker also offers an additional message of safety: if Kris or any LGBTQ student ever needed to talk to someone, about an issue at school or otherwise, they had a clear place to go. In this simple rainbow sticker, LGBTQ students saw themselves as safe to excavate their identities and extend themselves into the world.

As you read the stories of practice in this chapter, look for evidence of the dual processes of excavation and extension, and notice how the systems of representation at school affected middle school students, their developing sense of self, and their belonging in school communities.

STORY ONE: "Speaking Up: School Board Meeting" by Lisa Richardson

Living in the conservative community of Orange County, California, it was exciting to find that one of the school districts had permitted a middle school to have a "GSA" type club on campus. After several successful years on campus, the existence of the club came into question when a parent realized that his child had been attending the club against the father's wishes. The district was about to vote on whether or not the district should allow nonacademic clubs on campus in middle schools, and it proposed a change to the existing policy allowing middle school clubs on campus. Prior to that board meeting, only high schools were permitted to have nonacademic student clubs. The club had functioned without complaint for four years until a parent heard that a PFLAG Speaker's Bureau panel had been invited to the school to speak to the club at lunch. The panel took place under the supervision of teachers and counselors. This parent was enraged that the panel could take place without parent permission or notification. He sent out flyers asking people to come to the school board meeting and speak against the club. The board was set to discuss the possibility of allowing GSAs (and other clubs on middle school campuses) with the requirement of some type of parent permission slips. When several LGBT groups heard about the board agenda, they sent out a call for speakers.

The meeting was flooded with pro-LGBTQ speakers, students, parents, and allies. At the conclusion of the speeches, prior to voting on the proposal to allow the clubs and do away with the parent permission, one school board trustee stated,

> Before hearing everyone this evening and I've been enlightened, and for the reason in particular GSA, I am not for the permission slip because it absolutely will be a detriment. As you've all stated, there will be kids who won't come and that's what it's all about. So, I've changed my mind.

The board unanimously voted to do away with the normal review of the proposal and to take a vote right there and then, striking the requirement of parent permission slips entirely from the proposals and allowing nonacademic clubs on all middle school campuses in the district. The decision was unanimous. This is the speech I prepared. I gave only part of it due to time constraints.

School Board Meeting Speech 10/12/2017

My name is Lisa Richardson and I am the parent of two children who attended schools in this district from kindergarten through twelfth grade. My son is gay and recalls his time in middle school as the most painful years in his life. Not because he did not receive a good education or have opportunities there. He did, in fact he was the President of the PAL Club (Peer Assistance Leadership), but he was struggling with his gender orientation and sense of self. The frequent bullying and harassment he received caused him great stress, which resulted in the development of a serious digestive disease, anxiety, depression, and a major drop in his school attendance and grades. Had there been a GSA at his school at that time, his life would have been so very different.

Recently, I had an opportunity to visit the campus and, as a result of positive changes, it is now a very different school. Attending the school as it is now, with an environment free from discrimination, harassment and intolerance would have helped improve his self-esteem, feeling of safety and reduce his feelings of marginalization.

Organizations like GSAs provide a safe space for students to discuss issues like sexual orientation, gender identity, and gender expression, and equal rights, issues that for some students are crucial to address during this critical time in their psychological and social development. A large number of teens and pre-teens turn to the internet, drugs, and alcohol in order to come to terms with their sexual orientation and/or gender identities, and I for one feel strongly, in fact *I know!*, that a carefully moderated and well-run student organization is a much better way for students to deal with and address these issues than the resources students tend to seek out when there is no other arena for information and discussion.

The National Alliance on Mental Illness (NAMI) states that LGBTQ individuals are three times more likely than others to experience a mental health condition, such as major depression or generalized anxiety disorder. This fear of coming out and being discriminated against for sexual orientation and gender identities can lead to depression, post-traumatic stress disorder, thoughts of suicide, and substance abuse.

The Office of Disease Prevention and Healthy Promotion, at Healthy people.gov, states that the physical environment that contributes to healthy LGBT individuals includes:

- Safe schools, neighborhoods, and housing
- Access to recreational facilities and activities
- Availability of safe meeting places
- Access to health services.

Please allow students to continue with and create these vital, voluntary, student-run clubs in order to save our young people from possible suicide, depression and substance abuse.

Thank You

STORY TWO: "The Emotional Experience of LGBTQ Middle Schoolers" by Jey Ehrenhalt

When I was in middle school, I wanted desperately to be perceived as normal. In order to "pass" as cisgender and heterosexual, I denied the parts of myself that did not fit. I kept my queerness to myself, in hopes of assimilating into a social culture to which I would never easily belong. Many LGBTQ teenagers learn to keep their needs quiet and their desires a secret. Reflecting back on my own experience, I know that while I could have benefited profoundly from guidance, on the outside I made no such request; in fact, I appeared just fine.

I respect my younger self's decision to stay in the closet throughout secondary school. I needed a safe, supportive environment in which I could grow into my authentic self, and I came out as soon as I found it. Yet, looking back, I wonder if fewer years in hiding would have bred greater confidence in the long run. I wonder if, perhaps, I had been able to explore my own truth as an adolescent, I would enjoy more serenity in adulthood. As LGBTQ rights trudge stubbornly in the direction of progress, educators increasingly have the opportunity to provide safety and support in real time, when it's so often needed most.

Thus, I have interviewed queer adults who struggled with coming out in middle school and who ultimately came to identify as LGBTQ. I asked them about their emotional landscapes at the time. They reflected on their psychosocial experiences of being closeted in middle school and how it could have gone differently.

Educators may never know exactly what's happening in the maturing minds of their students. Still, middle school comprises three fragile years. Openness and affirmation may serve some kids more than we know. Queer and pre-queer students may never approach educators directly, but take it from these queer adults: they are listening.

Note: All following names have been changed.

Shame

One of the most prominent emotions queer adults report experiencing in middle school is shame. While their peers engage in socialized hetero-sexual dating rituals, queer youth may feel alienated, or excluded, from participating.

"For queer and trans kids," reflects Emily, age 34,

> the feeling of not belonging is more intense, in that you're excluded from things like gossip—talking about who's hot. Middle school is all about sex, and there's a particular confluence of queerness and sex that's especially poisonous, because that's what everyone cares about. Nothing else really matters.

As the social structure of middle school focuses on burgeoning sexuality, queer middle schoolers may respond by going into hiding. A sense of shame can also be triggered by a lack of older role models. Many schools lack any out teachers, staff, or students. This can perpetuate the instinct to deny, suppress, or push natural feelings away.

"It's hard to operate without a role model or someone to guide you," Emily explains.

> When you're that age, it's especially hard to be open about some-thing that no one around you is. For me, it was an environment

where the feelings I was having were being revealed to me as impossible, so there was nothing for me to do other than push them down.

For nonwhite queer middle schoolers, sexuality can exacerbate an already salient feeling of difference. Mercedes, age 32, reflects,

I didn't feel straight, I didn't feel feminine, I didn't feel white. I started going through puberty and that didn't help. People were meaner to me because I had Middle Eastern hair all over my body, and I looked more like a boy so my femininity was questioned. I thought, 'Don't let queerness be another thing I have to grapple with.' I remember praying to God every night, 'Please God, don't let me be a lesbian. I can't have another thing that makes me undesirable to my peers.' I just didn't want to be unhappy.

For transgender and gender-nonconforming teenagers, the element of gender gets added into an already complicated mix. As Faye, age 30, recalls,

I had pain in seeing the other boys going through puberty and realizing, that's never going to happen to me. The sexes were separating. These two worlds were being built in opposition to each other, and there were rules that didn't work for me.

For many, keeping feelings a secret becomes the simplest course of action. As Emily remembers, "I know there were so many kids out there who could have gotten together and talked about it if we were brave enough, but we didn't. We were totally silent."

Confusion and Denial

On the heels of an impulse to suppress or deny one's experience may come profound confusion and denial. Without access to vocabulary or language that conveys the nuances of identity and emotion, personal expression can be lost.

A lack of access to positive role models only worsens the confusion. "In middle school," Faye recounts, "being a happy thriving queer individual was not a possibility for something you could grow into. It wasn't on the menu of puberty. I had zero role models of older happy queer people."

As a result, internal meltdowns may occur. As Megan, 31, relays,

I remember being really confused all of the time, worrying all of the time, being like, 'Am I gay? Am I gay? Am I gay?' And then trying not to think about it and pushing those thoughts away, but still feeling anxious and upset all of the time.

This environment can be particularly disorienting for teenagers whose orientations do not fall on either end of the spectrum, or for those with fluid identities. "For me it was super confusing," recalls Mercedes,

because I wasn't gay and I wasn't straight. I didn't feel masculine or feminine. I was kind of white but also a person of color. I spoke English and Spanish. I always felt in the middle of those things, and I didn't understand which community to relate to.

This resistance to ambiguity can ultimately lead middle schoolers to remain in hiding for longer than they otherwise would. Liz, age 30, remembers the topic of queerness coming up in health class. Her teacher informed the class that people who were gay knew so right away. "Because I was never that sure," she says, "I stayed in the closet longer. I thought, 'gay people know for sure,' because that's what my teacher told us."

Nonbinary students deal with another layer of confusion around socialized gender norms. "I remember sitting in sixth grade," relays Faye, "studying how all of the girls crossed their legs, and feeling like I didn't want to cross my legs that way, but that I had to do it. I thought, 'I have to learn.'"

Lack of perspective as a young teenager aggravates the pressure to conform. "I felt like my middle school was the only place in the world," recounts Emily,

I had no sense of the outside world. You can't get out, but you really want to—you're trapped. You have to go through the motions of trying to fit in, and you feel like you're never going to get out. It's a very airless kind of environment.

Eric, age 51, remembers an attraction to substances as a way of coping with his confusing emotional pain. "I was in eighth grade health class," he relays,

when they told us to stay away from drugs, because they said it would lead to heroin, and that would take away all of our feelings. And I was like, 'Oh, this is the solution I've been looking for. Something to take away all of my feelings.'

Resilience and Strength

Some adults recognize a greater perspective they gained from their experiences as middle schoolers. Anne, now age 76, recalls, "Being marginalized led me to be able to have some idea of what it's like for others to be marginalized in different ways. It sparked my activism."

Liz describes a similar increase in empathy. "I'm white and middle class," she says, "so I saw myself represented in lots of other ways. Because of this one aspect of not seeing myself represented, I am more empathic when I hear of other people's concerns."

For others, an experience of not fitting in led to a natural allegiance to one's authentic self. "Early on," Mercedes shares, "I was able to shed the internalized hatred and decide to be who I am. I thought, 'I cannot want to die every single day. This is not sustainable. I actively refuse.' I moved away from thinking, 'I am the problem,' to see that there were external forces at play."

The experience of being closeted in middle school can, at the very least, lead to an increase in one's survival instinct. "There is something to be said for, 'OK, I survived this,'" cites Eric. "For a sense of, 'Since I survived this, I can really survive anything.'"

Ultimately, however, the experience could have been significantly more supportive for LGBTQ adults in their adolescent years. "There were things that I liked about middle school," asserts Liz. "But about being queer in middle school? There was nothing that I liked."

"It Gets...Tolerable"

First and foremost, queer adults agree that the direct path to improving the LGBTQ middle school experience is to be around other queer people. "If everyone who was LGBTQ had come out," affirms Emily, "it would have gotten a lot better. We needed people to be out."

To this end, the administration holds a critical responsibility to foster an environment where both teachers and students feel comfortable being open about who they are. As Lev, age 29, affirms, "What I would want to hear would be, 'Yep. Some people are gay.'"

"The idea of a gay adult who might be happy would've gone so far," agrees Eric. "I might not have said a word to that person, but I would have felt so much safer in the classroom. It could have made all the difference in the world."

LGBTQ adults point to mentorship as instrumental to supporting queer teens' healthy emotional development. "Some sort of authoritative figure," notes Eric, "who could say, 'There's another side to this. You're not the only one having this experience. Middle school doesn't last forever.' That was never said."

Megan, now a special educator in Providence, Rhode Island, points to the possibility of structured mentoring intervention when issues at school or with peers come up. "People could serve as mentors ad hoc when they're needed," she describes. "Kids could be allowed to do some self-selection for whom they trust and would be willing to talk to." This would provide a more private avenue for seeking help, when going to a teacher may put the middle schooler at risk for appearing to have ratted someone out.

Megan recollects a time in middle school when she was verbally assaulted while changing in the locker room for gym. She recalls,

> I needed advice from an adult on how to respond in a way that worked for me, rather than the adult directly intervening. I did not need anyone to storm in. I needed somebody who could say, 'OK, let's think about how you can respond next time.'

Access to resources is equally huge. Information provides a normalized take on pubescent confusion and acts as a reality check on urban myths and legends. As Eric relates,

> I thought I was the only one having my experience, but the experiences I was having were just a normal part of puberty. I needed resources that said, 'this is a normal part of life.' I needed to know that my straight peers were having some of the same feelings. I needed to know how to have safer sex, and how viruses get passed.

Furthermore, queer adults recommend emphasizing the ambiguity of sexuality and gender. "It's far more nuanced," says Faye, "than your health textbook suggests."

To this end, adults can highlight that it's okay to come out as questioning or fluid. As Liz points out,

> A lot of the conversation is: You decide alone. You come out when you're sure. But middle school's confusing for everyone, and staff can normalize that it's ok to come out even if you're not sure. The sense of isolation lessens through knowing that it's okay to talk about the questioning.

Moreover, for people with fluid identities, that sureness may never come. "Hearing you need to wait until you're sure may be damaging," emphasizes Mercedes. "You may think, 'Well I'm not sure, so I'm just going to stay in the closet forever.'" Normalizing the ambiguity allows the process to unfold in its own time.

Adults can also model compassionate response to difference. While school staff cannot control students' behavior, they can control their strategies for prevention, support, and response.

"Kids are sponges," Megan says. "They absorb what they see modeled. The most adults can be doing is modeling appropriate ways to talk about people who are different."

Furthermore, Megan supports research-based, anti-bullying social skills programs that integrate LGBTQ issues. This way, teachers can refer to a protocol even when they aren't sure of what to do. She suggests incorporating this initiative into the widely used Positive Behavior Interventions and Supports (PBIS) research as an appendix.

"Interacting with people who are different from you is a transferrable skill," she asserts. "If you equip kids with skills that allow them to be respectful to each other despite whatever differences they have, they'll be better equipped to handle the nuances of difference as they get older."

Past to Present: 2017

Finn, a tenth grader in Berkeley who came out as transgender in middle school, has experienced some of the benefits of a school's stronger focus on inclusivity. Finn took refuge in his school's GSA, where he found a strong network of social support. He formed a relationship with the GSA's sponsor, a queer role model who often checked in with Finn to see how he was doing. And the group met virtually no resistance when they chose to put on a school-wide assembly on the Day of Silence.

Yet Finn sat waiting in health class for queerness to be mentioned. "It was definitely disappointing," he recalls. "It wasn't brought up. It never came up once." His decision to come out, he says, was stalled when he heard his friends disclose that they thought it was wrong to be queer. And after coming out, Finn says a lot of his peers continued to use his female birth name, telling him they preferred it to his new one.

While we may glimpse progress toward LGBTQ inclusion and visibility in schools, conditions remain unpredictable and varied, especially in different regions throughout the country. As educators and school professionals, we still have a long way to go. Finn points to the danger of this complacency: "A lot of people think the queer rights movement should be over," he says. "They're like, 'Oh, you passed gay marriage. You're fine now. Why aren't you completely satisfied?' While there are trans people being killed every day."

In both these school board speech and memoir stories, adults look back on the challenges of middle school years and recognize that their identities, struggles, questions, and often unspoken dreams and desires became associated with shame, self-doubt, and personal pain. As they tell it, not seeing themselves reflected in their curriculum or campus culture played a large part in this pain and contributed to a nagging sense of difference and isolation. As teachers, staff, and administrators, we are required by state law and education codes to be inclusive in our curriculum, pedagogy, and school culture. We discuss the "how" of this inclusion in our next chapter on middle school and pedagogy.

Questions for Reflection

1. Reflecting on the poem "Coming Out in Spoken Word," where can you find examples of excavation and expansion in the speaker's identity development?
2. Remembering your middle school experience, how did your self-identity unfold, and in what ways did you find yourself engaging in excavation and expansion? How would you have liked things to be different in order to develop a more positive self-identity?
3. Recognizing that what is not said is just as significant as what is said, what aspects of LGBTQ and gender-diverse communities and experiences are missing from the representations in your curriculum and visibility on your school campus?
4. How do the representations in your middle school that exist portray marginalized groups, particularly LGBTQ communities or individuals (positively or negatively)? Can you improve or enhance those representations, or do they need to be addressed for their stereotypical portrayals?
5. In what ways might you display your willingness to be a safe space and/or mentor for LGBTQ and marginalized students in the school community?

References

Amelia. (2016, April 2). Middle school vs. my gay kid. *Huffington Post*. Retrieved from www.huffingtonpost.com/Amelia/middle-school-vs-my-gay-k_b_9588832.html

Burrill, A. I. (2017, January 31). LGBTQ principal comes out to her community through spoken word. *Huffington Post*. Retrieved from www.huffingtonpost.com/entry/lgbt-principal-comes-out-to-her-community-through-original_us_588f5716e4b06364bb1e27de

Caskey, M. M., & Anfara, V. A., Jr. (2007). Research summary: Young adolescents' developmental characteristics. Retrieved from www.nmsa.org/Research/Research Summaries/DevelopmentalCharacteristics/tabid/1414/Default.aspx

DeBord, G. (1967). *Society of the spectacle*. Black and Red Publishers. Retrieved from www.marxists.org/reference/archive/debord/society.htm

GLSEN. (2015). National School Climate Survey: The experiences of lesbian, gay, bisexual, transgender, and queer youth. Retrieved from www.glsen.org/sites/default/files/2015%20National%20GLSEN%202015%20National%20School%20Climate%20Survey%20%28NSCS%29%20-%20Full%20Report_0.pdf

Lee, N. (2001). *Childhood and society: Growing up in the age of uncertainty.* Buckingham: Open House Press.

Meyer, I. H. (2003). Prejudice, social stress, and mental health in lesbian, gay, and bisexual populations: Conceptual issues and research evidence. *Psychological Bulletin, 129*(5), 674–697.

Peterson, C., Matthews, A., Copps-Smith, E., & Conard, L. (2017). Suicidality, self-harm, and body dissatisfaction in transgender adolescents and emerging adults with gender dysphoria. *Suicide & Life-threatening Behavior, 47*(4), 475–482.

Swaim, S., Lounsbury, J., & Brazee, E. (2003). *This we believe: Keys to educating young adolescents.* Westerville, OH: National Middle School Association.

The Trevor Project. (2016). Facts about suicide. Retrieved from www.thetrevorproject.org/resources/preventing-suicide/facts-about-suicide/

6

MIDDLE SCHOOL CURRICULUM

A student has been visiting your middle school math classroom weekly at lunch, to eat, chat with you, and sometimes read a book. Today, without warning or introduction, the student confided, "I go by the pronoun, 'they.' I don't identify as male or female. I haven't told my parents. I have only told one friend. Can you call me 'they' at lunch? But only at lunch." You are not sure what to say or do. You have heard about other teachers in the district who have worked with trans and gender-expansive youth and their families, but this is the first time a twelve-year-old has shared their nonbinary gender identity with you. You try to build a safe space, but you have never directly talked about gender or other identities, communities, or histories in your classroom. What does identity have to do with middle school math? Why doesn't this student want to share their gender identity more openly? How can you build a more inclusive community among your students, so they feel safe, while teaching math at the same time? You are perplexed but want to reach out. You turn to them and smile. "Thanks for sharing with me. I can definitely use 'they' at lunch. Are there any other ways I can support you?"

After school, you start to brainstorm. You sign up to attend an LGBTQ (lesbian, gay, bisexual, trans and queer) Safe Space training with your district next month and secure a rainbow flag sticker to the corner of your classroom window. You understand that your student's identity is outside gender norms, and you are learning different terms like being nonbinary. You want to embrace this expansiveness as part of your classroom norm. But you are still uncertain how to build an inclusive space with a mathematics curriculum. You turn on the computer and start to search. You stumble upon a website called Radical Math and find several examples of ways to integrate social justice into various math topics. It feels a bit overwhelming. You are worried about drawing too much attention to students who are exploring their gender or sexuality, so you decide to integrate several social justice topics across the rest of the school year. Perhaps you could utilize data graphs and charts related to topics such as the school-to-prison pipeline, LGBTQ homelessness and dropout rates, and the impact of gender stereotypes in media. But it is simply overwhelming. You continue searching online and stumble upon a GLSEN example that seems like a perfect place to start (GLSEN, 2014):

> *Grade 7 — Statistics and Probability 7.SP*
>
> — *Use random sampling to draw inferences about a population.*
> — *Understand that statistics can be used to gain information about a popu-lation by examining a sample of the population; generalizations about a population from a sample are valid only if the sample is representative of that population. Understand that random sampling tends to produce repre-sentative samples and support valid inferences.*

SUGGESTED LGBT-INCLUSIVE LEARNING OPPORTUNITY:

> *Use GLSEN's 2015 National School Climate Survey in an activity to explore population samples as they relate to the experiences of LGBTQ students.*

The next day, your student comes in at lunch, and you talk to them about your idea. Your statistics unit starts next week. Your student asks you to talk generally but not mention them in particular. You nod in agreement, committed to whatever allied stance your student needs you to take. You are ready to get started!

The teacher in this vignette understands the relationship between a safe school environment, a curriculum, and the pedagogy of the classroom. While the teacher is not new to learning about students' gender and sexual identities, there is uncer-tainty about how to be inclusive during instructional time, particularly in content areas that are not directly or explicitly related to the study of society and culture.

Curriculum is a contested space through which many stakeholders respond to questions, like *what knowledge should be taught, and how? What are the goals for education more broadly in society and specifically for middle school students at the beginnings of adolescent identity development? Can/should we teach subject matter con-tent that is decontextualized from the social, cultural, political, and economic contexts in which our students, their peer groups, and their families live?* (Dillon, 2009). These questions demonstrate that curriculum is ideological, even when the content seems neutral or objective. What the curriculum omits, hides, or marginalizes also teaches us something about the society we live in and what it values and believes (Apple, 2013; Kelly, Luke, & Green, 2008). The statistics about mid-dle school LGBTQ youth beg us to understand their sociocultural contexts; the bias-based bullying they experience; and the unhealthy risk-taking, such as alcohol and substance abuse, they sometimes turn to when they feel unsafe or rejected (GLSEN, 2015). Disproportionately, LGBTQ middle school youth hear biased language from both students and educators; experience harassment and assault, and anti-LGBTQ discrimination; experience the effects of a hostile school climate on educational outcomes and psychological well-being; and have limited availability and utility of supportive school resources.

As teachers, we can address safety and inclusion through our curriculum, such as through positive representations of LGBTQ people, their contributions and accomplishments, and the evaluation of oppressions and inequities in history and today. Through curricular explorations, our LGBTQ students will feel seen, heard, and valued by everyone in the room. As teachers, we can work to be responsive to our students' cultural lives and be aware of the identities they work from and through in the classroom. GLSEN (2014) suggests guiding our reflection on the curriculum by asking,

- *How inclusive is my curriculum of LGBTQ people, history, and events?*
- *How can I provide a curriculum that has windows and mirrors for all my students?*
- *How can I ensure that the inclusion of LGBTQ-related curricular content is connected, contextualized, and inclusive of multiple intersectional experiences?*

In this chapter, we take a sociocultural approach to curriculum, asking educators to utilize real-life examples of social experiences as the textual content for discussions, activities, and assignments in middle school. A sociocultural approach also means scaffolding engagement so that all participants co-construct knowledge through meaningful exchanges of language using cultural tools (Eun, 2010).

For example, curriculum can include engagement with social policies, court decisions, and examples of lived inclusions and exclusions across cultures and histories. In language arts or social studies, we can look at the case of Loving v. Virginia (1967), which ended interracial marriage bans. We can write compare/contrast essays in relation to the Obergefell v. Hodges (2015) case, which decided that same-sex marriage is a fundamental right. Students can express their perspectives in written form or by using various multimedia tools that allow them to integrate video blogs and analysis of news media and popular culture. Additionally, we can look at the text of the Civil Rights Act of 1964, which enumerates protected classes that cannot be discriminated against, including ethnicity, religion, national origin, age, sex (including sexual orientation and gender identity), pregnancy, citizenship, familial status, disability status, and veteran status. We can compare/contrast public policies and civil rights activism before and after the passing of this act, such as through the graphic novel trilogy *March* by John Lewis, the *Black Lives Matter* manifesto, and the speeches and actions of undocumented feminist trans activist Jennicet Gutiérrez (Democracy Now, 2015).

We can also include video-based classroom discussions, such as "Race Visibility and Safe Spaces" (PBS Learning Media, n.d.), which explores how youth created safe spaces for themselves as gay and trans people of color through media production and community gatherings. We can examine what it means to build safe spaces, and then evaluate the safety of spaces at school and in our communities. We can ask students to evaluate the ways in which privilege and power impact their lives through the use of identity mapping and role play (Safe Zone Project, n.d.). We can use the Perspectives for a Diverse America database from Teaching Tolerance to help us select pieces of literature from LGBTQ authors, authors with disabilities, and authors of color that connect thematically with our discussions (Teaching Tolerance, n.d.). In whatever ways we decide to integrate students' lives, positionalities, and histories into the curriculum, we should work from an intersectional perspective and teach critical perspective taking.

Intersectionality

The aforementioned curricular examples attend to multiple identities, or intersectionality, such as those related to gender, sexual orientation, and race/ethnicity. When we teach from an intersectional sociocultural perspective, we consider both the identities that are present and absent in the curriculum, and how our students experience the curriculum through their own identities and in relation to multiple forms of bias, discrimination, or oppression. Intersectionality is a theory we can use to understand oppression in relation to identity differences. Bell (2016) provides this example:

> Ninth-grader Nicole is a mature, creative, hardworking student who gets along well with others. But she's always late for school, frequently misses her first-period class and rarely submits homework in any classes. Needless to say, her grades are suffering. Nicole's teachers know very little about her life. When they look at her, they see an African-American student who isn't doing well. They also see a typical example of the deep racial disparities that exist within absenteeism and dropout rates nationwide.
>
> But a teacher who took the time to peel back the layers of Nicole's identity would see another characteristic—her socio-economic status—and a more nuanced understanding would emerge. Nicole isn't just a black student; she's also a girl from a low-income family who bears the responsibility of taking care of her two younger siblings. To fully and adequately support Nicole, an educator must see her situation through an intersectional lens: recognizing that race-, gender- and class-related circumstances are contributing to her achievement issues.

When examining our curriculum and selecting new texts from an intersectional, sociocultural perspective, we should consider both the positionalities from which we view the world and the ways in which power is/has been leveraged in exclusionary and oppressive ways toward particular identities and groups via the curriculum (Krenshaw, 1991). We can affirm students' complex, lived identities and explore how bias impacts us on a daily basis at school and in the world. We can ask students to examine the role of language in shaping our values, beliefs, and ways of seeing the world.

For example, curriculum often contains binary-based, socially constructed categories of identity, such as through representations of disability/ability or masculinity/femininity in youth literature. We can examine these binaries in relation to multiple identity communities in order to inform our support of LGBTQ and gender diversity inclusion in school. Solis (2004) suggests,

> As teachers analyze the "legitimate" or "official" knowledge of the medical (deficit) model of disability, they will begin to uncover how those who position themselves as members of the "nondisabled privileged" use ableism discourses to produce disability. These disabled "Others" in turn are constructed as a homogeneous and powerless group that are either helpless victims and/or weak and undeserving.
>
> Therefore, I want to emphasize that the construction of the disabled subject can only result from recognizing disability as divergent from nondisability. If personal opinion is formed in terms of disability being manufactured in relation to the other or nondisabled, then in what ways do opinions fixed on the "other" empower the nondisabled other whom it privileges and disempower the disabled other whom it does not favor? And, how might we begin to reconceptualize a framework wherein nondisabled subjects do not necessarily or exclusively operate relative to their disabled others?
>
> *(screen 13)*

Binary-based categories privilege some to the disempowerment of others. As teachers, we can examine whose identities are being positioned at the center as the normative experience and whose identities are being Othered, marginalized, or constructed as abnormal in relation to the center (Crenshaw, 1991). When we construct queerness and disabled bodies from a deficit-lens—as not-the-norm—we are operating from a rehabilitation standpoint so as to bring these subjects/students/identities into closer alignment with the unspoken norm. These cultural messages and deficit orientations are often communicated through the curriculum.

We can explore language-based social constructions in many subject areas, such as in the analysis of stories that gendered and heteronormative language tell about the roles of men and women, boys and girls, masculine and feminine. For example, Campo-Engelstein and Johnson (2013) examined middle school science textbooks to determine how the concept of fertilization is explained, particularly in relation to gender-biased language constructing a "fairytale" about the active male sperm and the passive female egg. They cite The Biology and Gender Study Group (1988): "masculinist assumptions have impoverished biology by causing us to focus on certain problems to the exclusion of others, and they have led us to make particular interpretations when equally valid alternatives were available" (p. 62). In science and other subject areas, we can ask our students to become *textbook detectives*, analyzing the norms, values, and assumptions constructed in the curriculum's binary-based narratives (Bigelow, 1994). We can also ask what intersectional stories remain untold and what questions remain unasked or uninvestigated as a result of current textbook narratives.

In our efforts to reform and reenvision the curriculum, equity and queer literacy frameworks, described in Chapter 3, are also useful. Both frameworks begin with curricula that focus on the assets and identities students bring to the classroom. Equity literacy takes an allied stance toward multiple identity communities who have been impacted by inequitable policies and practices in schools and communities. A queer literacy framework asks us to deconstruct and dismantle rigid gender norms and heteronormative assumptions in our own thinking, in policies and practices of school, and at work in the curriculum.

Miller (2015) identifies five specific actions teachers can take:

- Refrain from possible presumptions that students are heterosexual or ascribe to an assumed gender
- Open up spaces for students to self-define with chosen (a) genders, (b) sexuality, (c) pronouns or names
- Engage in ongoing critique of how gender norms are reinforced in literature, media, technology, art, history, science, math, and so forth
- Advocate for equity across all categories of (a) gender and (b) sexuality orientations
- Ensure that students who identify on a continuum of gender and sexual minorities (GSM) will learn in environments free of bullying and harassment.

Relatedly, Wargo (2017) suggests working from a [q]ulturally sustaining pedagogy, in which normative sexual orientations and gender assumptions and expectations are "hacked," allowing the normalization of fluidity and continuum orientations toward identities. Such "hacking" means decentering power and taken-for-granted beliefs about intersectional identities. In this case, Wargo and his student teachers ask middle school students to interrogate and remix gender identities using classic fairy tale rhymes. In another study, Wargo (2017) works with LGBTQ students to construct their imagined and real selves through snapping selfies as identity texts and publicly displaying curated artifacts as life streams. In this project, the students utilize photography and Web 2.0 tools online to tell stories of self. The texts became spaces through which students could navigate memories of homophobia at school and accept themselves in this more fluid, expansive space.

In another example, San Ramon, California, middle school students and teachers created an LGBT Acceptance Week in April 2016. They developed a week-long activity about safety and respect, with a specific focus on LGBTQ students. While the week was met with some concern and contention in the community, it was implemented with success (Hollyfield, 2016). Leadership students at the middle school identified a concern for students' safety and wanted to create and implement curriculum to address it. Here is an example of the types of activities for a middle school Identity Week activity series:

IDENTITY WEEK AT THE MIDDLE SCHOOL

iWeek: Celebrating who we are

Day One: iDENTITY (express yourself)
- Dress up in clothes that say something about you
- Film Screening: *That's a Family*
- Workshops: Create a Selfie, "What are your dreams?"

Day Two: iMPACT (No Name-Calling Day)
- Film Screening: *A Place in the Middle*
- Workshops: Somos gente (learn a language).

Day Three: iNTERVENE (Be an Ally Day)
- Film Screening: *Let's Get Real*
- Workshops: Poetry Wall (build a selfie/poem mural).

Day Four: iNSPIRE (wear your school color)
- Panel of Americans assembly
- School community lunch palooza: Mix it Up Quotable Quotes and What Do We Have in Common?

Web Resource Links

A Place in the Middle: http://aplaceinthemiddle.org
Let's Get Real: https://www.groundspark.org/download/LGR_guide.pdf
Mix It Up: https://www.tolerance.org/mix-it-up
That's a Family: https://www.newday.com/film/thats-family
In these intersectional, sociocultural curricular examples, there is a strong relationship between curriculum and pedagogy: the interplay between the texts we choose to teach from, how we choose to engage with those texts, and the ways in which we center youth experiences during learning. We will explore one more curricular approach and then introduce two stories of practice from middle school educators for your reflection.

Critical Perspective Taking

One way to support LGBTQ and gender diversity inclusion is through teaching critical perspective taking. We can do this through a *critical media literacy* framework that helps us analyze popular media and its reinforcement of dominant ideologies that influence culture, oppress certain groups, and influence the purchasing of products (Chira, 2017). In particular, Kellner and Share (2005) suggest that critical media literacy teaches both about and through media, applying the following core principles:

- All media messages are constructed
- Messages are constructed using a creative language with its own rules
- Different people experience the same media message differently
- Media have embedded values and points of view
- Media are organized to gain profit and/or power.

Similar to taking on the role of textbook detectives, students can become *cultural investigators* as they decode popular culture (advertisements, music videos, political cartoons, films, and TV) images and their messages, and create counter images, messages, and narratives to articulate the relationship between self, others, knowledge, and power (Gainer, 2010). For example, Muslim youth slam poet Suhaiymah Manzoor-Khan comments on media-based efforts to produce antibias messages about Muslim people (Blumberg, 2017). She utilizes rhythm, imagery, and emotion to decenter media-based, antibias, and inclusion efforts, and shows the impact of a narrow focus on extraordinary examples of Muslim leadership and activism. She states, "If you need me to prove my humanity," she said, "I'm not the one who's not human."

To assist students as cultural investigators, the Critical Media Project is concerned about the ways in which media constructs oppressive binary categories that embed meanings about race and ethnicity.

Dominant	Subordinate
civilized	primitive
modern	backward
rational	irrational
order	chaos
center	margin
stability	violence
unmarked	marked
self	other
white	nonwhite
superior	inferior
majority	minority
citizen	illegal
insider	outsider

We can see how these binaries are also constructed in the media about gender. Trier-Bieniek and Leavy (2014) write,

> There are often representations of males in situation comedies where male characters are shown to be incompetent in childcare or housework, and this in turn becomes the source of comedy. Another common example is that female characters in films are typically obsessed with their romantic relationships and can even appear "psycho" as they try to land a man…
>
> *(p. 4)*

As cultural investigators, students can critically disrupt messages that limit, diminish, or erase experiences outside an assumed gender-binary, heteronormative center. Puchner, Markowitz and Hedley (2015) worked with middle school students to examine television commercials and print advertisements for gender stereotypes and sexist portrayals, including images or negative messages typically associated with men or women. Then they created video advertisements that challenged gender stereotypes in occupations. Similarly, Gainer (2010) worked with middle school students to read various media texts that related to adolescents and schooling. They analyzed messages about youth of color, interpreting them as narrow and stereotypical. Then, the students created counter media in ways that they viewed were more realistic and authentic to their lived experiences.

When examining popular media narratives like television and film, we can evaluate texts using both the tools of critics and students' own critical criteria for evaluation. For example, feminist cartoonist Bechdel (1986) created a rule for films with positive portrayals of women: *Do you, movie, feature two or more named women? Do they talk to each other? About something besides a guy?* If so, then the film passed the Bechdel test. Since then, Waldman (2014) notes that many critics, including Roxanne Gay, have elaborated on this rule to gauge if a film has strong gender-diverse character representation:

1. A woman's story is being told. She is not relegated to the role of sidekick, romantic interest, or bit player.
2. Her world is populated with intelligent women who also have stories worth telling, even if their stories aren't the focus of the movie.
3. If she must engage in a romantic storyline, she doesn't have to compromise her sanity or common sense for love.
4. At least half the time, this woman needs to be a woman of color and/or a transgender woman and/or a queer woman because all these women exist! Though she is different, her story should not focus solely on this difference because she is a sum of her parts. She is not the token. She has friends who look like her, so they need to show up once in a while.

5. She cannot live in an inexplicably perfect apartment in an expensive city with no visible means of affording said inexplicably perfect apartment.
6. She doesn't have to live up to an unrealistic feminist standard. She can and should be human. She just needs to be intelligent and witty and interesting in the way women, the world over, are, if we ever got a chance to really know them on the silver screen.

Relatedly, Common Sense Media has created a metric rating gender, specifically asking if films combat gender stereotypes. We can use this rating metric as a curricular tool in the classroom to help us raise questions about cultural production, including those identified by Chira (2017):

> How to strike the balance between overall quality and specific gender roles? What if a strong female character opts for a traditional role as wife and mother? Will recommendations that feature girls and boys reaching beyond traditional gender roles alienate some parents [or audiences more broadly]?

The Critical Media Project (n.d.) poses additional questions about sexual orientation:

> Have you ever wondered…why there aren't more gay and lesbian characters on television or in movies?…whether gay and lesbian characters are portrayed differently than their straight counterparts? …why stories about gay and lesbians tend to revolve exclusively around their sexuality and sexual orientation?

The Project also poses these questions about race and ethnicity:

• How are different racial and ethnic groups represented in entertainment, advertising, and news media?
• How are certain news stories covered or stories told based on the race and ethnicity of those involved?
• What specific images, words, and sounds contribute to our understanding of how a specific race or ethnicity is portrayed?
• Do the media make assumptions about what certain races do for work and for fun? Do the media assume that certain races only live in particular neighborhoods, drive certain cars, or listen to a single type of music? Does it assume that certain races predominantly seek government aid or commit crimes? Does it assume certain races are more openly sexual or sexually aggressive?
• What impact do these representations and assumptions have on the opportunities and possibilities for individuals of different races and ethnicities in their personal and professional lives? Do some groups experience social, political, and economic inequities more than others?

We can compare and contrast media messages in popular films and in independent documentaries like *Straightlaced: How Gender's Got Us All Tied Up* (Groundspark), *Gender: The Space Between* (CBS), and *The Gender Revolution* (National Geographic). We can further explore popular media messages in relation to films that encourage intersectional critical thinking about social justice and inclusion, such as *He Named Me Malala* (2015) and *Los Graduados* (2013).

In the following stories, we will see how a middle school teacher provides an opportunity for students to gain knowledge about gender and sexual minorities. In "Books Are Like Onions: Gender and Children's Literature," we see a lesson in which students analyze the gender roles portrayed in literature and critically define gender norms present in their own lived experiences. In both, teachers who identify as allies and LGBTQ in their communities speak from their own experiences.

STORY ONE: "Now who can tell me what transgender means? This one's a little tricky." by Julie Tarney

Originally published at: http://mysonwearsheels.com/2014/05/

As about 30 sixth graders filed into a classroom at PS/IS89 in lower Manhattan yesterday, my new friend Kalima, who just graduated from college on Thursday, drew a capital P on the chalkboard. Underneath it, one at a time, she added four more letters to read:

P

F

L

A

G

Next to each letter she wrote out the name of the organization that she, Susan and I were there representing: Parents, Families and Friends of Lesbian and Gay, Bisexual and Transgender People (PFLAG). Next to that she added another acronym: LGBTQ, for lesbian, gay, bisexual, transgender, queer/questioning.

This was my first PFLAG "Safe Schools" presentation, so I was there as an observer. It was foreign for me to see the terms of gender identity and sexual orientation on a classroom chalkboard. That never would have happened when I was in middle school in the sixties. I'd never even heard those words at that age. And I wished there had been volunteers like Kalima and Susan available to speak at my son's middle school in Milwaukee in 2001. I marveled at the progress of public education.

The desks in the room had been pushed back in a semi-circle around a large area rug so many of the kids were sitting comfortably on the floor when Kalima turned to face them. She introduced herself and asked for a

FIGURE 6.1 Kalima introduces PFLAG to a sixth-grade class. Photo by Julie
Tarney.

volunteer to read what was on the board. She explained that PFLAG was
an organization that comes to schools so that a parent or family member
of someone's who's gay, or a gay person, can tell his or her personal story.
"How many of you have had a conversation about anything regarding
this topic before?" Kalima asked. Most hands went up. But when she
asked if the subject had ever been discussed at school, some hands went
down.

"This is a space where we *can* talk about these topics, because it's not
really talked about in some homes or in a lot of schools. Here it's okay."

She told them she wanted to define the terms that were going to be
used in her story and in Susan's story as a PFLAG mom. And she asked
for volunteers to explain each of the words. A lot of hands went up. The
kids were smart, and Kalima helped them zero in on keys words for the
exact definitions. For example, a lesbian is a woman who's "attracted"
to another woman. After Kalima replied, "That's right" to the girl who
defined transgender, several voices popped up with "What?" or "What
was that?" And I heard one ask, "Plastic surgery?"

Kalima repeated the girl's answer: A transgender person is someone
who is born one gender but in your mind and your heart you feel like
you're the opposite gender. "Some may choose to have surgery to make
their outside match how they feel on the inside," she said. "Or they may
choose not to have surgery and just dress a certain way."

Susan then told her story as a mom of two boys, the youngest of whom grew up to identify as gay. She engaged the kids with questions about going to Toys R Us to illustrate society's unfair labeling of toys. She led them through the hurtfulness of name-calling and teasing and the sadness that resulted. They learned her youngest son had come out to her at age 14 and to his school at age 15. Their faces lit when she told them her son and his boyfriend were the first gay couple at the school's prom, and that all the kids and the parents who attended had applauded them.

Kalima shared what she described as a sheltered childhood, where she was taught that women married men and vice versa. She didn't know anyone who was gay growing up; she didn't even know what it meant. She did know she didn't have the same feelings about boys as her girlfriends, and she was confused by feelings she had for her best girlfriend. It wasn't before she'd withdrawn at school and wished she were invisible that Kalima realized she was gay. The first person she told was her best friend, who said she already kind of knew and it didn't matter; they were still best friends.

The kids' questions afterwards were great. They wanted to know if Kalima had a girlfriend. And they asked what Susan's youngest son was doing now. After each of two of the presentations, a boy came up to Kalima and asked if there was someone a friend could email with a question. "It's not me," both of them said.

I left the school energized and optimistic about this next generation of kids. They're the ones who will continue to shape the evolution of society's openness, understanding and acceptance of the LGBTQ community to be who they are and love who they love. And I was happy, too, with the addition of another descriptor for myself: I am a PFLAG mom.

FIGURE 6.2 PFLAG Mom Susan shares her story with the class. Photo by Julie Tarney.

STORY TWO: "Books Are Like Onions: Gender and Children's Literature" by Andrew Pegan

"Books are like onions," I said to the stunned silence of my middle school classroom. "No, seriously."

Moments earlier, my students had been laughing as Shrek (Mike Myers) explained to Donkey (Eddie Murphy) how Ogres were like onions, and yet I am met with total and complete silence.

> I'll prove it. Today we are going to read two examples of children's literature: *Brothers of the Knight* by Debbie Allen and *The Seven Chinese Sisters* by Kathy Tucker. We aren't just going to read them for comprehension, but instead we are going to look at how gender norms are represented, reinforced, and challenged in the stories. We are going to push far beyond the surface level and reach for something more.

Examining gender norms was not a new topic in my class. In the previous school year, we had read a novel that explicitly dealt with gender norms. The novel focused on a young Mongol Princess during the time of Genghis Khan who wanted to join the army and be a soldier. Throughout the book, characters frequently made reference to the main characters' rejection of traditional gender norms. This year, the stories we would analyze were not explicitly about someone defying gender norms. These were children's stories that had a rich subtext reinforcing or confronting gender norms.

"Before we start, there are a few vocabulary words you need to know." I provided them with definitions for norms, gender, and stereotypes. After defining the terms, I began a discussion about gender, norms, and stereotypes. "What characteristics do we associate with being a Male?" I ask. Hands shoot into the air.

"*Strong*" was one student's response. "*Brave*" was another's. We ended up with a list that also included *loud, short hair, big muscles, tall, goofy, handsome*, and *athletic*.

"What characteristics do we typically associate with being Female?" I continued. *Caring, nice, smart, long hair, shorter, less muscular, compassionate*, and *pretty* made the list.

"What kinds of activities do we associate with Males and Females enjoying?" was my next question. According to my students, males like sports, video games, and hanging out with their friends while girls prefer cooking, cleaning, and talking on the phone with their friends.

With a solid representation of traditional gender norms established, we read the two children's stories. These lists remained present on the whiteboard as we read, a reference point for my students to remind them of their characterization of gender norms.

As we read, we took notes on key events in each story and on times when gender norms were confirmed or challenged by different characters. In summary, *Brothers of The Knight* focuses on a group of brothers whose greatest passion in life is dancing, and *The Seven Chinese Sisters* is about a group of sisters who have to fight off a dragon that is endangering their youngest sister.

After reading the stories we began our next discussion. I asked, "How did the stories reinforce the gender norms we listed earlier?"

"Well in *The Seven Chinese Sisters* a couple of the sisters cooked and cleaned which is something girls do," one student offers.

"The Brothers lie to their father and sneak out at night, which seems like something that boys would do," offers another student.

"Good. How do the stories challenge gender norms?"

A half-dozen hands shot into the air. "Well the girls are really aggressive and fight off a big dragon which is not something I would think of girls doing," says one student. "And the boys like dancing which is something I would have thought girls like more."

The conversation continued like this for several minutes, with students continuing to come up with examples of challenges to gender norms. Then I asked, "What skills are required to be a good baseball player?" My students listed several qualities, including lots of practice, following the coach's directions, and good hand-eye coordination. "What about being a good baker?" I asked. This list includes lots of practice, ability to follow recipes exactly, and good at measuring.

"So," I said, "If the skills are roughly the same why do we associate the jobs to different genders?" My students talked among themselves for a few minutes, and eventually, we collectively arrived at this: "That is how we see them on TV."

"Interesting. So where do gender norms come from?" The list was long, but mostly, the students focused on mass media (books, TV, movies, and magazines), their peers, and adults in their lives (parents, extended family, and teachers). I then asked, "How can gender norms influence young people like yourselves?" Some students offered some positives, like norms help you know how to act or how to dress. However, most students found gender norms limiting and confining. They said that it could keep someone from doing something they really want to do or keep them from being themselves.

One student also mentioned that it is really hard for transgender people who feel pressured to look and act a certain way even though that is not who they are. The students reacted very tentatively to this new thought as it was not one we had spent much time previously discussing. Several students who are members of our schools Kaleidoscope Club (a club that focuses on creating a safe space for all students) came to dominate this portion of the discussion, offering up some additional thoughts by seeking to educate their peers about what being transgender means and how gender norms impact transgender people. Their insights were based on activities and discussions that took place during the Kaleidoscope Club meetings and served to provide the rest of the class with a deeper understanding of the topic.

To close the lesson, I described what a rich and thoughtful conversation we just had based on two children's stories. I explained that any story, when examined through the right "frame," can become the foundation for a deep and critical analysis.

"Books have layers," I say, "Just like onions." And people.

Questions for Reflection

1. How will you evaluate your curriculum to ensure that it provides windows and mirrors that include representations of all your students' identities as well as the larger community? Which identities are present, and which are missing in the curriculum?
2. Is your curricular content inclusive of multiple intersectional experiences?
3. In what ways can you frame the textual content for discussions, activities, and assignments in your classroom to ensure that they include real-life examples of social experiences?
4. What kinds of bias, discrimination, or oppression do your students experience? How will you obtain that information? How might you counter that through your curriculum content?
5. Which Equity and/or Queer Literacy framework might you use to guide you in deconstructing rigid gender norms and heteronormative assumptions in your teaching and when working with the curriculum?

References

Apple, M. (2013). *Knowledge, power, and education: The selected works of Michael W. Apple*. New York, NY: Routledge, Taylor and Francis Group.

Bechdel, A. (1986). *Dykes to watch out for*. Ithaca, NY: Firebrand Books.

Bell, M. K. (2016, Summer). Teaching at the intersections. Honor and teach about your students' multiple identities. *Teaching Tolerance*. Retrieved from www.tolerance.org/magazine/summer-2016/teaching-at-the-intersections

Bigelow, B. (1994). *Rethinking our classrooms: Teaching for equity and justice.* Milwaukee, WI: Rethinking Schools.

Blumberg, A. (2017, July 5). If you need me to prove my humanity, I'm not the one who's not human. *Huffington Post.* Retrieved from www.huffingtonpost.com/entry/suhaiymah-manzoor-khan-slam-poet_us_595d26c9e4b0da2c7326cf5c

Campo-Engelstein, L., & Johnson, N. L. (2013). Revisiting "the fertilization fairytale:" An analysis of gendered language used to describe fertilization in science textbooks from middle school to medical school. *Cultural Studies of Science Education, 9*(1), 201–220.

Chira, S. (2017, June 20). A new rating for TV and movies tries to combat gender stereotypes. *The New York Times.* Retrieved from www.nytimes.com/2017/06/20/arts/common-sense-media-ratings-gender.html

Crenshaw, K. (1991). Mapping the margins: Intersectionality, identity politics, and violence against women of color. *Stanford Law Review, 43*(6), 1241–1299.

The Critical Media Project. (n.d.). Retrieved from www.criticalmediaproject.org/cml/topicbackground/lgbt/

Democracy Now. (2015, June 25). *Undocumented Trans Activist Jennicet Guiterrez Challenges Obama on Deportations at White House* [Video File]. Retrieved from www.youtube.com/watch?v=ER9_M002aQY&feature=youtu.be

Dillon, J. (2009). The questions of curriculum. *Journal of Curriculum Studies, 41*(3), 343–359.

Eun, B. (2010). From learning to development: A sociocultural approach to instruction. *Cambridge Journal of Education, 40*(4), 401–418.

Gainer, J. S. (2010). Critical media literacy in middle school: Exploring the politics of representation. *Journal of Adolescent & Adult Literacy, 53*(5), 364–373.

The Gay, Lesbian & Straight Education Network. (2014). *Developing LGBT-Inclusive Classroom Resources.* Retrieved from www.glsen.org/sites/default/files/LGBT%20incl%20curr%20guide.pdf

The Gay, Lesbian & Straight Education Network. (2015). *National Climate Survey.* Retrieved from www.glsen.org/article/2015-national-school-climate-survey

Hollyfield, A. (2016, April 11). Controversial LGBTQ acceptance week begins at San Ramon school. *ABC 7 News.* Retrieved from http://abc7news.com/education/lgbtq-acceptance-week-begins-at-san-ramon-school/1285765/

Kellner, D., & Share, J. (2005). Toward critical media literacy: Core concepts, debates, organizations and policy. *Discourse: Studies in the Cultural Politics of Education, 26*(3), 369–386.

Kelly, G., Luke, A., & Green, J. (2008). What counts as knowledge in educational settings: Disciplinary knowledge, assessment, and curriculum. *Review of Research in Education, 32*(1), Vii–X.

Miller, sj. (2015). A queer literacy framework promoting (a)gender and (a)sexuality self-determination and justice. *English Journal, 104*(5), 37–44.

PBS Learning Media. (n.d.). *Race, Visibility and Safe Spaces* [Video File]. Retrieved from https://ca.pbslearningmedia.org/resource/fp17.lgbtq.space.racevissaf/race-visibility-and-safe-spaces/#.We4wvhNSzLY

Puchner, L., Markowitz, L., & Hedley, M. (2015). Critical media literacy and gender: Teaching middle school students about gender stereotypes and occupations. *Journal of Media Literacy Education, 7*(2), 23–24.

Safe Zone Project. (n.d.). *Privilege for Sale(+) (Gender ID Focused Ed).* Retrieved from http://thesafezoneproject.com/activity/privilege-for-sale-gender-id-focused-ed/

Solis, S. (2004). The disability making factory. *Disability Studies Quarterly, 24*(1). Retrieved at http://dsq-sds.org/article/view/851/1026

Teaching Tolerance. (n.d.). *Educating for a Diverse Democracy.* Retrieved from www.tolerance.org/

Trier-Bieniek, A., & Leavy, P. (2014). *Gender and pop culture: A text-reader.* Rotterdam: Sense Publishers.

Waldman, K. (2014, January 7). The Bechdel test sets the bar too low. Let's write a new one. *Slate.* Retrieved from www.slate.com/blogs/xx_factor/2014/01/07/the_bechdel_test_needs_an_update_we_ve_set_the_bar_for_female_representation.html

Wargo, J. M. (2017) "Every selfie tells a story…": LGBTQ youth lifestreams and new media narratives as connective identity texts. *New Media & Society, 19*(4), 560–578.

7

MIDDLE SCHOOL PEDAGOGY

*As you enter the parking lot of the local middle school, you quickly notice the rainbow col-
ored "Safe Space" posters hanging from the windows of several classrooms. Upon entering
the office to sign in, you see posters of students in multicultural settings and phrases such
as "All are welcomed here." It is refreshing to see that, in the critical middle school years,
students are being surrounded by positive, inclusive messages.*

*You just started teaching social studies here, and a colleague has invited you to attend
the PFLAG (Parents and Friends of Lesbians and Gays) Speaker's Bureau as part of
the Gay–Straight Alliance (GSA) beginning-of-the-year activities. You are excited to see
that several counselors, the group's teacher advisor, and another teacher are using their
lunchtime to participate in an effort to educate themselves as well as support students in the
GSA as you all learn more about the LGBTQ (lesbian, gay, bisexual, transgender and
queer) community. The classroom is so packed with students that the custodian brought in
extra chairs, and then stayed to listen!*

*Each PFLAG speaker shares a personal story, and then asks who feels safe at school.
The audience is comprised of students who identified as gay, lesbian, transgender, and
straight allies. Most raise their hands. The speakers then lead a discussion about "gender
binaries." You participate in a brainstorm, associating words, traits, jobs, roles, and other
ideas with the words "Boy" and "Girl" written on a T-chart. The students call out
words like "pants" for the "Boy's" side and "dress" for the "Girl's" side, then blue/
pink, tough/sensitive, and so on. The facilitator then talks about how these words are
gender stereotypes that do not reflect our lived experiences: for example, an individual
can be a boy and wear dresses and like to play soccer or dance while being attracted to
the same and/or opposite sex. The group also discusses the differences between biological
sex, gender identity, gender expression, and sexual orientation or desire, and the fact
that each of us can fall anywhere on each spectrum. This concept is new to some of the
participants, including you. (Note: see definitions in Chapter One and in the book's
Appendix).*

At the conclusion the workshop, the GSA advisor asks for resources that he will add to the student collection. As a new teacher on campus, you are in awe of the incredible work that is being done at this school to be inclusive and welcoming. You also learn about the school's gender-neutral dress code and its webpage's links to LGBTQ resources and "How We Strive to be Bully Free." You are really excited to start the year. First stop: talk to the GSA advisor!

This vignette illustrates the possibility that middle schools can effectively implement safe school practices and thrive as inclusive spaces. The community organization Gender Spectrum (2017) suggests that to build safe havens for LGBTQ youth in middle school, we must do the following:

- Seek knowledge and perspectives
- Create openings in conversations
- Respect and affirm what students tell us about themselves
- Assure students that their safety and well-being is our priority
- Work with allies
- Assess the current school climate
- Connect gender inclusion to education objectives.

In the vignette, the school sought to increase their knowledge by inviting PFLAG speakers to their campus. The GSA was a focal point of community engagement and student-driven activism to build more inclusive school spaces (Mayo, 2013). The speakers shared personal stories, which created openings for new conversations. By hosting a GSA student club, the school assured students that their safety and well-being was a priority and that they were respected and affirmed on school campus. We don't know from the story whether the school regularly assesses its climate, but we do know from the show of hands at the PFLAG panel that most students felt safe at school. One step that the GSA advisor at this middle school might take is following up with those students who did not raise their hands and finding out why, then identifying improvement strategies, not only for school climate but also for curriculum and pedagogy.

In this chapter, we focus on pedagogies in middle school that support LGBTQ youth, that are caring and critical, and that build spaces of belonging through learning. You may typically associate *pedagogy* with procedural strategies for engagement in classroom activities, such as a project, experiment, or problem-set. In this chapter, we examine middle school pedagogy from inclusive, community-based, and critical vantage points. We suggest that, first and foremost, *pedagogies* are practices of belonging through which all academic learning occurs. Schools and classrooms must center pedagogies of relationship in order to redress oppression of LGBTQ youth and youth of color. To do this, schools may use restorative justice practices and/or responsive, mindful processes of self-care and relationship building. Further, relationships must unfold in relation to curricula, such as through ongoing disruptions of rigid, narrow assumptions about social relationships and singular knowledge canons. We close the chapter with two stories of practice that explore these critical, caring approaches to pedagogy.

Pedagogies of Belonging

Building an LGBTQ-inclusive middle school requires pedagogies that value the knowledge and contributions of communities that are traditionally marginalized or omitted from the school curriculum. In this chapter, we investigate relational practices grounded in queer, anti-racist perspectives, and in social relations grappling with power and oppression. For example, we can reflect on heteronormative assumptions about gender, bodies, and sexuality in the ways in which we structure relations among students and between teachers and students. We can also open classroom spaces to explore counter-narratives and fugitive knowledge as core to learning (Beer & Mackenthun, 2015; Mickell, 2013). Counter-narratives and fugitive knowledge are those stories and ideas that have resisted being controlled and retold through dominant ideologies and normative identities. Queer and anti-racist critiques of commonplace assumptions, stories, and knowledge are pedagogically necessary. The dispositional act of being curiously critical means examining our own thought processes; our valuation of curricula (traditional or counter/fugitive); and our ways of engaging young people in discussion, analysis, and other knowledge production.

As conscious, wide-awake educators, we grapple everyday with how oppression and segregation impact our views of the world and our interactions at school as well as how these worldviews and identities impact our students and their families (DiAngelo, 2016; Greene, 2000). As three middle-class, cisgender educators, the authors are keenly aware that our positionalities and the resulting erasures, assumptions, and mistakes we make impact our LGBTQ students and students of color on a daily basis. Being caring educators means using this dispositional awareness to build new pedagogical practices of inclusion and belonging.

Our vision is that pedagogical practices are relational and critical, both to intervene in the reproduction of oppressive ways of seeing ourselves, each other, and the world, and to offer hope for sustaining queer, anti-racist schools. bell hooks (2003) talks about this process as a pedagogy of hope in which the deep purpose of our teaching is communicated through our pedagogical strategies. In her narrative style, bell hooks models how to combine critical thinking about race, gender, class, and nationality with autobiographical narratives and everyday situations of learning. A pedagogy of hope resides in the possibilities we envision and then enact in our classrooms: through an examination of inclusions and exclusions, and a repositioning of counter-narratives into the center of the curriculum.

Further, relational pedagogies emphasize teacher warmth and instructional relevance that decenters whiteness and straightness, which is of particular importance for LGBTQ youth and youth of color (Booker & Lim, 2016). Additionally, for white and heterosexual middle schoolers, our relational, critical pedagogies model being empathetic, inclusive, and actively anti-oppressive. Through presence, strategic language, and actions, this pedagogy is about mattering (Love, 2015). Our relationships will ensure the sustenance of all students' identities, languages, cultures, and ways of being and knowing. Indeed, Paris and Alim (2017) argue for asset-based pedagogies with explicitly pluralistic outcomes that also call out the harms of singular notions of success, academic achievement, and goodness that have too often impacted our queer youth and youth of color.

CLASSROOM SNAPSHOT: 'CURIOUSLY CRITICAL' PEDAGOGY

A middle school language arts teacher uses "Once Upon a Time" cards to build a classroom community and introduce narrative structure. The cards contain fairy-tale images (such as gold coin, bird, and castle), and the students create a collaborative story with the cards. One group tells a story with male characters and narrates their story ending card, "They married, and lived happily ever after." Most of the class nods, some cheer, and one student says under his breath, "That is so gay."

The teacher intervenes, saying, "We don't use language to hurt each other or our ideas. And being gay is the way some people are. It is ok." Then the teacher continues,

> I think this is a great opportunity to discuss the origins of fairy tales, how they have been structured in different places and times, and how those structures have changed. This is a great opportunity to examine our assumptions about what 'happily ever after' has meant in stories. A fairy-tale ending has traditionally depended on a heterosexual narrative about a man and woman, a prince or princess, at least in European fairy tales.
>
> Yet there have been many social changes since those original fairy tales, including marriage equality for gay men and lesbians. The narrative now is about love, that 'love is love.' I would like you in small groups to research how social norms have changed over time based on the civil rights struggles of a particular group of people, such as LGBTQ communities, communities of color, or communities with disabilities. And I would like you to identify one story that reflects these changes to share with the class. Two examples based on changes in fairy tales are *King and King* and the *Paperbag Princess*. We will share our findings on Friday in class.

The teacher then sets out to identify a structure for the research and record some discussion questions on the board.

Hacking Norms and Culturally Sustaining Pedagogies

In the aforementioned classroom snapshot, the teacher identifies a pedagogical opportunity to disrupt bias and create a space for new learning based on honoring multiple narratives and the life experiences of oppressed communities. This is an example of Britzman's (1998) suggestion that we pedagogically open texts as "sites for enacting 'deconstructive revolts', with their potential 'for unhinging the normal from the self in order to prepare the self to encounter its own conditions of alterity'" (p. 85). The class in the snapshot was given the space to deconstruct the fairy-tale structure and its origins in heteronormative social relations, and then explore the destabilization of norms as narrative content, using multiple perspectives, perspective-taking, and critical analysis.

As a pedagogical strategy, this destabilization process must also consider the ways in which teachers may unintentionally "Other" gender diversity, LGBTQ, or nonwhite experiences when discussing characters, stories, or events that feature those identities. For example, Dinkins and Englert (2015) found that often

1. the school environment and classroom context positioned students as heterosexual;
2. students and teacher positioned gender performance and sexual identity as *other*; and
3. while the text acted as both a window and a mirror, the teacher and students consistently framed different, and sometimes contradictory, views for each other.

In this way, when teachers ask students to think about multiple perspectives, we must cautiously observe our wording and positioning: whose perspective(s) are located at the center of the questions we ask? Whose perspective(s) are positioned as different from the center or assumed norm? And how often are those normative (re)positionings occurring in the classroom?

Wargo (2017) suggests that, to build a culturally sustaining pedagogy with our students, we must shift the cultural capital we value by expanding the perspectives we include, the norms we question, and the texts we utilize. Working with new middle school teachers, Wargo modeled questioning gender norms with the book *Parrotfish*, asking teachers to conceptualize gender on a continuum, and then place character traits on that continuum with stickies. During the discussion, the teachers moved the stickies based on emerging thoughts about gender and gender identity and expression. They also used this strategy to discuss their own identities. Then they examined gender binaries in "The Princess and the Pea" and utilized collage techniques to remix expectations of heteronormativity in the tale and illustrate alternative story endings. Using literature with LGBTQ characters and themes (such as gender nonbinary and trans characters, gay relationships, and queer families) helps build safe havens for LGBTQ youth in our middle school classrooms.

We can also use pedagogies of mattering to examine the impact of positioning and Othering through the messages we send about students' lives. Too often, student-generated texts and popular media texts are devalued as "low culture," marginalized to introductions in a unit of study about canonical texts and other textbook-sanctioned knowledge, or given grammar-based feedback and evaluation to the exclusion of noticing the life themes and concerns these texts communicate (Ives & Crandall, 2014; Kinloch, 2017). For example, working with struggling adolescent writers of color, Kinloch (2017) shifted her feedback away from editing (word choice, misspellings, departures from the topic) toward seeing what students conveyed through narratives of resistance and coded messages of alienation and miscommunication. Pedagogies of mattering shift from deficit readings of youth and youth culture to readings of possibility: how do youth assert their identities and sustain their self-worth, and how can we as teachers engage these possibilities as the center of classroom interactions? The integration of LGBTQ literature, student-generated identity-based texts, current events, and cross-disciplinary intersections with LGBTQ themes provides a pedagogical shift toward complicated conversations about gender norms and biases, gender identity and expression, and sexual and gender diversity as central to learning (Blackburn, Clark, & Martino, 2016).

Restorative Practices, Mindfulness, and Trauma-Sensitive Pedagogies

Pedagogies of mattering and belonging are about nurturing relational dispositions of care and critique, decentering exclusionary norms and assumptions, and repositioning counter-narratives and multiple identities at the center of our pedagogical interactions with students and engagement with the curriculum. One pedagogical shift related to building safe, welcoming, inclusive school spaces for LGBTQ youth is toward addressing when harm, bias, and bullying occurs, particularly through community-building restorative practices. We must be aware that LGBTQ youth often experience trauma and learn to inform our pedagogies through a trauma-sensitive lens. We must remind ourselves of why LGBTQ youth deeply need these restorative practices as part of their regular, anticipated days at school. As WestEd (2013) suggests, "The connection between trauma, mental health and co-occurring disorders such as substance abuse, eating disorders, HIV/AIDS and further violence has been well-documented" (pp. 2–3). Written for counselors and community wellness providers, the publication provides several principles that can also inform our work as educators in understanding the relationship between LGBTQ youth and trauma:

Principle 1. For youth struggling with issues of sexual orientation and gender identity, exposure to harassment and violence is frequent.

Principle 2. Provide physical and emotional safety to ensure that [student] needs are being met, safety procedures are clearly established and communicated, the environment is predictable and respectful relationships are fostered.

Principle 3. Adapt [school] policies, procedures, forms and regulations to maximize inclusion of GLBTQ clients while also minimizing re-traumatization.

Principle 4. Foster a participatory culture in which [students] participate in program design, individual service planning and the creation of policies and procedures (WestEd, 2013).

One way to involve students in programs that redress harm and are trauma-sensitive is to utilize restorative practices. Restorative justice approaches can support our pedagogies when people and relationships are violated (Smith, Fisher, & Frey, 2015). Morrison and Vaandering (2012) suggest that schools need

> a responsive regulatory framework supports pedagogy, praxis, and discipline such that relational school cultures are nurtured; wherein, behavior is understood in social context, individuals are recognized as being part of a social web of relations, and building, maintaining, and repairing relationships become priorities.

Restorative practices are not punitive but rather focus on how to redress hurt through prevention classroom circles; intervention mediation with small group circles; and reentry for students who have been suspended, truant, or incarcerated (We Are Teachers, 2013).

For example, in 2006, Oakland first introduced the program at Cole Middle School (Sumner, Silverman, & Frampton, 2010). District leaders planned to close the school due to low test scores when it started a restorative justice pilot program. In the three years since embracing the practice, suspensions dropped by 87 percent, violence decreased dramatically, and expulsions became nonexistent. Punitive practices do not deter young people from unwanted behaviors at school. Relationship building that occurs through restorative practices is effective as a prevention and intervention process.

In another example, Jewlyes Gutierrez, a 16-year-old transgender girl, was charged by the Contra Costa County California District Attorney with battery for defending herself against bullies at her school in 2016 (Garcia, 2014). Her story is indicative of a wider trend: harsh school discipline policies disproportionately impact students of color, students with disabilities, and students who identify as LGBTQ (Anti-Defamation League, 2017). Punitive discipline policies punish students regardless of context, while restorative practices focus on repairing relationships.

GSA NETWORK STATEMENT ON RESTORATIVE PRACTICES

GSA Network (GSA Network, 2013) believes that the GSA movement and LGBTQ students across the country would benefit significantly from shifting school climates away from a culture of punitive school discipline, including when responding to incidents of anti-LGBTQ bias, harassment, and bullying. Effectively meeting the needs of LGBTQ youth requires creating supportive learning environments for all students, which can be achieved through various models, such as restorative justice, peer counseling, and mediation. These solutions bring students and educators together to collaboratively and proactively address the root cause of conflict, thereby allowing schools to address and correct student behavior without denying students valuable instructional time. Numerous studies show the potential for restorative practices to prevent and significantly reduce suspensions, expulsions, and alternative school placements. Restorative justice approaches to school discipline offer the best solutions for LGBTQ youth in schools.

Restorative practices support the overall well-being of the school and teach implicitly and explicitly that dignity and relationships are at the center of learning. Teaching mindfulness is a key component of a restorative school community. As we teach young people to develop awareness of their thoughts and feelings; the conditions of the environment; and the connection between their breath, thoughts, and actions, we can help them develop a sense of presence and focus. Pizzuto (2016), a middle school teacher, conveys that she made mindfulness a classroom routine: helping students to relax, visualize, take deep breaths, and center themselves each day. These mindful practices support non-judgment and self-acceptance as well as expansion of the creative, imaginative self. As an example of the social justice impact of mindfulness, Toomey (2017) found that utilizing mindfulness practices with Latino/a LGBTQ youth at school, as well as with trans youth and their caregivers in counseling, helped youth develop increased self-compassion. Not only does mindfulness build a classroom community, but it also creates a shared experience of self-care.

One of the book authors, Chappell, writes poems to support mindful self-healing practice. She remembers an exchange with her father in college. Upon telling him about her own questioning sexual identity, he responded, "I don't care if you are a lesbian, just don't turn my son gay." Chappell often remembers this moment as one of many dismissals of herself as less valuable or worthy of dignity. In the midst of these memories today, she deliberately rejects the negative disciplining of her body and her identity. Then she writes to heal, to create a radical acceptance of body and identity, through mindful breath and writing. As you read Chappell's poems below, imagine how you might use mindfulness and restorative practices as a pedagogical tool with your students.

Once
I have come and gone
A body standing, once thick and strong
Now dashed and fallen
I am gone, please come
A body standing, now thick and strong

Enough
I must begin with myself.
I must look at those parts of my physical body
that I have been taught to hate:
the jiggles in my stomach, the wrinkles on my face,
the cellulite in my legs.
This body gives me life.
These parts are me make everything possible.
I touch the corners of my eyes.
give my belly a rub.
hug my thighs, especially on the dimples
You are enough, I whisper.
Staring straight into the mirror,
I am
Enough

Touch
I want to caress life, so when I am
Riding up s that reach an infinite blue
The sweat on my palms glistens and
I sweep them across my hips
I dry them and feel the skin, fat, muscle.
I am gentle in my thoughts and touch.
I have given this body to many brutal words
I am gentle
I touch myself
I make it a habit
I live in the caress.

Unbound
I am in an opening,
feeling the knotted, gnarling, root-bound tree
sitting on my hips.
The memory doesn't want to leave,
it screams out in pain.
I wait.
Breathe

slowly
I stretch and release a fist of memories.
Haunting, held years
surprise me,
I let the bending tell new stories.

Consider the principles of belonging at work in the chapter. As teachers we can seek knowledge and perspectives; create openings in conversations; respect and affirm what students tell you about themselves; assure students their safety and well-being is your priority; work with allies; assess the current school climate; connect inclusion practices to education objectives (Gender Spectrum, 2017). The following are two stories of practice exemplifying LGBTQ-inclusive pedagogies that build safe, welcoming, and inclusive middle schools. As you read, reflect on how these principles operate in each story.

STORY ONE: "Rainbow Warriors" by Veronica Reinhart

Just like a family, a school can be happy and cohesive, or grumpy and dysfunctional. Unfortunately, my school has not always been as happy and cohesive as it is today. Several years ago, my school was in a dark spiral. Imagine us the "Shameless" family of public schools. We had students refusing to attend class, excessive tardies, drug use on campus, fights, and rampant bullying. Many students had no respect for faculty, staff, or each other. One of the bleakest moments occurred when Andrew, one of my eighth-grade students, almost had his hair lit on fire in the locker room for being openly gay at school.

I was not a stranger to LGBTQ bullying before this happened. Growing up in the "Bible Belt" as a non-Christian with a lesbian mom had taught me about the intolerance of others at school and in the community. However, I felt that I had escaped much of that by moving to California. Although not perfect, California was a much more progressive state than the one I had grown up in.

I was not prepared, however, for the aggression displayed by my students in middle school. After Andrew's assault in the locker room, I approached my administrator at the time to talk about starting a GSA at our school. I felt something must be done to give our LGBTQ students support and to educate other students about homophobia. She was horrified. "What will the parents say?!" She was already trying to keep a sinking school afloat. Why would I give her another issue for parents to complain about?

Unfortunately, during the time in which I had this conversation, I was not fully educated about laws regarding LGBTQ students. Had I known about the Federal Equal Access Act and California's AB 537, I would have fought harder to get a GSA at my school. Our school was imploding, and California's Proposition 8 had just passed the year before; I did not have much hope of change.

I had many openly out LGBTQ students that same school year when Andrew was attacked. In my journalism class, many of these students wanted to write opinion pieces concerning Prop 8. Of course, these pieces were also denied publication by our administrator. A few months later, I had another student, Olivia, try to commit suicide by swallowing pills. Olivia had broken up with her girlfriend and could find no solace for the loss of both a friend and a lover. Luckily, Olivia survived this attempt.

Our downward spiral continued for two more school years. Finally, my fellow teachers and I had had enough. We could no longer accept the tardies, truancies, fights, and bullying from and among students. Our school had become a hostile environment—not only for teachers but for students. The staff tried as best as possible to reinforce the positive behaviors of students and to manage our own discipline within our classrooms, but there was no administrative support past what we could immediately handle ourselves. Our administration failed to reward "good" or positive behavior, and there were certainly no consequences for misbehavior other than suspension. Suspensions were useless to deter negative behavior from most students. Instead of making students reflect upon their behavior, suspensions give most students a day off from school. We used our union to file a "hostile work environment" complaint against our district.

Local publicity, a lengthy investigation, an administration change, support from our school district, and additional funding helped get our school back on track. But the damage was done. Parents, especially those of GATE and honors students, pulled their students out of our school. Our enrollment dropped from almost 1400 to 950 students. We also lost several great teachers to other schools in the district. Elective programs were cut, including journalism, weight lifting, and yearbook. Our grades and test scores were extremely low, and we were ranked as the worst middle school in Orange County. Students were scared of each other. While many of them participated in the chaos by taking the opportunity to skip class or not complete work, they also feared instability; the school's hostile climate made them feel unsafe and unsure. The other consequence: our LGBTQ students were unwilling to be openly out at school.

When we finally had a new, permanent administrator, some closeted students approached him about starting a GSA. Luckily, I was in his office during this conversation, and I quickly volunteered my services as an advisor. By this time, I had gained a full understanding of the laws supporting LGBTQ students. I knew that he could not deny the students a GSA club as long as there were other types of extracurricular clubs on campus, and I was hoping he'd say yes. (It's much easier to come to work when your administrator approves of you and your work.) He said yes.

My dreams of a GSA were finally realized.

Four years later, with the help and guidance of the LGBT Center OC, my school now has a thriving GSA called Rainbow Warriors. We average 20–30 students at each weekly meeting. Our students and staff proudly wear Rainbow Warrior T-shirts around school. We have "Safe Zone" and "It's Okay to be Gay" posters prominently displayed in class-room windows and hallways.

Here is one of the poems written by a Rainbow Warrior.

"My Advice as a Bisexual Person"
By Yahaira, middle school student

We were all born to be who we are.
We are all beautiful people with a beautiful dream ahead of us.
Stop judging each other based on their looks, body, shape, skin
tone, culture,
'Cause no matter what, we were born like that, and we should love
one another.

No one can stop you from being you.
No one should bring you down because of what they think of you.
We also can't stop them, but we can control our thoughts.
Negative thoughts lead to negative actions.

We are all human beings.
We are all perfect like that.
We are all perfect at being or doing what we do best—and that's
being us!
So smile and thank God for giving you one more day of life,
One more day of giving what you want.

I am bisexual.
I am an LGBTQ ally.

For the past two years, our school has hosted the LGBT Youth Conven-ing sponsored by the LGBT Center OC. The Convening is a conference hosted by LGBTQ youth for LGBTQ youth and their allies, families, teachers, and supporters. This year, during October, our students and staff celebrated National Coming Out Day by wearing colorful stickers that said phrases such as "Out and Proud," "I Support Rainbow Warriors," and "I am Against LGBTQ Bullying." We also asked the student body to sign pledges standing up for LGBTQ students at school. The GSA arranged these pledges to create a giant "LGBTQ" wall. And this year, for the first time ever, we have a pansexual student body president. She is an active member of the LGBTQ community and Rainbow Warriors (Figure 7.1).

We have found that when a school recognizes and stands up for its most marginalized members, it uplifts us all. Because of the work that Rainbow Warriors and our school as a whole have done to be more welcoming for LGBTQ students, all students feel safer. While there will always be more work to be done, I know that our school climate has changed dramatically. Now we have at least 20+ students at Spurgeon who are "out" openly at school. Gay eighth-grade males are reporting back how the school has become much safer and more open since their sixth-grade year, and I hear many calling out classmates for accidentally using "gay" in a derogatory fashion.

And the parents? In the four years of Rainbow Warriors, we have received three complaints. Once parents find out that we support ALL students, whether they are LGBTQ, English-language learners, immigrant and undocumented children, minorities, or disabled, they are grateful

FIGURE 7.1 Spurgeon Middle School's Rainbow Warriors Wall. Photo by Veronica Reinhart.

that their child will be attending a school with such inclusion. For instance, we are a middle school that has both a GSA and a Bible Club. A few members of Rainbow Warriors attend the Bible Club because they no longer feel comfortable attending church with their families. Additionally, we have S.U.C.C.E.S.S. (systematic utilization of comprehensive strategies for ensuring student success) classes for students with autism, co-teaching mainstream inclusion programs for Special Education students and English Language Development classes specifically designed to support immigrant students.

When I meet teachers and faculty from other schools who are lamenting about their school environments, I remind them that any school can change, but it takes work. The whole school must be involved, including administration, staff, teachers, and students. When our middle school hit rock-bottom four years ago, everyone knew that it had nowhere to go but up—even the students. Everyone invested in the change; we participated in stakeholder meetings to ensure that everyone's interests were being taken into account. Many parents and staff see LGBTQ issues as only affecting a small percentage of a school. They need to be reminded that a school can only succeed if its most marginalized populations are seen as central to the rich diversity of the school. Otherwise, elements of discontent build from these marginalized groups and conflict can only grow from there.

Additionally, instruction must be made available to students about vulnerable populations, such as the LGBTQ, disabled, English-Language Learners, and immigrant and undocumented communities. Simply put, policies of "don't do that" don't work. Most bullying occurs because students are ignorant of what it means to have a particular identity or be a member of a particular community. Teaching about bias and discrimination, its history, and its present manifestations is necessary. Telling a student "not to bully" is not effective, but teaching the "bully" about their victims does. We hold mediations between students who have engaged in bullying or have been victims of bullying (sometimes these students have been in both roles) rather than suspending them as part of our restorative justice practices. We have found that suspension does very little to build empathy and understanding between students.

We also have educated our administration and staff. At least once a year, the staff have had professional development meetings concerning LGBTQ issues at school. The last such training covered all of the California laws that support LGBTQ students in schools. Furthermore, many of our staff have also attended trainings in restorative justice, Welcoming

Schools, and Positive Behavioral Intervention and Support (PBIS) to help foster a safe environment at our school.

If our middle school—a Title I urban, public school with over 97 percent minority students and over 87 percent of students on free and/ or reduced lunch—can change, any school can change. It takes work, commitment, care, and honesty. Problems can no longer be the elephant in the room or be swept under the rug like a dysfunctional family. Once everyone is committed together to making a change, education can really be the vehicle to transform student lives. [t16] As a current student said, "School is the only place I can be myself. If I didn't have my friends and be here, I don't know what I would do."

STORY TWO: "Atlas of a Northeastern Trans/Queer Educator: Or How We Must Acknowledge the Strength of LGBTQ Students" by James Shultis

Across the country, LGBTQ young people are demanding acceptance and validation of their identities. Their resiliency shows in the interactions they have with friends and their continued push for change in the face of resistance. Often challenged by society for who they are, many of the youth we see today are thriving because they have created space where they can be their full selves. Having "school-based resources, such as supportive student clubs (e.g., Gay-Straight Alliances, or GSAs), LGBT-inclusive curricula, supportive school personnel, and comprehensive, enumerated policies for addressing bullying, harassment, and assault, may help create a more positive school environment for LGBTQ students" (Kosciw, Greytak, Giga, Villenas, & Danischewski, 2016). As educators, students, community members, and families, we know all too well that to have an inclusive school environment fosters better outcomes for students. These spaces are integral to student growth and their overall well-being. Not just for LGBTQ students but for everyone.

Over the last 15 years, I've worked in various capacities advocating for LGBTQ rights, especially as they relate to transgender and gender-nonconforming people. This work has been mainly centered in the Northeast, primarily in Massachusetts, New Jersey, and New York. For five of those years, I worked at an LGBTQ community center, with a catchment of ten counties in the upstate New York area, and served in a volunteer capacity for a local chapter of GLSEN serving eight counties in upstate New York GLSEN, a national organization with over 40 chapters, "envisions a world in which every child learns to respect and accept all people, regardless of sexual orientation or gender identity/expression". Throughout that time and subsequently, I also worked as an independent trainer providing professional development to K-12 educators in schools and youth-serving organizations focused on LGBTQ youth. In these positions, I visited over 300 schools throughout the Northeast and was able to connect with educators and students to hear how I might best approach LGBTQ identities in their communities.

Imagine boarding a plane blindfolded, having the plane take off and land, getting off the plane, then taking the blindfold off. Often going from one school to the next throughout the Northeast felt like this. I would typically get a phone call or an email from either the principal or a school counselor stating something along the lines of *We have a student who is transgender. We want to help them out but aren't sure how.* Or perhaps something like *One of our teachers connected with us. They have a boy in their class that is asking to be called "so and so," and we aren't sure if that's okay.* Or sometimes it might be *We have an issue with one of our students who identifies as gay. They are being bullied and we think we should have a conversation about it.* I could sense from the requests, that many of the schools were afraid to address these issues head-on, let alone mention the language of sexual orientation or gender identity/expression with their students.

Before I was an educator, I was a young person, navigating the choppy waters of middle and high school in Central New Jersey. Where I grew up wasn't the Jersey people always think of. There were farms and forests, and I rode my bike everywhere. There were the stereotypical strip malls and diners I would go to once I was older and started hanging out with friends who drove. We'd go to them every chance we got. Thinking back, while I was growing up in the mid-90s, I had very few examples of what it meant to be gay, let alone any positive transgender role models. The experience was isolating. And I know now, not uncommon. "[LGBTQ] students also described persistent patterns of isolation, exclusion, and marginalization that made them feel unsafe or unwelcome at school" (Human Rights Watch, 2016).

On my drive to one school, I pass more cows than I do houses or people, fields of wheat moving with the afternoon breeze. Another time, I'm immersed in a large city where I need to feed the meter before crossing a busy intersection to the school entrance. In each of these instances, I'm reminded how vastly different each young person's experience is in school and in the world. What might it be like to step off the school bus (if there is one) and head into your school?

"Every day I sit behind a bunch of guys in their camo gear and confederate flag hats, I don't really feel safe," said a self-identified trans feminine youth at a GSA meeting in New York, 2016.

"Me and [their friend] just eat in the auditorium since we don't want to be targeted if we went in the lunchroom," said a self-identified gay youth at workshop in Massachusetts, 2017.

"I just want to wear what I want, like sparkles and stuff, and that just wouldn't be okay here. Even though they say there's a anti-bullying policy, it's not enforced," said a self-identified gender nonconforming youth at workshop in New York, 2016.

Each time a conversation like this occurs, the room turns electric, with young people simultaneously sharing and supporting one another. Even in the midst of crisis, LGBTQ young people have each other's backs. I remember that feeling as a young person too. It was empowering. I imagine it's where so many youth leaders get their start.

Many of the student workshops I do are with young people, in middle or high school GSAs or at local community centers that serve as safe havens for LGBTQ youth. Youth share candidly what it's like in their schools, often jumping in on each other's shares to reply that their experiences have been similar to their peers. This is consistent with statistics showing, "The vast majority of LGBTQ students (85.2 percent) experienced verbal harassment (e.g., called names or threatened) at school based on a personal characteristic, most commonly sexual orientation (70.8 percent of LGBTQ students) and gender expression (54.5 percent)" (Kosciw, Greytak, Giga, Villenas, & Danischewski, 2015).

A friend of mine once asked, *do you get nervous going into some of these schools as an out, transgender person?* It's a hard question to answer. For one thing, I'm not in high school anymore. I have the ability to move in and out of those spaces. As a trans teen, that wasn't an option. Or if it was, I didn't know it. I also "pass," which is when

> Either some people are visibly marked in such a way that it is impossible to conceal the trait in question, even if they wanted to. But other traits are less visible, or completely unnoticeable, to other people in most situations…some people are more visibly [trans]— that is, they are often recognized or 'read' as [trans]—while other [trans people] are sometimes or almost always, perceived as cissexual, even though they are not.
>
> *(Serano, 2013)*

The bulk of schools I've worked in, the administrations have been predominantly headed by white men, which mirrors my whiteness and my masculinity. Recognizing this has been helpful, and often, I use it to my advantage to have difficult conversations about the types of professional development that could be run and/or student resources that could be created or further supported. At the same time, I understand the consequences that may exist for being found to be trans.

My experience, however, can never be that of a trans woman of color. Her experience and vulnerability are and have been so disproportionate to mine. In 2016, there were 27 transgender women of color murdered in the USA. Transgender women and transgender people of color are much more vulnerable to violence, especially at the hands of law enforcement. Transgender people of color were more than two and a half times more likely to experience police violence and six times more likely to experience physical violence from the police compared to white non-transgender LGB respondents (GLAAD, n.d.).

It's important to recognize our vulnerabilities as well as our strength. Despite the violence and stigma, trans and gender-nonconforming individuals are fiercer than ever. This is doubly true for trans and gender-nonconforming youth.

Today, with more ways to access information about LGBTQ identities (with the access and ability to do so), youth can get online, find community through social media, articles, YouTube, and so forth. However, these young people are still traversing the tricky terrain of adolescence. Some of the top reasons for which LGBTQ students said they were not planning to graduate or were not sure if they would graduate were mental health concerns, such as "depression, anxiety, or stress, as given by 86.3 percent of those who provided reasons for leaving high school…[followed by] academic concerns (67.5 percent), including poor grades, high number of absences, or not having enough credits to graduate…[and] over half of LGBTQ students (60.5 percent) explicitly reported a hostile school climate as being factor in their decision or doubts about finishing high school" (Kosciw, Greytak, Giga, Villenas, & Danischewski, 2016).

Ensuring that youth have access to adequate mental health resources that are respectful and knowledgeable of their identities is key, along with having other inclusive resources/curriculum, student groups, and enforced antidiscrimination and harassment policies that include sexual orientation and gender identity/expression.

I'm hopeful that LGBTQ educators, whether they are the youth themselves or adults, continue to encourage and inspire one another. For me, meeting others who were interested in interrupting homophobia, transphobia, and dismantling racist systems was incredibly validating and saved my life. When we are able to see successful LGBTQ role models, especially trans and gender-nonconforming ones, we are able to envision a life for ourselves too.

If I were to look back and meet my adolescent self again, I might say to them, *You are capable of so much. Whether or not that has been acknowledged or actualized. You are making a difference. You are needed here. I love you.*

Questions for Reflection

1. Reflecting on your own middle school experience, what assumptions about gender, bodies, and sexuality did you experience? How did those assumptions affect your school performance and social experiences?
2. Thinking about your curriculum content, when might you use counternarratives and fugitive knowledge to disrupt and decenter the heteronormative assumptions that exist?
3. When deconstructing or destabilizing content that is gender-biased, think about the ways you incorporate gender diversity. How might you unintentionally "other" those who identify as differently gendered?
4. What improvement strategies can you initiate to create a more welcoming and inclusive school climate, curriculum, and pedagogy?
5. How will you intervene when you overhear incidences of bias-based bullying? What language will you use to respond in a way that educates rather than punishes?

References

Anti-Defamation League. (2017). School discipline and the school-to-prison pipeline. *Anti-Defamation League*. Retrieved from www.adl.org/education/resources/tools-and-strategies/table-talk/school-to-prison-pipeline

Beer, A., & Mackenthun, G. (2015). *Fugitive knowledge: The loss and preservation of knowledge in cultural contact zones*. Münster: Waxman Verlag.

Blackburn, M., Clark, C., & Martino, W. (2016). Investigating LGBT-themed literature and trans informed pedagogies in classrooms. *Discourse: Studies in the Cultural Politics of Education, 37*(6), 801–806.

Booker, K., & Lim, J. (2016). Belongingness and pedagogy: Engaging African American girls in middle school mathematics. *Youth & Society*.

Britzman, D. (1998). *Lost subjects, contested objects*. Albany, NY: State University of New York Press.

DiAngelo, R. (2016). *Seeing the water: Whiteness in daily life*. Video. University of Washington. Retrieved from www.youtube.com/watch?v=2Lv3xoiuDtM

Dinkins, E. G., & Englert, P. (2015). LGBTQ literature in middle school classrooms: Possibilities for challenging heteronormative environments. *Sex Education: Sexuality, Society and Learning, 15*(4), 392–405.

Garcia, O. (2014, March 27). #GSAs4Justice campaign empowers LGBT teens. GLAAD. Retrieved from www.glaad.org/blog/gsas4justice-campaign-empowers-lgbt-teens

Gender Spectrum. (2017). Retrieved from www.genderspectrum.org/blog/asca-safe havens/

GLAAD. (n.d.). *Understanding issues facing transgender Americans.* Retrieved from www.glaad.org/sites/default/files/understanding-issues-facing-transgender-americans.pdf

Greene, M. (2000). *Releasing the imagination: Essays on education, the arts, and social change.* San Francisco, CA: Jossey-Bass Inc.

GSA Network. (2013, October 2). GSA network statement in support of restorative approaches to school discipline. *GSA Network –Trans and Queer Youth Uniting for Racial and Gender Justice.* Retrieved from https://gsanetwork.org/news/gsa-network-statement-support-restorative-approaches-school-discipline/100213

hooks, b. (2003). *Teaching community: A pedagogy of hope.* New York: Routledge.

Human Rights Watch. (2016). *Like walking through a hailstorm: Discrimination against LGBT youth in US schools.* New York: Human Rights Watch.

Ives, D., & Crandall, C. (2014). Enacting a critical pedagogy of popular culture at the intersection of student writing, popular culture, and critical literacy. In P. Paugh, T. Kress, & R. Lake (Eds.), *Teaching towards democracy with postmodern and popular culture texts* (pp. 201–220). Rotterdam: Sense.

Kinloch, V. (2017). Reading the world as text: Black adolescents and out-of-school literacies. In R. K. Durst, G. E. Newell & J. D. Marshall (Eds.), *English language arts research and teaching: Revisiting and extending Arthur Applebee's contributions, Chapter 8.* New York: Routledge.

Kosciw, J. G., Greytak, E. A., Giga, N. M., Villenas, C., & Danischewski, D. J. (2016). *The 2015 national school climate survey: The experiences of lesbian, gay, bisexual, transgender, and queer youth in our nation's schools.* New York: GLSEN.

Love, B. L. (2015). Imagining mattering: Hip hop civics ed, intersectionality & black joy. *Georgia Educational Research Association Conference.* Retrieved from http://digital commons.georgiasouthern.edu/gera/2015/2015/1/

Mayo, J. B. (2013). Critical pedagogy enacted in the gay-straight alliance –new possibilities for a third space in teacher development. *Educational Researcher, 42*(5), 266–275.

Mickell, C. (2013). Using fiction to research silenced or counter narratives of lives in-between contested race, class, and power in the South. *Journal of Curriculum Theorizing, 28*(3), 168–180.

Morrison, B. E., & Vaandering, D. (2012). Restorative justice: Pedagogy, praxis, and discipline. *Journal of School Violence, 11*(2), 138–155.

Paris, D., & Alim, S. (2017). *Culturally sustaining pedagogies: Teaching and learning for justice in a changing world.* New York: Teachers College Press.

Pizzuto, D. (2016, December 12). Mindful in middle school—One teacher's experience incorporating mindfulness into her middle school curriculum. *George Lucas Educational Foundation.* Retrieved from www.edutopia.org/article/mindful-middle-school-daria-pizzuto

Serano, J. (2013). *Excluded: Making feminist and queer movements more inclusive.* Berkeley, CA: Seal Press.

Smith, D., Fisher, D., & Frey, N. (2015). *Better than carrots or sticks: Restorative practices for positive classroom management.* Alexandria, VA: ASCD.

Sumner, M. D., Silverman, C. J., & Frampton, M. L. (2010). *School-based restorative justice as an alternative to zero-tolerance policies: Lessons from West Oakland*. Retrieved from www.law.berkeley.edu/files/thcsj/10-2010_School-based_Restorative_Justice_As_an_Alternative_to_Zero-Tolerance_Policies.pdf

Toomey, R. (2017, February 9). Deep dish—Cultivating mindfulness and compassion among trans youth and their caregivers: Preliminary findings from a pilot study. *Institute for LGBT Studies −University of Arizona*. Retrieved from https://lgbt.arizona.edu/events/deep-dish-cultivating-mindfulness-and-compassion-among-trans-youth-and-their-caregivers

Wargo, J. M. (2017). Hacking heteronormativity and remixing rhymes: Enacting a [Q]ulturally sustaining pedagogy in middle grades english language arts. *Voices from the Middle Voices from the Middle, 24*(3), 39.

We Are Teachers. (2013). *Restorative justice: A different approach to discipline*. Retrieved from www.weareteachers.com/restorative-justice-a-different-approach-to-discipline/

WestEd. (2013). *Practice guidelines for the delivery of trauma-informed and GLBTQ culturally-competent care*. Retrieved from www.air.org/sites/default/files/downloads/report/Trauma-Informed%20and%20GLBTQ%20Culturally%20Competent%20Care.pdf

PART III

High School

8

HIGH SCHOOL ENVIRONMENT

We begin this chapter with student reflections on identity and acceptance at school. Jadesola M. Ajileye, writing for the Los Angeles Times High School Insider blog on October 2, 2017, has graciously given the book authors permission to reprint her opinion piece here. Ajileye writes,

No pronoun belongs to any certain sex, meaning pronouns aren't assigned to, or just for, males or females. In short, all pronouns are gender neutral. This belief has gained popularity as more schools and workplaces try to meet the needs of the genderqueer and transgender community. This year, our school, Daniel Pearl Magnet High School (DPMHS), has become more open in asking students their preferred gender pronoun as to avoid misunderstandings and because it would be a disservice to some students otherwise.

"It is a reflection of the needs of our students," Magnet Coordinator Nicole Bootel said. "We would like to treat people the way they want to be treated. I think that people want to be referred to in a manner that's comfortable to them. It's a simple enough adjustment."

These changes are the result of recent campaigns for gender-neutral bathrooms. DPMHS is ahead of the curve, having these accommodations in place for four years now, ahead of any other high school in LAUSD.

Gender identity for most people is the same as their biological sex or their gender expression fits enough into traditional norms that people can correctly assume their pronouns are either "he" or "she." However, for those that don't fall into this category, assumptions can be considered rude and limiting.

"Pronouns are an unavoidable fact of the English language, and people deserve the common decency of being referred to in a way that reflects who they are and how they identify," said Tatiana Fiermonte, a representative of the LGBT National Help Center, in an interview. "It isn't a question of respect or kindness, it is a minimum standard of decency."

Other pronouns like "they," "ve," "ze" and "xe" exist, all are gender neutral pronouns the LGBT community approves of and utilizes so it is courteous to practice asking someone how they identify to avoid confusion.

"You can't always tell someone's gender or what they prefer to be called by appearances so, by asking you put the ball in their court," said an anonymous representative of Equality California, an LGBTQ organization in Los Angeles, in an interview. "Support people by dignifying how they perceive themselves and their own gender. Be polite and try to empathize, imagine you were in someone else's shoes and people judged you by how you look."

By not jumping to conclusions, you're modeling respectful pronoun use for others and promoting tolerance. The use of preferred gender pronouns in schools is progressive and a great way to promote inclusion and support students.

"The ideal method is to create an environment where people feel comfortable declaring for themselves how they identify," Fiermonte said. "And maybe ask globally rather than asking specific individuals. It creates an atmosphere that is inherently more welcoming and understanding of the diverse experiences of gender [that] people have."

It's a privilege to not have to worry about which pronoun someone is going to use for you based on how they perceive your gender. If you have this privilege, yet fail to respect someone else's identity, you're being oppressive.

"You should correct yourself when you mis-gender someone on purpose or not," an anonymous freshman said. "Transgender people deserve respect just as any other human being. PGPs are important because trans people need a voice to be heard; because we feel disrespected, invalidated, and dismissed, when they're not used."

In this blog, Ajileye emphasizes the importance of high schools' embracing student's agency in shaping their own identities and opening social practices toward increased gender diversity and inclusivity.

Reconceptualizing High School Environments: New Metaphors and Practices

In this chapter, we discuss the high school environment, exploring ideas and practices that imagine campus spaces as an "open text" through which a variety or repertoire of meanings and belongings may emerge (Yon, 2000).

Yon highlights how our various identities are negotiated in and through the social processes and practices that we engage in. Such engagement is particularly salient for young adult high school students as they search for self and meaning—a search to *be* and to *know* that continues into adulthood. In this sense, student identities are never already "there," static and fully formed, but rather are produced, negotiated, emergent, and always in-process in the environment of school (Yon, 2000).

Campus cultures, as a reflection of student identities, form through similarly organic and dynamic processes. School environments are likewise not already there—static and fixed—but are produced, negotiated, emergent, and always in-process. In contrast to older institutional discourses that imagined school climate as both a result and reinforcement of universal, uniform, and systematized educational goals and values—a symptom of the same outdated Fordist model discussed in Chapter 2—this *emergent* model sees school community members, students, staff, and educators alike in dialogue with one another, responsible to each other and for creating their learning community. This chapter looks at how a reframing of school climate and environment as an emergent space where students and educators share in responsibility for its values, practices, and aims can work to ensure that LGBTQ (lesbian, gay, bisexual, transgender and queer) students, and all students, thrive and develop to their greatest possible potential. We begin with a story by a Teacher of the Year who experienced the impact of a school environment. As you read each story in the chapter, reflect on how you are integral to your own school environment and the ways in which you might advocate for gender diversity and LGBTQ inclusion on your campus.

STORY ONE: "Teacher of the Year" by Brett Bigham

Most people know me as the gay Teacher of the Year. But there is much more to my story, and the truth is, although I did get fired, it was because I decided to stand up for LGBTQ students, and it was worth it.

As a kid, every time I was called a "faggot," my skin got tougher. For each round of bullying I went through, my tongue got sharper, and my resolve to stand up for myself got stronger. I grew up in a very religious community and week after week, month after month, I was caught between my Christian friends and my Mormon friends. Each group was certain that only their church was the right church. The only thing they seemed to agree on was that I was going to burn in hell.

And somehow, instead of withering under this constant attack, I grew to welcome the ugliness, and I began to fight back. I wasn't a social justice warrior back then, just a kid trying not to get beat up but refusing to be anything but myself.

I refused to be crushed because I had learned a very hard lesson my sophomore year. My best friend, Mark, came out to me, which was like someone throwing me a life preserver. Like most gay kids in that era, I thought I was alone, but suddenly, I had a gay best friend. It was an amazing feeling. It was also short-lived. That same week, Mark killed himself. I was devastated and more alone than ever.

It had never occurred to me that someone would choose being dead over being gay. I wondered if that would be my future.

—

The turning point was the bubblegum-pink Izod polo shirt. I'm a child of the 1980s, and jaws dropped when I walked into Canby High School in that pink shirt. It seems a ridiculous statement by today's standards, but that shirt was my gay flag. It was my way of saying, "Yeah, I'm gay, what are you going to do about it?" What the biggest school bully did was punch me in the face and call me "faggot" again. I drove into Portland and bought an even brighter pink shirt.

From then on, when I was called a fag, my response was "takes one to know one." That got me punched a few more times, but the bullying died out as I got taller and bigger.

When I became a teacher, I met a lot of kids who were victims of bullying. It broke my heart to see how deeply hurt some of those young people were. I made sure I always had time for the shy kids and the outsiders. At recess duty, I would find myself surrounded by the kids who didn't mingle with the others. It reminded me of my own childhood in many ways. There are always kids who don't fit in.

It was this pathway that led me to be such a strong advocate for LGBT youth. My first job after finishing my teaching program was in a small Oregon town. Every day, I would hear homophobic remarks, one right after another. I knew if I was hearing them, the gay kids in the school were hearing even more. This was before Gay–Straight Alliance (GSA) clubs; this was before safe spaces and staff trainings. This was only a few years after the Oregon Citizen's Alliance, a right-wing hate mob, tried to pass a law that stated gay people would not be allowed to work in schools. Coming out in a small town in rural Oregon was scary. It still is.

But I could not let the hate speech and homophobic slurs become the way the gay kids in that district defined themselves. I decided to do what I could. It was with shaking hands that I stuck a rainbow sticker on my car bumper. I remember driving to school that first day with my newly "rainbowed" car. I went to school early and parked where every kid coming off the buses would see it.

By fourth period, the braver kids were asking me if I was gay. By sixth period, the mean ones were starting to make comments. I had the same reply for all of them, "I don't talk about my personal life at school," but the sticker was saying it all for me. Regardless of the words, the message to the LGBT students was clear: you are not alone.

Ever since that year, I have been open about my sexuality but have never had the need to discuss it with my students. The truth is, as a special education teacher working with young people who have profound disabilities, most of my students will not have the life trajectory of growing up, falling in love, and raising kids in the typical "American" fashion. For many of them, a sexual relationship is probably not in their future. Because of this, my own sexuality was never a topic of conversation.

———

That all changed when I was named Teacher of the Year. I am not the first gay person to be chosen by a state for this amazing award. There are a few, here and there, sprinkled around the country. Many of them remain quiet, a few have spoken out, but mostly, their sexuality has been ignored. My hope was that I wouldn't have to talk about it, but the photos of me with my partner at the White House would send the message for me.

However, that's not the way things happened. A few months into 2014, I was told by my supervisor and head of my department that I was no longer allowed to say I was gay in public. In her words, "If you keep saying you are gay, someone is going to shoot you in the head." Strong words that she followed up with "Someone is going to kill you if you keep saying that." At first, I thought she was trying to protect me, but the truth came out later, and I realized she was serious. She told my coworkers that what I was saying was going to bring shame on the district and that I had to be stopped.

Just before my visit to the White House for the Presidential Honoring Ceremony, the district sat me down and gave me a new set of rules. I was not allowed to say anything, 24 hours a day, seven days a week, unless I gave the district everything I was going to say in advance for their approval. I was told I could not answer questions at a speech or with the media unless they approved of my answers in advance. I was told I could not write anything unless I turned it in to be vetted, and the district demanded that I bring my personal mail from home for them to read and vet before I would be allowed to mail it.

Later, they added that I could not speak to any person unless the district approved of the person or group. That same month, I was told I could not meet with a high school GSA club. In writing, the district said, "Meeting with those students has no value to this district."

On May 1, 2014, I was honored at the White House. I attended with my partner. Following the ceremony, the White House International Press Corp asked if any teachers wanted to make a statement. I hesitated. I stood there, clenching and unclenching my hands. All I could think about was being fired if I stepped forward and spoke. It is one of the few moments of my life where I can honestly say I felt despair.

Then Mark's face, my best friend from high school, came into my mind. And all those years of missing him welled up inside of me. His parents' faces followed his. And that horrible pain that is left from a suicide roared up inside of me like a wave of misery. That is the simple fact about LGBTQ—and all teen—suicide: the surviving friends and family have a life's worth of pain that pools up like a reservoir in their hearts. We slowly dam it up and hide it away, but it never leaves, and it keeps filling up one drop at a time.

As I stood there at the White House, my dam broke. All of that pain and loss would be someone else's when their best friend, or son, or sister killed themselves.

"Pardon me," I said as I stepped by the teachers from Minnesota and Georgia, "I'm coming out of the closet."

I stepped up to the microphone and stood up for LGBT youth. I stepped up to stop some suicides. I stepped up to keep people like me from having to carry a lifetime of sadness over their dead LGBT friends. While I was speaking, I knew I was going to be fired. I knew my life was about to be turned upside down.

And I knew I was going to save a few lives.

—

From that moment on, I didn't look back. A few weeks later, gay marriage became legal in Oregon, and Mike and I were married on that first day. The story was carried all across the state. My wedding vows, said in front of a room full of TV cameras, violated my district's orders.

Soon after that, Mike and I were the first gay couple to ever ride in the Rose Festival Parade. For that entire parade route, in front of 400,000 people, Mike and I waved as the speakers blared out, "Riding with him is his husband," every two blocks. The parade was broadcast live on local stations.

The district did fire me. I fought back as hard as I could, and the teacher's union stood firmly beside me and got me my job back. Eventually, the district fired the superintendent, and my supervisor soon followed; in the same month, they were trying to fire me for a second time, and an election put three new board members on the school board. The investigation by the state showed that the district had acted in bad faith.

The head of human resources, the legal counsel, and the Head of Special Education are all gone from their positions.

I never wanted that kind of fight. I just wanted some LGBT kids to know they were valued and loved. However, the actions of my district amplified the message. The *London Daily Mail* published a full page on my story. It was picked up around the globe and even ran in the *Nigeria Times*. In Nigeria, they are executing gay people, but one morning, the gay people in that country looked at the news and saw Mike and I riding in the Rose Festival Parade. They saw a gay couple, yes, but more importantly, they saw the people lining the streets, waving, clapping, and cheering for the gay Teacher of the Year. I can imagine what that felt like to them, but I do know that the price I paid to be in their newspaper was a very small price for giving comfort to so many.

It is hard to explain the emotions of that parade and the day at the White House. I never thought, in a million years, that I could send such a message to so many LGBT youth. You have a future. You can meet a president, you can be a teacher, you can be a husband or a wife to your partner... you can just be.

But mainly, loud and clear, they heard the message I wanted them to hear more than anything. You are not alone.

Perhaps the most significant shift marking adolescence in high school as distinctly different from earlier school years is an increase in independence and agency. Through these final years of K–12 education, school culture begins to become more actively shaped by the now-adult and near-adult students themselves. This is certainly not to say that educators have lost their influence but rather that students become more like partners in creating campus culture during these late teen years. This can make for many powerful learning opportunities and create new possibilities for personal growth—both for students and for us as educators.

The *Los Angeles Times* award-winning student-written article that we begin this chapter with, taken from Daniel Pearl Magnet High School's (DPMHS) *Pearl Post*, provides one example of how educators can, and do, work with their high school students to create shared norms, values, and practices that recognize, respect, and celebrate LGBTQ and gender diversity. These practices continue to evolve in conversation with students' awareness of themselves, each other, and changes in the larger culture. This article and Brett Bigelow's Teacher of the Year story illustrate the importance of gender- and queer-expansive learning spaces and the role of inclusivity in opening such possibilities.

To offer some additional context, 2017, the year in which this book was written, was the first year in which DPMHS' Principal Deb Smith formally asked teachers to inquire about students' preferred pronouns. (Some teachers at this model-inclusive high school had already been asking variations of this for years.) Keeping with best practices for ensuring student privacy, teachers did this through a questionnaire issued in the first week of class that also asked about the students' strengths as learners and community members, and their goals for the upcoming academic year. This new practice to query students on preferred pronouns and names did more than just allow individual students to assert and affirm their gender identities—it also set a new priority within the school as a learning community, a priority that the students themselves felt was important enough to highlight through the school's newspaper.

As a magnet high school for journalism, DPMHS may be more aware than most of the significance of student/faculty partnerships in the co-creation of campus cultures. As a Teacher of the Year, Brett Bigelow is well aware of his status and responsibility as a leader for ethical and inclusive treatment of LGBTQ youth and teachers. As such, his individual actions as a teacher and DPMHS' pronoun initiative provide us with great models.

We now turn to a story of practice by DPMHS' Principal Deb Smith. From measures as seemingly small as an open office door, to actively and vocally cultivating a faculty and staff ethos that seeks to acknowledge and support students' diversity in all its forms, and settling for nothing less, Principal Smith's story about supporting trans students offers important information for educators and demonstrates what it means to honor student agency proactively and with empathy at the high school.

STORY TWO: "Becoming Johanna" by Principal Deb Smith

J looked like any other student enrolling at my school, but I knew there was a bit of a back story. J had faced expulsion from the school district for "assault on a school employee," so I was charged with informing my faculty of his prior behavior and ensuring his safety at school as well. Safety for him? Why would he be in harm's way? But J had a big secret, and his prior attempts to reveal his secret, or at the least get an adult to ask him what was wrong, had gotten him into big trouble, ranging from causing a disruption on school property and willful defiance to an "assault against a school employee." J was struggling with his gender identity and didn't have the tools to come out, instead choosing to act-out to get attention, hoping an adult would ask about him. Instead, the adults saw his behavior as aggressive, defiant, combative, and noncompliant. I knew some of this before J enrolled. I was a brand-new principal and, as you can imagine, very concerned about how I would manage all of these factors.

From this point forward in the story, I will use she; her; hers; and J's name, Johanna.

I was tasked with supporting this young person as the principal of my school but was also venturing into uncharted waters, not having any idea exactly how to go about helping Johanna navigate all that would come of this transition, supporting her and her mother in the process, supporting my faculty and the other students, as well as all stakeholders in the school. This was a multifaceted, complex issue with some known consequences as well as unknown and unintended consequences, ranging from addressing school records and state IDs, to providing support for her mental health as well as for the family, teachers, and students. I had no manual for this, no district policy bulletins to refer to. I had a boss who had no idea how to proceed, but I had a kid in front of me who needed help to become her authentic self, and I was not going to let her down. I would find a way.

After Johanna came out to me and I received her permission to inform the school community, I made it clear to the faculty and students that Johanna was to be referred to by her preferred gender pronouns, or PGPs: she, her, hers. She would use her chosen name and the restroom of her identity, the girl's room. I waited for the fallout, the conflict, the district calling to let me know that students, parents, and staff were complaining. I waited. I waited some more. Days and weeks went by and nothing, not one peep. And so it went, Johanna was just Johanna and that was that. She began to wear makeup, dressed in feminine clothing, engaged with the other girls at school, giggled and talked about girl stuff, and looked at fashion magazines, and Wonder Woman was still her hero.

The students and most of the faculty just went with the flow, not really seeing the big deal of it all. The students themselves never questioned it, never came to me to complain, never bullied or teased her. One of my other students, Ari, who also was trans but not out (all of the students believed Ari to be a boy from birth though he had been originally assigned female), reached out to her and assured her that this school was "cool like that," that she would be fine, but if there was a problem, he had her back. He would defend her and stand up to anyone who might have challenged her.

I had one teacher though who just couldn't get it, and although he adhered to my expectations regarding the way in which he would publicly address her, it was clear he was struggling and that this was against his personal beliefs. Johanna, being a very savvy and intuitive young lady with plenty of experience of veiled unacceptance, did not back down. She did not like being in this teacher's class, she challenged him constantly, did not put effort into her assignments, often falling behind, and in his PE class, she basically refused to participate. I knew this would become my problem and that I would have to find a way to support this teacher and at the same time support Johanna. I explained to Johanna countless times that she had to pass his classes in order to graduate and that this was not a battle she should pursue. I encouraged her to do the bare minimum to earn passing grades, but she had experienced so many teachers like this before him and saw him as the enemy. She showed open disrespect for the teacher, was often kicked out of his class, and then showed up in my office with all the raw emotion of a wounded child—angry, hurt, defiant.

It was my job to support Johanna and help the teacher to set aside his own personal views and beliefs, and create a safe space for Johanna in his classroom. I set the expectations, provided him with guidance, shared reading material that was also faith-based, had speakers come and present to the school about topics related to homophobia and discrimination, and further explained that Johanna had a right to be safe in his room. I also communicated that if he could not do this, I would sign his teacher-initiated transfer to another school. I would not tolerate anything less than a safe space for this student.

I also expressed my expectations of behavior to Johanna, often resulting in outright rages on her part, including profanity directed at me. Regardless of her behavior, which I felt were attempts to reject my acceptance of her in the face of her own self-hatred (especially given that her mother had turned her over to the foster system), I was responsible for her as a student at my school. My belief that no other school could do better than "us" drove my determination that I would not transfer her, I would not reject her. I communicated that I would accept her even when she couldn't accept herself. I often remind people of a common saying, "I'll believe it when I see it," but point out that this puts the onus on the other person to change. If I am the instrument of change, as I believe I am for my students, I have to see it as "I'll see it when I believe it"—a subtle but completely different mind-set about honoring young people's identities.

Other challenges in supporting Johanna came along as the years passed: she was placed in foster care; attended a summer school that did not have her chosen name on the class role; registered for college and found they were using an old account with her birth name attached, thus not allowing her to enroll with her new legal name; and worked on aligning all of her state-testing records with her new legal name and changing all of her identifying IDs. All of these examples, and more, point to how frustrated a young trans person can be, contributing to their lack of emotional constitution, lack of ability to manage very difficult, adult problems. All of this when students only need to focus on is being present in the classroom, achieving to the best of their ability, and just being young.

These very real issues, made apparent to me during my time with Johanna, illustrate the paramount importance of being mindful that, as educators, we don't know everything about the lives of our students. We are most often not privy to their trials and tribulations: students do not wake up in the morning with the sole intent to make a teacher or school employee miserable. Rather, our students face each day with a renewed hope that today will be better. Things will be different. Better.

Every time Johanna was faced with one of these significant challenges, she would come to me and would look at me and say, "I cannot do this anymore, I cannot tell another person about me; I am tired of explaining this, telling my story, I just want to quit." I would reassure her that I would help, that I would talk to whoever we needed to talk to, that it would be OK. We navigated the hurdles together. School systems, student information systems, state ID systems were not set up for people like Johanna at that time, and I suspect it is still difficult for trans youth today.

When I reflect back on my years with Johanna at school, I think about the system, the district, the legalese, the policies, and the human aspects of working with students who identify as trans, gender-nonconforming, or in any other way that is not normative. I realize how complicated much of it is for them. At the end of the day, my goal is to provide an education in a safe and welcoming space for any student who comes into my school. Johanna was just one of many students that I have had over the past 40 years of my career, and she was a precedent-setting student in the district when it came to the legal aspects of her enrollment documents, testing documents, and state and district IDs. However, Johanna was for me just another kid who wanted an education, who wanted to be valued and respected for who she was, and ultimately wanted to be her authentic self. She deserved this, all of it.

I am often asked how I do it, how do I create a safe and welcoming school for my students, a place for all students to thrive and grow. For me, it is hard to come up with answers to these questions because I really don't think about it; I just know that the students who enter my school are to be treated with respect, dignity, compassion, and fairness. I work at being mindful, at withholding judgment based on a student's behavior or how they present. I work at taking a step back to breathe and observe the situation before I make decisions. I remind myself that I don't know everything about a particular student or situation that may be impacting what is happening. I remind myself that the best way to understand is to listen.

One of my favorite examples of this (what I suggest my teachers try when a student is needing support) is to ask the student directly, "How can I help you right now? What do you need from me? Is there something I can do for you that would make it better?" These are such simple questions and yet so rarely offered to students.

It is my expectation that all students in my school will feel welcomed, that they will feel worthy and capable of great things. I am clear with my faculty and staff of my expectations. I will not tolerate anything less than safe spaces for kids to thrive, learn, achieve, and—if anyone on my faculty or staff cannot do this—I will gladly sign a transfer. I lead by example, provide training and resources for my staff to be informed as social changes happen, sometimes at a very rapid pace. I bring in a monthly speaker or an assembly for the student body to address social issues related to discrimination, anti-bullying, empowerment, or any topic that is relevant to what might be happening on campus. I make myself available at all times to all of the members of my school community—my stakeholders. My office door is always open. I will drop what I am doing to listen to a student, parent, or teacher, and I often tell people that my priority is first to my students, then teachers, then parents, and the district comes last.

When I transferred to my current school, Daniel Pearl Magnet High School, one unintended consequence of the school facility's structure is that I do not have a counter and a secretary that separate me from anyone. My office door is in the main hallway—no one must seek permission or clearance to enter my door, and although this can cause numerous interruptions throughout the day (impromptu parent conferences, teacher complaint sessions), it also provides me real-time, moment-to-moment interactions with the school community. My students, teachers, and parents see me as an active participant in the daily comings and goings of the school, and I believe this is one of the most crucial elements of my work with my students, families, and staff.

My experiences over the years with students who identify or have yet to come out as LGBTQ, who have "lived in the margins" of a school community, whether they are vivacious and active or are quiet and tend to stay by themselves, have been some of the most rewarding in my career. I have learned so much from this group of students and their families. I have learned to meet all students where they are without preconceived notions of who they are or who they will become in the future. I let them know I am a safe person, that I respect them and honor their experiences, that I value the diversity they bring to school. I post messages around my campus that my school is a safe and welcoming space through the use of supportive and inclusive posters, stickers, bulletin board displays, and a wide variety of print material in my office and the school library related to the LGBTQ community. Students notice these things, and as little as they may seem to you or me, they are important. Such a simple thing like posting "safe zone" stickers on doors, in hallways, and in classrooms conveys to students that they are welcome and will be supported, valued, and respected. It is up to us, the adults in the school, to set the tone for the students. We must model acceptance and a welcoming attitude. We must authentically believe it in our hearts, in order to convey to all members of the school that school is a place where kids can be who they are, can feel safe about it, and can focus on their education.

Social-Emotional Learning in Practice

When school environments are understood less as institutional, rigid, static, and, normative, they can become more negotiated, co-constructed, emergent, and in-process. We see this process in Principal Deb Smith's story as she highlights the social and personal responsibility of everyone at school for the co-creation of supportive learning spaces. However, she notes that it is the adults' responsibility: administrators, teachers, and staff to create safe, welcoming environments so that all students feel affirmed and valued, and willing to take up their role as a co-creator of the learning spaces.

While there will always be important procedural, legal, and program-related guidelines and mandates through which we as educators must tailor our interactions and policies, these need not stop us from recognizing and responding first to the very human and emotional lives that are always a part of our learning spaces. Hamedani & Darling-Hammond (2015) suggest that excellence in learning proceeds from and within our students' emotional and social lives, a process that is integrated and never separate from one another. As high school educators, we must learn about and engage our students on these social and emotional levels, teaching them emotional literacy: a language to describe their interior experiences in relation to the social world. Social-emotional learning (SEL) means that we work on:

> developing young people as whole human beings who are socially and emotionally aware and skilled, who engage a growth mindset that enables them to persevere when challenged, who learn to be mindful, conscientious, and empowered, and who develop a sense of social responsibility about making positive contributions to their school community and the wider community beyond… the missing piece in accountability-driven practices.
>
> *(Hamedani & Darling-Hammond, 2015, p. 1)*

When school systems are rigidly focused on standardization, institutionalization, and normativity among students and in learning, students often miss learning about themselves, who they are, and how they feel about the world as well as how to build responsible relationships with one another. This is of particular importance as students witness bias-based bullying, cyberbullying, and relational aggression. For example, LGBT youth experience three times more bullying and harassment online than non-LGBT youth (GLSEN, 2013). However, they also find communities that offer great acceptance, peer support, access to health information, and opportunities to participate in civic and political causes.

The Collaborative for Academic, Social and Emotional Learning (CASEL) identifies five competencies that educators can explicitly teach to prevent bias-based bullying, both in person and online, with high school youth. These include self-awareness, self-management, social awareness, relationship skills, and responsible decision-making (CASEL, 2017). Utilizing these competencies in instructional and cross-curricular activities on campus, social emotional learning can become the foundation for social justice work in schools. Hamedani & Darling-Hammond (2015) identified several programs that work to support students learning about self and relationship, including at Fenway High School in Boston where teaching faculty developed an Unsung Voices elective. This elective included

> A different way to look at LGBT issues, promotes understanding for Fenway's LGBT community members, and engages students in social awareness and multicultural literacy. An example of a question discussed in the class is: Why is being gay and gay marriage a "White issue?" On the day we visited the class, students were learning about Bayard Rustin, a gay African American who was a leader in the nonviolent Civil Rights movement. The class viewed a film on the subject and talked about the challenges that Rustin experienced as a gay civil rights leader in the 1940s and 1950s. Other topics covered in the class include: biographies of famous LGBT people, LGBT issues in the hip hop community, sexuality norms among athletes, coming out in African American and Latino communities, marriage and family, and gay culture. While this course provides ample opportunity to engage students around this timely social justice issue, it also tailors its content to the student population by focusing on how LGBT issues importantly intersect with race and ethnicity.
>
> *(p. 87)*

Social-emotional learning competencies guide us to develop "Habits of Mind" with our students. At Fenway, students learned:

- *Perspective: What points of view are given?*
- *Evidence: What proof is there?*

- *Relevance: Why is it important?*
- *Connection: How are things related?*
- *Supposition: What if…? (p. 88).*

These Habits of Mind help us to position multiple perspectives at the center of our relationships, policies and practices, and instruction at school. They allow us to see how seemingly willfully defiant behavior in students like Johanna stems from her having to either ignore her identity and the growing self-awareness she had about herself or assert it and risk rejection and erasure. Having SEL-focused habits of mind at the center of school practices allows us to examine student behavior from a restorative lens. What happens when schools are not safe, welcoming or inclusive, and what if they were? Would LGBTQ students like Johanna approach their environments and interactions differently?

Social-emotional learning is a vital component of the identity development of all students and of particular importance to those historically marginalized, shamed, or hurt by relationships, policies, and practices at school. Returning to Principal Smith's story, if she as a school leader had ignored the role of social-emotional learning in academic development, her student Johanna could have been dismissed as "deviant," and by way of this failed by a system that could not enact the immediate nonnormative changes necessary even to simply allow her to access the appropriate restroom. Safe, welcoming, and inclusive schools for LGBTQ students require the strong role of a school administrator, particularly in relation to homophobic and transphobic bullying. The Gay and Lesbian Equality Network (GLEN) (2013) identifies that the school principal should oversee the formulation and implementation of anti-bullying policies as they specifically impact LGBTQ youth, support staff in the implementation of prevention education and strategies, and serve as the liaison with the school board and parents and guardians. Principals should communicate the following to school staff:

- Promotion of anti-bullying policy
- Relationship between laws and policies
- Positive school culture in which differences in sexual orientation and gender identity are welcomed
- Communication with parents and guardians about positive approaches to sexuality
- Education and prevention strategies that benefit everyone (GLEN, 2013, pp. 32–33).

In our third story from the field, another high school principal offers a picture of the range of experiences and concerns of LGBTQIA students in high school and what a response aligned with SEL goals might look and feel like in each case.

STORY THREE: "LGBTQIA in High School: Brave Students and Brave Spaces" by Melissa Rivers

As a Title I high school principal where 85 percent of the students live at or below the poverty level, are primarily Mexican American and Mexican, African-American, and immigrants, I have had joy and heartbreak in working with many LGBTQI (lesbian, gay, bisexual, transgendered, questioning, intersex) high school students. Our interactions include the coming-out process, relationships, dealing with hostile families, being displaced, and sharing community resources and safe spaces. The students are incredibly brave and yet vulnerable as they share their stories with me, all the while undertaking the challenges and memory-making moments of being a high school teenager. The following are a few of the most memorable moments I have shared with my students. All names are pseudonyms, with the exception of Tyler Clementi, the Rutgers student who committed suicide in 2010.

When returning to P-12 education five years after earning my doctorate, I was purposeful in wanting to find a position at a school inclusive of all students, including LGBTQ students. This became important to me after I learned of the number of queer students committing suicide, not too long after Tyler Clementi ended his life in 2010. I knew that with the expansion of programs across the country, such as GLSEN and GSAs, safe spaces in and outside schools were much more prevalent than they were when I was teaching. I became deeply committed to the belief that students need to know there are adults who are safe and there are spaces where they do not have to fear who they are. While designated safe spaces are important, a school culture where students can hold their same-gender boyfriend or girlfriend's hand without fear was very important to me. I wanted to lessen the chance that one of my students would become another statistic.

I knew that regardless of the school, as a principal, I would be confronted with the reality of student-on-student harassment, and I knew that some of my LGBTQI students would be kicked out of their houses or experience violence simply for being gay. The statistics are undeniable. In the following paragraphs, I share some of the stories of my interactions with students, all of whom are Mexican or Mexican American and identify as LGBTQI. I am focusing on several aspects of LGBTQI students' experiences that I have come to understand as critical to us as educators, working to create safe learning environments for all students. My focus includes public displays of affection between LGBTQI students, the coming-out process, the needs of transgender students, and the importance of LGBTQI-affirming school clubs and organizations. I conclude with a brief discussion of why creating brave spaces that honor LGBTQI students is also important for LGBTQI faculty or administrators.

Public Displays of Affection

Disciplinary measures concerning public displays of affection (PDA) between two same-gender students require a great deal of thought on the part of educators. For these students, typical disciplinary procedures have implications well beyond those of their heterosexual counterparts. For example, the usual approach of reporting to parent(s)/guardian(s) that their child was "making out" with another student can create a life or death situation for queer students. This fact was never explicitly discussed in any of my education programs nor in the one I taught in. However, I have since learned through firsthand experience and observation that educators must think before "outing" or revealing a student's sexuality to their parent(s)/guardian(s). In one situation, the assistant principal told both students' parents their children were violating the school PDA rule with a student of the same sex. While neither of those students was kicked out of their homes, both were subjected to shaming by their parents and one was forced by her parents to stay away from the other and switched out of all classes with that student.

Coming Out

The process of "coming out" is a critical moment in any person's life, regardless of age. However, this process may have an exacerbated impact on teenagers since they rely on their parents or guardians for support financially, physically, and emotionally. For many high schoolers, revealing that they do not conform to the gender binary or heteronormativity, the potential for danger, whether perceived or real, is extremely high. The following three stories illustrate some of the most common perils faced by students when "coming out" to their families. These stories are drawn directly from my experiences as a school administrator.

Selena:

Selena was an 18-year-old student who was living with her dad and his wife, her stepmother. Selena's biological mother had passed away five years prior, and she did not have a close relationship with her dad or his new wife. Selena came to my office after she was kicked out of her house for being gay. She stated to me that her dad found out she was dating a girl and stated that did not want her influencing her younger sibling (half-sister). Her father then told Selena she would have to leave the home and kicked her out with only her clothes. She understood I had to call Child Protective Services (CPS) because I saw the bruises and explained that I was required by law to call CPS if a student was being harmed. However, because Selena was 18 and a legal adult, she refused to talk to CPS or the police because she "just wanted to be out." Selena spent a month "couch surfing" at a friend's house before coming out to her grandparents and finally moving in with them.

Julio:

Julio was an undocumented senior, who came to talk to me a week before graduation because he was scared. Julio had begun to attend Valley One-in-Ten meetings. Valley One-in-Ten is an organization that seeks to support LGBTQI youth through social programs, teaches healthy choices, and provides resources for the teen LGBTQ community. At this time, Julio's mom started checking his phone to find out where he had been going. Through looking at his text messages, Julio's mom began to question him about his sexuality. Julio's mom told him if she found out he was gay, she would bring his older brother back from Texas to "beat the gay out of him." No son of hers would be gay. Julio cried and said he would have to hide who he is and, when he could save enough money, move out. I shared with him the community services that provided housing for LGBTQI youth and other housing options. I never heard from him after graduation.

Celia:

Celia was a 17-year-old who came to me the summer before her senior year. Celia's mom asked if she could talk to me about her daughter's schedule and a concern. Over the summer Celia's mom found out she was dating another student, a young woman. I met with Celia and her mom, who wanted to make sure that her daughter would not be scheduled in the same classes as her girlfriend. Mom was in tears because she could not understand how her daughter could be gay. They were a "good Catholic family," she explained. Celia's mom was considering having her daughter transfer schools or sending her to New Mexico to live with her Aunt. We talked about her fears and how her vision for her daughter was different than her daughter's view. Celia's mom did not want her daughter to commit suicide over being gay; she did not understand how she as a mother had caused her daughter to be gay. Being gay was not acceptable to her.

I believe it was rooted in culture and religion. We talked about whether being gay was a choice or not. I shared a story from a colleague about when her first-generation Mexican-American brother came out and how their mother was upset until her brother explained that just as she had no choice of being born in Mexico, he had no choice about being gay. We discussed how parents have dreams for their children when they are born. Celia's mom worried that her daughter would not be able to get married or have children. We talked about Pope Francis's statement about LGBT people and what it meant when he asked, "Who am I to judge?" I explained that while I could switch Celia's classes, the school would not monitor Celia and her girlfriend or in any way keep track of whether the two were talking to each other or eating lunch together. Celia was able to stay at our school and graduate.

Transgender and Transitioning Students

Bathrooms and transgender students have been at the forefront of LGBTQI concerns in recent years. But there is much more than bathrooms and locker rooms to consider when creating a safe space for gender-nonconforming, trans, or transitioning high school students. This story is about the first transgender student I worked with at our school.

Carla:

Carla was a 14-year-old first-year student, whose sister I knew well and who graduated from our school. Carla asked to talk to me on registration day. She told me that her sister had told her it was okay. We went into my office, and Carla put her head down and quietly asked if it would be okay for her not to be called Carla by her teachers. I asked her what would she like to be called. Her reply: Carl. He further explained that he is transitioning from female to male and had just told his family of his true gender identity over the weekend. I let him know that it was not a problem and that I would talk with the faculty and staff about it. I asked Carl which restroom he felt safe using, and he replied that he was not sure. I let him know he can use the faculty/staff bathrooms until he figured it out. Carl used both the faculty/staff and girl's restrooms. He did not feel comfortable yet using the boy's restroom. While it was difficult to switch pronouns when talking with him, and I admit I still slip on occasion, I was amazed at the strength Carl had to talk to his new principal about such a difficult thing. I felt if he had the strength to share his story, the least I could do was to make sure I was doing everything I could to support him.

All of Carl's teachers agreed to call him Carl, not Carla. However, two months later, he came to me very upset. He was put into a student group in class where his email was shared publicly. Because the school had not changed his email (a complete oversight, not intentional) from Carla to Carl, he felt "outed" as a biological female, causing him great concern that his gender identity as a young man might also now be questioned. I immediately had his email changed to reflect his name, Carl, and his gender identity. However, according to state law, we are not able to change his name on his report card to reflect his gender identity.

At the end of the semester, Carl asked to talk to me about his schedule. He wanted to see if it would be OK if he did not take a physical education class until he was a senior. I told Carl that would not be a problem and put a note in his file. I asked why, and he explained to me that, by the time he was a senior, he would probably be okay about changing his clothes in front of his peers since he would be through more of his transition by then. As a principal and a leader, I have learned a great deal from Carl. Most importantly, I learned that I do not have to know it all: if I am willing to listen to my students, they will tell me what I need to know to support them and to create a safe learning environment for them.

LGBTQ Clubs and Student Organizations

I always believed our school was a safe space for queer students, but questioned that belief when a student asked to create a GSA. Same-gender couples felt comfortable and supported to hold hands at school. We always had same-gender couples at dances and prom, with no issues. Beatriz said she wanted all students to have a safe place where they could have allies and talk about what they were going through. She did not think LGBTQ students had that space. So, I connected her with GLSEN. Over the summer, she attended a GLSEN training to learn how to start a GSA. Currently, our GSA meets weekly and has a consistent group of 20 students.

This past year, Beatriz and I had several conversations about the GSA and how things were going. The day after the presidential election, Beatriz was in the office and I asked her how she was doing. When she looked up, I noticed a tear dripping down her face. We went into my office and I asked what was wrong. The tears began streaming as she shared her worry that she would never be able to be herself at home. Her parents had voted for Trump, which made her feel that she would never be able to come out as bisexual. The reason why she started the GSA was not just for other students to feel safe, but for her to have a safe space as well.

Schools have to be safe spaces for all students, especially for our most vulnerable. This requires purposeful action. It requires having courageous conversations with bus drivers who may try to separate a couple from sitting with one another on the bus because they are holding hands and are the same gender, arguing that it is against God's law for them to be together. It includes talking to prospective employees about what being inclusive means. It requires the whole school to be dedicated to this mission, even if they may not understand what the student is going through. It requires listening to students and building relationships with them as one of Melissa River's students asks us to do in this art work.

In Conclusion

Creating a safe space for all students has always been important to me. When I returned to K–12 education, I knew I would be confronting LGBTQI issues differently than when I was a teacher. I knew my students' stories would affect me. However, I did not realize just how much it would affect me emotionally.

Meeting with a student in August 2015, after the Supreme Court decision legalizing gay marriage, I was asked my thoughts on the ruling. I shared how great I thought it was and that it was about time. I add this because I am a lesbian educator. I am not out to my students, nor to all of my staff. When seeing queer couples dancing at prom, I cried, not ever expecting to see that in my lifetime: three queer couples could be dancing with all the straight couples, and not one rude comment was said to them. I did not tell the student that I cried my eyes out after the Supreme Court decision, or that my partner and I got married the day after the decision. I wear my wedding ring on my middle finger. I struggle with the idea of being out at school and not being out. I worry that I am not being a good role model to my students, that I am perpetuating the idea they must be silent to be accepted.

I have experienced hate for being queer. I have had bottles thrown at me when walking down the street hand in hand with a girlfriend. I have had epitaphs carved into my office door, calling me a F★&★ing Dyke, my office broken into and trashed, even though I was not out at school. The principal did not believe it was a hate crime, nor did he think it was important to call the police, in spite of my asking for it. He told me to clean up my office and get over it. I learned to keep my private life, private.

I live and work in a state that does not believe in my rights as a lesbian. Many of my students come from very conservative, religious backgrounds. I believe they would not keep their students at our school if they knew I was gay; therefore, I am not out. However, I know some students have figured me out. After meeting with Selena about where she would live, how to talk with her grandparents, giving her resources, and the book *It Gets Better,* she was surprised at how much information I gave her and asked how I knew about all of these things. I told her it was because I had several friends who were gay or had queer children. Later that day, Selena saw me alone in the courtyard, came up and asked, "Doc, are you gay?" My response was, would it make any difference if I were? Her reply, "It's ok, doc, I won't tell, I've got your back" and gave me a hug. Knowing that I am their safe space is enough.

As illustrated by these three brave practitioner stories, and the student journalism article that opened this chapter, the critical reframing of high school environments as constantly emergent and in-process. We view this reframing as be both vital and hopeful. If school environments are less institutional, regimented, and static—depending on old rigid gender binaries and heteronormative assumptions about relationships—educators can negotiate, co-construct, and make emergent newly safe, welcoming, and inclusive policies and practices. We are in-process. This framing keeps us focused on the kind of future horizon that is responsive to our student population and social justice changes in the larger culture. We recognize that this is a significant shift from more traditional framings of high school campus cultures. However, emergent spaces, guided by social emotional learning practices, encourage educators to recognize students in all their complexities and intersectionalities. We can embrace the environment as both shaped by, and shaping, the practices and policies of school.

Questions for Reflection

1. Reflecting on your high school's environment, how can it become less institutional and normative and more emergent and formative? What are some first steps you can take? How will you ensure the continued evolution of your school climate?
2. How can you involve the administrators, teachers, and staff in the co-creation of supportive learning environments?
3. How might you incorporate the five competencies of Social and Emotional Learning into your instruction and campus activities?
4. Which school activities are in need of modification and which need to be eliminated in order to create a more welcoming and inclusive environment?

References

Ajilese, J. M. (2017, October 2). Opinion: Students accepted through preferred gender pronouns. *High School Insider, Los Angeles Times.* Retrieved from http://highschool.latimes.com/daniel-pearl-magnet-high-school/opinion-students-accepted-through-preferred-gender-pronouns/

CASEL. (2017). Core SEL competencies. *CASEL.* Retrieved from http://casel.org/core-competencies/

GLEN. (2013). *Being LGBT in school: A resource for post-primary schools to prevent homophobic and transphobic bullying and support LGBT students.* Gay + Lesbian Equality Network. Retrieved from www.education.ie/en/Publications/Education-Reports/Being-LGBT-in-School.pdf

GLSEN. (2013). *Out Online: The experiences of lesbian, gay, bisexual and transgender youth on the internet.* Gay Lesbian Straight Education Network. Retrieved from www.glsen.org/press/study-finds-lgbt-youth-face-greater-harassment-online

Hamedani, M. G., & Darling-Hammond, L. (2015). *Social emotional learning in high school: How three urban high schools engage, educate, and empower youth.* SCOPE: Stanford Center for Opportunity Policy in Education. Retrieved from https://edpolicy.stanford.edu/sites/default/files/publications/scope-pub-social-emotional-learning-execsummary.pdf

Yon, D. (2000). *Elusive culture: Schooling, race and identity in global times.* Albany: State University of New York Press.

9

HIGH SCHOOL CURRICULUM

In high schools across the country, you notice that student clubs often implement LGBTQ (lesbian, gay, bisexual, transgender, queer) activities related to school climate. You make a list of the most frequent activities to suggest to your school's recently formed GSA (traditionally known as a Gay Straight Alliance), which the students call the Gender and Sexuality Alliance. They started the club last year, using the GSA Network's (2009) "10 Tips for Starting a GSA." Now that the students are organized, they want to start implementing some activities you made note of. You are excited to think about how school climate actions can become an informal curriculum at your school. The GSA wants to implement an Ally Week, the Day of Silence, and a School Climate Survey, and then reflect on the outcomes. They learned about each of these events on GLSEN's (2017) website. You are amazed and excited for the learning that will take place!

Ally Week: A national event occurring in fall that focuses on conversations about what LGBTQ students need from their allies.

Day of Silence: A national event occurring in the spring to raise awareness about LGBTQ bullying and the silencing effect of LGBT name-calling.

School Climate Survey: A downloadable survey for middle and high schools to distribute locally to their campus. The survey includes a focus on bias, bullying, and harassment. Students can analyze the data from this survey about their campus.

Additionally, you wonder how you can encourage LGBTQ inclusion in the high school curriculum and coursework. You know that many teachers have a limited understanding of LGBTQ-related concepts, such as the gender binary and gender on a continuum, the relationship between gender and sexuality, creating a safe space, intervening in bias-based bullying, supporting transgender youth, understanding naming and the role of pronouns, identifying behaviors that help and behaviors that hurt, addressing privilege and marginalization, and discussing bias and microaggressions. Yikes! The list is long. At some point, you hope the GSA can develop resources and a speaking event to help educate the high school faculty and students on these ideas. But you realize this may be quite a challenge and will definitely take some time, especially in relation to the very traditional ways that academic disciplines are taught on your campus.

This vignette highlights the power of youth-driven change at schools and the role informal and unsanctioned curriculum can play in that change. High school is a space where youth are not only learning complex disciplinary content but also learning about what society values and how society sees and respects them, and their experiences. High school students need to see their lives and the social world as available for curricular study.

LGBTQ inclusion in curriculum is challenging for high schools and colleges because courses are more deeply and broadly discipline-specific. Most academic disciplines are traditionally not inclusive of multiple perspectives on gender and sexuality. We begin this chapter with an examination of the role of curriculum theory in the construction of knowledge so that we may then deconstruct and re-center multiple epistemologies in the high school curriculum. In disciplinary and interdisciplinary teaching teams, we can ask key questions: *whose curriculum, for what purposes, to whose benefit?*

In the USA, curriculum is often taught from a Western tradition of hegemonic disciplinarity, which means that discipline-identified knowledge, skills, and readings have not often been inclusive of marginalized or oppressed experiences or perspectives (Osborne, 2015). The discipline's function has been to normalize or normatize a selective tradition of canonical knowledge for the purpose of communicating official knowledge in that discipline. This official knowledge then acts as a filter for curricular decisions (Luke, Cooke, & Luke, 1986). Such a selective tradition can be viewed as "cherished knowledge" in the sense that it is the stuff we have always taught and still hold on to intellectually, even emotionally. (Jupp, 2017). The problem is that these canons have often utilized ideologies that include, or are even driven by, biases about race, class, gender, and sexuality, both in terms of texts chosen and perspectives included.

Young (2014) suggests that the core question guiding curricular decisions should be *how does (the curriculum) promote conceptual progression?* While this question does not inherently attend to the biases at work in disciplinary selective traditions, Young pairs it with a critique of the "knowledge of the powerful" and the ways in which knowledge has been utilized to cultivate the elite in this country. Young proposes that curriculum become "powerful knowledge," which ensures that there are resources for learning explanations, critiquing, and thinking of alternatives. In this way, as teachers, we can expand our curricular texts, epistemological beliefs, and ontological ways of knowing the world outside the canon. As we examine the curriculum's conceptual progression, we can include "difficult knowledge," those narratives that disrupt binary notions of normal and abnormal, and move toward a study of human variation. If we open up the curricular conversation to include an analysis of its exclusionary or inclusionary functions toward minoritized communities, families, and youth, we can begin to identify unsanctioned and fugitive knowledge, such as counter-narratives, that will enrich both disciplinary and interdisciplinary learning.

We propose having curricular conversations (Burke & Collier, 2017) among your high school's disciplinary faculty and across disciplines in professional learning communities to grapple with content-based LGBTQ inclusion. We can ask *who is the curriculum for, for what purposes, and to whose benefit?* We can examine the skills, competencies, behaviors, knowledge, and capacities built through the curriculum. Finally, we can introduce a new question: *how can we integrate the specific experiences, perspectives, histories, and contributions of minoritized communities into all our courses at the high school?* A place to start is James Banks's (2001) framework for multicultural curriculum integration. Originally applied to analyzing curricular inclusion of cultural diversity, particularly race and ethnicity, this framework can be utilized to think about all identity-based communities' histories and perspectives that have been marginalized or minoritized in society and in the curriculum.

JAMES BANKS'S FRAMEWORK FOR MULTICULTURAL CURRICULUM INTEGRATION

The contributions approach (Level 1): Focuses on heroes, holidays, and discrete cultural elements.

The additive approach (Level 2): Content, concepts, themes, and perspectives are added to the curriculum without changing its structure.

The transformation approach (Level 3): The structure of the curriculum is changed to enable students to view concepts, issues, events *from the perspectives* of diverse cultural groups.

The social action approach (Level 4): Students make decisions on important social issues and take actions to help solve them.

Vecellio (2012) applied Banks's framework to California's FAIR (Fair, Accurate, Inclusive and Respectful) Education Act's efforts to include LGBTQ community/history in the K-12 curriculum. The author provides examples at each level of the framework. Through a *contributions approach,* students would study citizens like Harvey Milk, Gertrude Stein, Bayard Rustin, and two-spirit Native Americans. Additionally, schools might include "celebrations" like LGBT Pride Month (June), LGBT History Month (October), and National Coming Out Day (October 11). Through the *additive approach*, students would experience content focused on the roles that LGBTQ people and communities have played in society, like an examination of changing gender roles and family structures over time; the history of LGBTQ civil rights struggles; and the influence of media and comparison of court cases and laws. Through the *transformation approach,* students would examine how diverse identity communities comprise US culture. Banks (2001) states,

> The emphasis should be on how the common U.S. culture and society emerged from a complex synthesis and interaction of the diverse cultural elements that originated within the various cultural, racial, ethnic, and religious groups that make up U.S. society.
>
> *(p. 235)*

In the transformation approach, Vecellio (2012) applies cultural synthesis to an examination of the perspectives of LGBTQ people in relation to US society, and asks us "to examine things as they are and seek to determine how the LGBT community had some influence on what that thing has come to be" (p. 172). Vecellio suggests that students ask, "what is missing from our view of a given concept, issue, or event because the LGBT influence, perspective, or experience has not been adequately accounted for?" (2012, p. 172). Finally, with a *social action approach*, students ask, *what should we do with the information we have learned?* This approach requires both an examination of the curriculum and decision-making about how to act in the world, such as taking up a cause and writing letters about anti-LGBTQ legislation, participating in a community organization like the It Gets Better Project, or presenting at a school board meeting to advocate for greater inclusion of LGBTQ literature in school libraries.

The following are some disciplinary content-based examples of LGBTQ curricular integration at varying levels of the Banks's framework (from the contributions approach to the social action approach). After reading the examples, we end the chapter with a teacher's story exploring the opportunities for LGBTQ inclusion and visibility in high school.

Disciplinary Content Examples of LGBTQ Integration

Social Studies

When studying the impact of colonialism and westward expansion on Native American tribes, social studies teachers address the displacement of tribes onto reservations and indigenous children being forcibly removed from tribes and placed in federal boarding schools. During this study, teachers can address how these oppressive policies and practices drastically altered Native American social structures, including governance, gender, and family diversity. For example, the California History Social Studies Framework revisions (2016) identify that students will learn how the breaking of Native lands led to "displacing elements of female and two-spirit authority traditionally respected in many tribal societies." Students can compare and contrast third-gender peoples in multiple societies across the world, including the Muxe in Mexico, two-spirit people in Native American tribes, the Mahu in Hawaii, the Sakalavas of Madagascar, and the third-gender Incan god Chuiqui Chinchay (Independent Lens, 2015).

English and Theater Arts

The disciplines of English and theater arts can explore LGBTQ youth lives and perspectives during class, through a performance, and using queer texts for analysis. Chappell (2016) reviewed the play *The Year We Thought of Love*, which was devised by LGBTQ youth in Boston and shown to local high school students in an assembly format. The documentary film features LGBTQ youth doing devised theater about their lives. As the stories unfolded, Chappell found herself identifying with the young people's struggles: to understand themselves, to claim the right to name themselves, and to be loved and love in the world. The teens explore themes of being and becoming: who they are at different points along their journeys of gender and sexuality, and who they want to become:

> *"I love attention."*
> *"I am creative."*
> *"I am in love."*
> *"I am gender queer."*
> *"I am somebody."*

The goals of the devised theater work and its performance for high school audiences include:

- Sharing stories of LGBTQ youth, primarily of color, in their own voices
- Demonstrating the power of theater in finding one's voice and claiming and sharing one's story
- Reducing isolation by hearing stories from LGBTQ youth who advocate for themselves
- Encouraging the seeking of support from other youth and adults
- Modeling the work of LGBTQ artists and activists
- Increasing empathy and understanding of LGBTQ youth
- Empowering viewers to provide support to LGBTQ youth
- Acknowledging the power and wisdom of LGBTQ youth to advocate for themselves.

English and theater arts courses can explore these goals by featuring stories of LGBTQ youth during textual analysis and engagement with world events and community lives. Films like *The Year We Thought About Love* help us reflect on questions like: how were schools impacted by the True Colors performances and post-show discussion with the actors? How can teachers and administrators reflect on the ways in which their schools might contribute to the discrimination and marginalization of LGBTQ youth? What policies and practices do schools need to change (curriculum, pedagogy, school climate and procedures, family supports and resources) to become more responsive to their own LGBTQ students? How can the inclusion of LGBTQ youth narratives in the high school curriculum become an educative experience not only for students but for the adults in the room?

Science

A school administrator, Mary Hoelscher (2017), shares her thoughts on LGBTQ inclusion in high school science, including the impact of not seeing herself in the curriculum as a bisexual, genderqueer person. She identifies the impact of these omissions on LGBTQ youth, most of whom do not enter STEM (science, technology, engineering and mathematics) fields. Hoelscher advocates for including the lives of LGBTQ scientists in STEM curriculum and addressing LGBTQ themes in the study of science, such as in biology:

> Nature *loves* gender and sexual diversity. In addition to there being more than two biological sexes, there are even animals who change their biological sex, individual animals with two sexes, and animals that have sex roles reversed from the stereotypes I had been raised learning. And same-sex mating is just the beginning of the diversity of sexual behavior in the animal kingdom. Sex, in nature, just as within human populations, has purposes far beyond reproduction that provide real benefits for individuals and their communities.
>
> *(Screens 2–3)*

An LGBTQ-inclusive science class would address this wonderful ecological and human diversity as part of the context for studying STEM.

Mathematics

The national organization GLSEN provides an example of integrating LGBTQ-focused topics in mathematics through statistics and data analysis. High school youth can examine LGBT demographic trends as reflected in the 2010 census results. They can work in small groups to create a chart or graph illustrating national or state-level trends on a specific topic (e.g., number of same-sex couples, number of same-sex couples raising children, number of adopted or foster children in LGBT-headed households, etc.). Importantly, the chosen data should not tokenize, exoticize, or victimize LGBT communities, such as trans or nonbinary people (Harbin, 2016). Further, when analyzing data, teacher and students should avoid asking a trans or queer student to explain the data or overgeneralize about individual LGBTQ experiences based on the demographic trends. These can be points of discussion with the class.

Athletics and Physical Education

High school coaches and PE teachers can have conversations with their students about the importance of athletes being aware of social issues (Jaklitsch, 2017). The coach can begin with a discussion of Colin Kapernick's #TakeAKnee movement, which began to point attention toward trends of racial violence committed by police officers as well as the subsequent NFL discussions about the role of social justice in sports (Goldman, 2017). Further, the coach can discuss other social issues that sports should attend to, such as supporting the well-being of LGBTQ athletes. The students can read and reflect on articles like the NCAA's *Mind, Body and Sport: Harassment and discrimination— LGBTQ student-athletes* (Rankin & Weber, 2014). Importantly, coaches and students should avoid asking a trans or queer student to explain the article or represent *the* LGBTQ experience based on current events or demographic trends.

Media Production

Throughout the year, the film/video/media teacher can address social justice issues in media studies and popular culture. Students can investigate questions like: how inclusive is the entertainment industry? How do gender stereotypes and biases impact representation in advertising? What should a commitment to diversity in media entail? What responsibility do I have as an individual to redress the "inclusion crisis" about issues of race, gender, and difference in media? They can read articles about representation issues, like this one published by the Annenberg Foundation and University of Southern California (Public Affairs Staff, 2017).

Health

The Human Rights Campaign (HRC) (2015) suggests that "Lesbian, gay, bisexual, transgender, queer and questioning (LGBTQ) youth need and deserve to learn in settings that are inclusive of their experiences and that give them the education necessary to stay safe and healthy." This means that schools should offer comprehensive sex education in addition to integrating LGBTQ topics throughout health classes and well-being health services offered at the high school. As the HRC points out, "The GLSEN 2013 National School Climate Survey found that fewer than five percent of LGBT students had health classes that included positive representations of LGBT-related topics. Among millennials surveyed in 2015, only 12 percent said their sex education classes covered same-sex relationships" (Jones & Cox, 2015). Health teachers can share these statistics in order to advocate for an inclusive health programs in high school. Such inclusive programs would:

- help youth understand gender identity and sexual orientation with age-appropriate and medically accurate information
- incorporate positive examples of LGBTQ individuals, romantic relationships, and families
- emphasize the need for protection during sex for people of all identities
- dispel common myths and stereotypes about behavior and identity (HRC, 2015, p. 1).

One example is the Health Connected Curriculum aligned with California's recent passage of grades 9–12 Comprehensive Sex Education policy (Health Connected, 2014). In this curriculum, among many topics, students talk about multiple identities and analyze the film *Straightlaced: How Gender's Got Us All Tied Up* (GroundSpark, n.d.).

From the aforementioned multidisciplinary curricular examples, we hope to illustrate the ease with which gender diversity and LGBTQ inclusion can be operationalized across the high school disciplines. To begin, we recommend that you initiate curricular conversations with your colleagues on campus. As an LGBTQ ally and advocate, your voice is important. In these conversations, you can analyze the official knowledge in the disciplines that has been "cherished" over the years, in particular how this knowledge may marginalize or erase the perspectives, ways of knowing and being, and histories of particular communities. You can pose the question *how can we integrate specific experiences, perspectives, histories, and contributions of minoritized communities into all our courses at the high school?* You are welcome to share the examples of LGBTQ integration from this book as well as James Banks's multicultural curriculum integration framework. Initiate conversations about what the levels of curricular inclusion might look like, including the contributions of LGBTQ individuals and communities, additive perspectives, transformation of the curricular center, and social action projects.

In the stories that follow, we read about curricular integration of students' lives, which leads the teacher to reflect on LGBTQ inclusion. Drama teacher John Newman shares his experiences navigating a restrictive political environment to create LGBTQ-inclusive spaces through strategic actions in his drama classroom. Then English teacher Dan Krack shares how he struggles with the lack of mentoring for LGBTQ youth in schools, and the silencing effect of this lack of visibility on his own teaching and identity, as well as on the identities of and relationships with his students. In part, we can solve these challenges through curriculum change.

STORY ONE: "A Silent, Safe Haven in Drama" by John Newman

I taught and directed high school theater in Salt Lake City, Utah, between 1991 and 2010. By the time I left my high school teaching position, the school hosted student clubs that included a GSA as well as everything from culture-based groups like the Hispanic Club and Polynesian Club to interest-based groups like the Simpsons Fan Club and the Salt Lake Lawnchair Rewebbing Society.

However, the GSA was not always allowed at the school. In February 1996, the Salt Lake City School Board voted to eliminate all non-curricular clubs rather than allow a GSA club to meet at one of its high schools. After a lengthy legal battle, the ban was reversed in October 2000.

During my district's 1996–2000 ban on non-curricular clubs, I continued to advise the school's drama club. Since drama is a core subject in the state curriculum and Utah requires 1.5 fine arts credits for graduation, the drama club I advised was considered a "school club," rather than a "student club," and was exempted from the ban on extracurricular clubs. The drama club members were accepting of students who came from different belief systems as well as from different socioeconomic classes and backgrounds. The inclusive nature of the drama club allowed it to serve as a safe haven for LGBTQ students, even though their issues could not be openly discussed or presented on stage.

There were always a number of students in the drama program who were openly gay. As far as I could observe, from my outside adult perspective, these students were welcomed and accepted by the other students. The drama program represented a wider religious, ability, and economic diversity than other arts programs at the school. I believe that this was one reason that LGBTQ students participated in greater numbers in the drama club than they did in other arts-based clubs on campus.

While I do not advocate beliefs and practices generally accepted in the LGBTQ community, I consider myself an ally to those whose beliefs differ from my own. A central tenant of my religion is that we claim the right to worship according to the dictates of our own conscience and allow others the same privilege. Where I take a further leap is to extend the idea of "worship" to "belief." That allows me to assert the rights of my students in the LGBTQ community without necessarily agreeing with all of their stances. While I may not have been advocate for their cause, I could be a supporter of LGBTQ students whose belief systems varied from my own.

I should clarify that the drama club was only one facet of my co-curricular program. I taught theater classes during the day and directed productions after regular school hours that were not considered functions of the drama club. However, the drama club was the student-run organization and served as the social network of the larger theater program. The members of the club elected student officers and undertook, as its central project, an annual production of student-written, student-directed, student-acted one-act plays.

The following are some of my philosophical approaches to theater education and my observations of their impact on LGBTQ inclusion in the high school. What I describe about the theater program as a whole was generally true about the drama club and the student productions it presented.

Inclusive Casting

The drama program at our school was less popular with students than other arts programs. My audition pool was never exponentially larger than the number of roles I could cast in musicals and plays, but during the 1990s, I gradually moved toward an "all-comers" casting approach. With plays, this meant that I would need to direct one play and recruit a guest director for a second show that was rehearsed during the same time frame, or I would expand the cast of a single production in order to offer a meaningful role to all who auditioned.

Rather than increasing the popularity of the play productions, I found this policy tended to reduce the total number of auditioners. There is an elitism that many students subscribe to that they don't want to be a part of something if everyone can be a part of it. However, while I may have had fewer students auditioning for my productions, those who did audition knew from the outset that they would be welcomed and included. I believe that an inclusive atmosphere was encouraging to those who were concerned about being accepted by their peers, including LGBTQ students participating in the theater productions and the drama club.

Finding Outside Venues for Student-Written Plays

Since district and state policies explicitly forbade discussion of homosexuality in health courses, those policies were interpreted by administrators to implicitly forbid the presentation of homosexual relationships and gender fluidity in performing arts productions in the schools. One year, a student playwright had written a play that dealt with homophobia in what I considered a sensitive and realistic way. Two young male characters, who seemingly identify as heterosexual, struggle against the fact that if two men are close friends, they must always be concerned that others will misconstrue their relationship as being sexual when it is actually platonic.

I took the play to our site administrator who ruled that its subject matter was unacceptable for production at our school. Ironically, he refused to read the play that he found offensive. The student did not take no for an answer and took the script to the district office. I was surprised to receive a conference call one afternoon from the district's human sexuality committee. It was made clear to me that the play must not be produced, and it was implied that if I produced the play against their prohibition, it could put my job in jeopardy.

I followed the mandate from the district but worked with the student playwright to find another venue where his play could be presented. We looked at performing it for the GSA, which would have required signed parent permission forms for all student audience members. I ultimately was able to connect the student with a local theater company that could produce his script. Even when a school is unable or unwilling to present controversial material written by student playwrights, a theater teacher may connect a student writer with outside producers who have greater latitude in the plays that they can produce.

Presenting Established Plays that Explore Gender Fluidity

During the final year of the club ban, we produced the musical *Peter Pan* and Shakespeare's comedy *Twelfth Night*. Both plays require a woman to play the role of a man, and yet both are almost universally accepted in the cannon of family-friendly theater. We chose to produce those scripts based on their own merits, the former because it was an ideal musical to perform for all the sixth graders in the district and the latter because it was the preferred Shakespeare title of the guest director. However, when my administrator objected to producing *Twelfth Night* because of its gender-bending elements, I defended the play as a well-accepted piece of classical theater. Other Shakespeare plays, such as *As You Like It* and *Cymbeline,* and non-Shakespeare plays, such as *Charlie's Aunt,* may allow schools' theater programs to examine gender issues while staying within the bounds of the accepted repertory.

Discussing and Challenging Gender Roles and Expectations in All Plays and Musicals

Because I always had more women auditioning than men, I would often make some male roles female and play them as female. Doing so allowed us to discuss whether or not women would have been able to play particular roles in society, how they might have filled those roles if they had been allowed, and to what degree our society continues to maintain gender barriers. Even a musical like *Fiddler on the Roof,* in which the roles of women, girls, men, and boys are rigidly defined in the opening number, provides opportunities to discuss how the roles of mamas, daughters, papas, and sons have or have not transformed over time and what gender rigidities persist in our own society.

It is also possible to look at more universal issues, such as individual difference, silenced voices, and subtle and overt oppression, which are presented in many scripts that even the most conservative administrators would deem acceptable. Exploration of these issues may allow students who are different, silenced, and oppressed to consider how others have dealt with those dynamics, even if the characteristics that set the characters apart may not be the ones that distinguish individual students in the theater program, including those who identify with the LGBTQ community.

Developing New Plays with Playwrights in Residence

In addition to producing an annual musical and Shakespeare play, my program produced more than a dozen premieres of new plays by award-winning writers of plays for young audiences and actors. Some of these plays challenged traditional gender roles, such as the strong female protagonist in Sandra Fenichel Asher's *ARK 5* and the sensitive male protagonist in Elise Forier's *The Hawk Prince.* All of those plays invited discussion with the playwrights, who participated in workshop development, about the ways that male and female characters were presented in the scripts. Those discussions invited students to interrogate and challenge how gender roles are defined and presented in the plays that they perform.

Restrictions of discussion and presentation of LGBTQ issues that currently exist in many public schools will not last forever and are subject to legal challenges and court rulings that may reverse them in the near future. I told my students, when the school restricted their plays on LGBTQ subjects, there would likely come a time when such plays would not only be allowed but could not legally be prohibited. In the meantime, theater teachers, even in the most conservative school environments, can explore issues of difference and discrimination in other contexts and lead inclusive programs in which all students can feel safe, accepted, and respected.

STORY TWO: "They Need More than Gaga" by Dan Krack

This is a story that, until now, I have reserved only for close, trusted friends. While the telling of this story publicly is potentially dangerous for me, I seize this opportunity to share it as a leap forward in my commitment to advocating for my LGBTQ students. I am confident that the potential benefits of sharing my story outweigh the risks I take in telling it. I believe that LGBTQ people are more visible these days, thanks to more widespread representation of LGBTQ people in the media. For instance, popular television shows including *Modern Family, Scream Queens, Grey's Anatomy,* and *The Real O'Neals* all feature LGBTQ principal characters that disrupt the previously heteronormative prime-time television landscape. Additionally, the debate over state and federal laws regarding LGBTQ issues including civil rights, marriage equality, and transgender bathroom use have also had an impact on LGBTQ visibility by bringing the argument of LGBTQ civil rights from the margins into the mainstream. However, despite the increased visibility, LGBTQ young people are still part of an extremely vulnerable population. In this story, I offer my voice to the cause of helping young people to accept themselves, especially when it seems that no one else values, respects, or loves them. I want to be able to help students gain a sense of belonging and to be able to tell them that it can and *will* get better for them. However, as a teacher, I often feel powerless. And, at times, invisible.

I teach high school English near Pittsburgh, PA, and I often utilize an art project as a first-week-of-school activity. My students create what I call "bio-collages" by cutting images, words, and phrases from magazines and pasting them to the cover of their writer's notebook. The artwork becomes a visual representation of themselves that I use as a springboard for conversation and personal narrative writing. The activity also allows me the opportunity to get to know the students more personally. Through their collages, some students allow me to glimpse into their private lives. The images curated by some students indicate clues to socioeconomic status and even learning disabilities. The collage project often reminds me that even in my seemingly mono-cultural teaching context, there is a broad range of diversities within my classroom that aren't always visible or immediately apparent (Figure 9.1).

FIGURE 9.1   Student Journal Cover. Photo by Dan Krack.

One year, I noticed that a student's bio-collage featured a rainbow as its focal point, with the phrase "Be yourself" beneath it. The individual letters were of mismatched fonts, sizes, and colors so that they looked like the letters of a ransom note. Pictures of Lady Gaga, Adam Lambert, Ellen DeGeneres, and Rosie O'Donnell were affixed to each corner of her construction. I immediately interpreted these images as symbols of her sexual identity, but I refrained from asking her about it directly. Instead, I tried to make a connection with her by commenting on the images she selected for her collage.

"Ellen? I saw her stand-up act a while back. She was hysterical! Gaga's new album is pretty good. Have you heard it yet? And Rosie? A friend of mine from college was on Broadway with her," I said hoping that she'd understand that I was decoding her collage.

"Cool," she mumbled as she clipped away at a magazine, avoiding eye contact with me.

As I reflected on my exchange with the student, I grew frustrated with myself for missing an opportunity to learn more about her sexual/gender identity. I was nervous to ask more direct and pointed questions because I was afraid of encroaching on her privacy, even though she seemed to put—as I interpreted it—her sexual identity on display. I felt that I was crossing a boundary as a teacher to inquire about her interior feelings and identity. What if I had misinterpreted the images on her collage and the student was offended that I was questioning her heterosexuality? What if the student turned around and asked me about *my* sexual identity? Would asking this student about her sexual identity be outing myself in some way? I was nervous that asking her more direct questions could result in the loss of my job. The irony of this is that my heterosexual colleagues enjoy the privilege of never having to hide *their* sexuality. I, on the other hand, must hide my true identity and perform what Adrienne Rich refers to as "compulsory heterosexuality" in order to preserve my livelihood.

Every year that I've used the bio-collage activity, I've observed a handful of artworks that could be read as an expression of LGBTQ identities. I am struck by the courage that it takes for these teenagers to express their sexual identity in such a public way. I am happy that some of my students feel confident to reveal their identities and tell their stories through the bio-collage; I often wonder what gives them such courage. Perhaps the confidence comes from a supportive group of friends that make the student feel safe and accepted. Perhaps the confidence comes from a supportive home life and families who love and encourage the child unconditionally. Or perhaps the confidence comes from the student's strong sense of self and a desire to resist and reject heteronormativity and/or stereotypical gender roles.

However, I know there are other students who do not feel as comfortable with being public about their sexuality or gender identification; I wonder how they navigate the heteronormative space of school. What is the essence of their discomfort? Are they wrestling with coming to terms with their LGBTQ identities? Do they feel uncomfortable or unsafe in educational, social, and/or domestic contexts? Do they feel connected to the school community? Are they being bullied? Do they feel like they fit in? Do they have the support of friends and family? Do they have anyone to whom they can talk? We can ask these same questions in relation to any group of marginalized students who might feel invisible. Speaking strictly from my personal teaching experiences, public schools do not often encourage critical discussions of race, religion, class, and ability, let alone gender and sexuality. The silence surrounding topics of difference does not help to encourage social justice, but instead works to further social inequality.

When I consider the struggles of some of my LGBTQ students to find their place within the school environment, I can't help but think of some of my ethnic minority students who have endured similar struggles. A former student of South Asian descent once told me that she used to cry every day after school because there wasn't anyone who looked like her in her class. She went on to explain that she often felt lonely because, outside of her immediate family, she didn't meet many people who looked or spoke like her in her community or on television. Additionally, she felt further alienated by the school's curriculum that was largely centered on the Anglo literature and experience. The experience of this former student is parallel to the experiences of some LGBTQ students I have taught.

I remember what school was like for me growing up in the 1980s. On the outside I was a popular and successful student in high school, but on the inside, I kept my sexuality a secret and suffered in silence with depression and anxiety. As a teenager, there were virtually no visible role models for me to look up to, only the images that mainstream media published, which served to marginalize and oppress the LGBTQ community. Today, however, popular culture offers an array of openly gay celebrities and athletes that serve as positive role models for gay teens. For example, many performing artists such as Lady Gaga are strong, vocal LGBTQ allies and advocates, and openly LGBTQ actors such as Neil Patrick Harris, a married gay man with children and Laverne Cox, an out trans actor, are featured prominently on stage and screen. Today, more than ever, LGBTQ teenagers are finding their identities represented positively on television shows, such as *Glee, Orange is the New Black*, and *Empire*. I believe that popular culture has helped make LGBTQ issues more acceptable within mainstream discourse, and, therefore, it is necessary and imperative for LGBTQ celebrities and their allies to be open and visible.

However, Lady Gaga, Neil Patrick Harris, Ellen, and Laverne Cox are not sufficient enough role models for LGBTQ youth. While their messages are empowering, celebrities are simply too far out of reach. Yet individuals such as teachers, coaches, doctors, counselors, and parents who *should* serve as LGBTQ role models are often silenced by our system of education that prohibits free and open discussion of sexuality in the classroom.

I can't help but imagine the impact that openly LGBTQ teachers and administrators could have on *all* of the students they teach! For the students who feel marginalized and alienated by heteronormativity and homophobia, an LGBTQ teacher can serve as proof that life does get better after high school. For the other students (and teachers) in the school, an open and visible LGBTQ teacher can help combat the ostracization, alienation, oppression, discrimination, marginalization, and demonization we sometimes face. The unfortunate reality, though, is that many LGBTQ teachers don a cloak of invisibility when we get ready for school in the morning. We do this to preserve our jobs, our livelihood. We do this, so we can continue to do what we are passionate about—to help young people blossom and grow as we advocate for *all* of our students. But if we remain invisible, are we really doing all we can to help liberate our LGBTQ students?

In my school district, the ubiquity of Trump/Pence campaign signs still displayed throughout the community (and even feet from the school's main entrance) a month after the election is a constant reminder of the community's unabashed alignment with Trump's brand of conservative values. Frustration boils within me because I feel that since I am an educator in this conservative district, my identity as a gay man is expected to remain hidden. As a result, I often feel the clash of my private and professional identities and the constriction of institutionalized oppression.

As I write this story, I am reeling from a collision of my identities that occurred in class today. I walked over to collect test papers from a couple of male students I will call Tom and Steve. On his scratch paper, Tom drew a rainbow with the words "Steve is gay" written above an arrow pointing to Steve who was seated next to him.

"Tom, so what if he is? What's wrong with that?" I asked as he stared blankly at me.

"Yeah! Well I'm offended!" Steve said as he grabbed the paper off of Tom's desk. "I'm not gay! I'm offended that he said I am!"

"Why would you be offended to be called gay? Do you even know any gay people?" I retorted.

"I dunno. I'm sure I do. I'm probably talking to one right nnnn...," Steve answered, trying to prevent the words from falling out of his mouth.

What I *wanted* to say was "Hey, Steve! *I* am offended that you find being gay offensive! And yes! You *are* talking to one right now!"

But I didn't say what I wanted to say. Instead, I gave in to Steve's homophobia by allowing him to have the last word. I am angry that my heterosexual colleagues enjoy the privilege of being true to themselves by not having to be continually aware of how they perform their heterosexual identities. Heteronormativity permits (and perhaps requires) my colleagues' private, heterosexual identities to overlap with their professional identities. This is evidenced by the way my straight colleagues can display pictures of their families on their desks and the way they can talk openly about their spouses and children without the fear that someone is listening. I am angry that I allowed Tom and Steve to leave the classroom today laughing at the row they created. Laughing at my identity. Laughing at who I am.

At the end of the day when the last student left the room, I straightened the desks, silently bundled myself up in my stifling cloak of invisibility, and headed home where I knew I'd be able to breathe again.

Questions for Reflection

1. Referring back to James Banks's levels of multicultural curriculum integration, where do you see yourself in integrating the experiences, perspectives, histories, and contributions of the LGBTQ community into your curriculum and courses?
2. What resources will you use to ensure that you are educated on terminology, histories, issues, and contributions of the LGBTQ community?
3. Is there already a GSA at your school? If not, who will you approach and how can you go about helping students to form one and invite members to join?
4. If you do have a GSA, how might you facilitate and empower members/students to educate teachers and other students about LGBTQ related topics, such as:
   - Gender binary versus gender on a continuum
   - The relationship between gender and sexuality
   - Creating a more welcoming school and safe spaces
   - Intervening in biased-based bullying
   - The role of pronouns and names
   - Discussions of bias and micro-aggressions.
5. How will you schedule times to meet in professional learning communities for the purpose of discussing content-based gender diversity and LGBTQ inclusion?
6. How might you use the social action approach in your classroom to further goals of gender diversity and LGBTQ inclusion at your high school? In which activities will you have your students engage in order to apply their learning to the world around them?

References

Banks, J. (2001). *Multicultural education: Issues and perspectives* (4th ed.). New York, NY: Wiley.

Burke, A., & Collier, D. R. (2017). 'I was kind of teaching myself': Teachers' conversations about social justice and teaching for change. *Teacher Development, 21*(2), 269–287.

California History Social Studies Framework. (2016). LGBT Revisions. Retrieved from http://clgbthistory.org/wp-content/uploads/2010/09/Accepted-2016-Framework-LGBT-Revisions.pdf

Chappell, S. (2016). *A review of* The year we thought about love: Behind the scenes of the nation's longest running LGBTQ youth theater, directed by Ellen Brodsky. *Youth Theatre Journal, 30*, 184–186.

GLSEN, Inc. (2017). Ally week. *GLSEN.* Retrieved from www.glsen.org/allyweek

GLSEN, Inc. (2017). Day of silence. *GLSEN.* Retrieved from www.glsen.org/day-of-silence

GLSEN, Inc. (2017). Local school climate survey. *GLSEN.* Retrieved from http://localsurvey.glsen.org/

Goldman, T. (2017, October 17). NFL players and owners have not resolved controversy over anthem protests. *National Public Radio.* Retrieved from http://kbia.org/post/nfl-players-and-owners-have-not-resolved-controversy-over-anthem-protests#stream/0

GroundSpark. (n.d.). Straightlaced curriculum guide. Retrieved from https://groundspark.org/our-films-and-campaigns/straightlaced/straightlaced-curriculum-guide

GSA Network. (2009). 10 steps for starting a GSA. *GSA Network – trans and queer youth uniting for racial and gender justice.* Retrieved from https://gsanetwork.org/resources/building-your-gsa/10-steps-starting-gsa

Harbin, B. (2016). Teaching beyond the gender binary in the university classroom. *Vanderbilt University – Center for Teaching.* Retrieved from https://cft.vanderbilt.edu/teaching-beyond-the-gender-binary-in-the-university-classroom/

Health Connected. (2014). *Health connected curriculum: Sex ed starts here.* Retrieved from www.health-connected.org/curriculum

Hoelscher, M. (n.d.). Why (and how) STEM curriculum needs to be LGBT inclusive. *GLSEN.* Retrieved from www.glsen.org/blog/why-and-how-stem-curriculum-needs-be-lgbt-inclusive

The Human Rights Campaign. (2015). A call to action: LGBTQ youth need inclusive sex education. *The Human Rights Campaign.* Retrieved from www.hrc.org/resources/a-call-to-action-lgbtq-youth-need-inclusive-sex-education

Independent Lens. (2015). *A map of gender diverse cultures.* Retrieved from www.pbs.org/independentlens/content/two-spirits_map-html/

Jaklitsch, D. (2017, Summer). Factors affecting the experiences of LGBT students in physical education and sport – A synthesis of the research literature. *Kinesiology, Sport Studies, and Physical Education Synthesis Projects.* Retrieved from http://digitalcommons.brockport.edu/cgi/viewcontent.cgi?article=1028&context=pes_synthesis

Jones, R. P., & Cox, D. (2015). *How race and religion shape millennial attitudes on sexuality and reproductive health.* Washington, D.C.: Public Religion Research Institute.

Jupp, J. C. (2017). What learning is needed for white teachers' race-visible teaching? Racialised curriculum recoding of cherished knowledges. *Whiteness and Education, 2*(1), 1–17.

Luke, A., Cooke, J., & Luke, C. (1986, December). The selective tradition in action: Gender bias in student teachers' selections of children's literature. *English Education, 18*(4), 209–218.

Osborne, P. (2015, September). Problematizing disciplinarity, transdisciplinary problematics. *Theory, Culture & Society, 32*(5–6), 3–35.

Public Affairs Staff. (2017, March 30). From C-Suite to characters on screen: How inclusive is the entertainment industry? *USC Annenberg.* Retrieved from http://annenberg.usc.edu/news/faculty-research/c-suite-characters-screen-how-inclusive-entertainment-industry

Rankin, S., & Weber, G. (2014). Mind, body and sport: Harassment and discrimination – LGBTQ student-athletes. *NCAA.* Retrieved from www.ncaa.org/sport-science-institute/mind-body-and-sport-harassment-and-discrimination-lgbtq-student-athletes

Vecellio, S. (2012). Enacting FAIR education: Approaches to integrating LGBT content in the K-12 curriculum. *Multicultural Perspectives, 14*(3), 169–174.

Young, M. (2014). Curriculum theory: What it is and why it is important. *Cadernos de Pesquisa, 44*(151), 190–202.

10
HIGH SCHOOL PEDAGOGY

While eating breakfast before class, you read through social media posts and stumble across a link to the California Endowment's Youth Action initiative. You read the words of Kristian Morgan (2017), a high school junior, who writes about the role of June's Pride Month in the lives of lesbian, gay, bisexual, trans and queer (LGBTQ) youth:

> *Unfortunately, not everyone has the privilege of celebrating Pride Month. To some, June is simply the month of June. They are not allowed to sport brightly colored rainbows or kiss their partner while on dates or protest for their rights as individuals. Some environments are unsafe for such expeditions and they must endeavor to create their own space or to find a space in which they can face this dangerous reality and finally be free to be openly and pridefully themselves.*
>
> *Sometimes, folks in our community are not even able to express themselves at home. In unaccepting homes, individuals who are LGBTQ cannot hang a rainbow flag by their window or buy a "gay agenda" shirt from Spencer's. In this situation, the person must put on a mask and hide their true identity from the world. They are forced into a life of stealth.*

You also read a blog entry from the Australian youth group Ygender (Hawkins, 2017). The youth share stories about being nonbinary:

Arlo (they/them)
> *For me being non-binary means that I don't exclusively id as male or female. Learning about non-binary identities was a game changer for me because it gave me the words to articulate something very integral to me that I didn't have the language to describe for a really long time. Interacting with my gender often feels like a very*

personal, intimate experience. I would describe my gender as in flux, and whilst it sometimes had ties to elements of femininity and masculinity, exists for the most part entirely outside of that.

George (they/them)

[Being non-binary] means to me to identify outside of today's social norms or gender. Recently my dad started using my pronouns and that made me really happy!

Erik (he/him)

I'm a non-binary trans masculine person. Being non-binary is different for everyone. To me, it means that some days I am a boy, some days I am not entirely a boy and other days I am not a boy. This doesn't mean that my gender has any elements of being a girl. My gender fluctuates between being a boy and of a gender that is entirely beyond the girl-boy binary. Being non-binary is a very important part of my identity that I would never want to be different in any other way.

After reading the two blogs, you are struck by the diversity of identities that these young people have shared in their writing. Listening to our students, you think, is such an important job. I have to ensure they know that their voices are heard and that they are visible in the world of school and my classroom. During the summer, you research many pedagogical strategies you would like to try that celebrate student voices. You feel ready to start the school year!

This vignette illustrates how teachers in their daily lives often notice youth stories, and then conscientiously reflect on how these stories apply to their teaching practice. This chapter focuses on high school pedagogies that encourage and embrace student voices and identities, particularly toward LGBTQ inclusion. We begin by describing active learning strategies with social justice goals, including naming and identity work, self and community mapping, historiography, and youth participatory action research. We end with stories of pedagogical practice and discussion questions for you to utilize individually or with a professional learning community toward the goals of gender diversity and LGBTQ inclusion at school.

Active Learning

Active learning pedagogies often promote small, collaborative learning communities. These collaborations can enhance social integration in the classroom, particularly through teacher-scaffolded interactions with students across diverse identities (Cooper & Brownell, 2016). Yet such scaffolding requires that teachers exercise cultural competence, an awareness and respect for diversity, and the social contexts that students navigate during their interactions. In the following textbox, the Suicide Prevention Center has developed a checklist for school-based LGBTQ cultural competence. You can use this checklist to assess your school and classroom climate, and the efficacy of our selected pedagogical strategies.

LGBTQ CULTURAL COMPETENCE SCHOOL ASSESSMENT BY THE SUICIDE PREVENTION RESOURCE CENTER (2018)

Individual Staff Member or Teacher

- Has knowledge of LGBTQ issues, including victimization, difficulties accessing services, and ineffective providers
- Has awareness of heterosexism and discrimination against transgender individuals
- Models appreciation for all youth, condemns any discrimination, and plays advocacy role
- Gets support from other staff when exploring values and developing empathy
- Assesses and respects youth's decision about disclosing to others.

School

- Has explicit policies prohibiting discrimination on the basis of gender identity and sexual orientation
- Has explicit policies prohibiting discriminatory language, bullying, and physical violence
- Has a Safe Zone program and a Gay-Straight Alliance (GSA) or similar group
- Provides information about LGBTQ suicide risk in staff awareness education
- Has programs about LGBTQ issues and invites young teens and preteens
- Trains faculty and staff in LGBTQ culturally competent services and includes this in supervision and performance reviews
- Offers informational programming for families on issues of sexual orientation and gender identity
- Offers extracurricular programs that reflect diversity
- Has openly LGBTQ students, teachers, and/or staff members
- Establishes a welcoming environment through outreach and in front desk, classroom, and other school spaces that reflects support and inclusion
- Addresses LGBTQ issues throughout curricula, including in health education, and has examples of LGBTQ individuals
- Uses forms for parents and students that allow for a range of sexual orientations and gender identities as well as a diversity of households
- Offers LGBTQ-inclusive resources and services for referrals
- Provides easily available, accurate information and library and media resources that provide LGBTQ information and authors

- Reviews school print and media materials with LGBTQ people
- Supports staff who play an advocacy role
- Has unisex bathrooms and inclusive dress code.

For example, Cooper and Brownell (2016) found that although LGBTQ students in a biology class did not observe explicit discrimination during active learning activities, they still felt that the peer group was not welcoming or accepting of their identities. LGBTQ students observed peers making transphobic and homophobic remarks during group activities, which led LGBTQ students to struggle internally about whether to defend themselves and/or refute the harassment. However, the researchers also found that active learning environments, such as small group discussions and activities, sometimes provided opportunities to negotiate social identities and social inclusion in positive ways.

As teachers begin to utilize more active learning strategies and develop cultural competencies that promote social inclusion and respect for diversity, we can take up themes of personal relevance to our students, such as naming and identity, voice and silence, and conflict pedagogy. By high school, LGBTQ youth eagerly hope that teachers will make queer identities visible in class. Kulke (2016) interviewed a high school junior who was studying Walt Whitman, and noticed that the teacher omitted mentioning that Whitman was gay. The student reflected, "I was like, 'Hey, why didn't you mention his sexuality? It was super important to all of his art.' And he was like, 'You know, the funny thing is, I knew that he was queer. I knew that, and I didn't share that with the class. And I don't know why.'"

While this student bravely talked with her teacher about her concerns about the visibility of LGBTQ identities, experiences, and mentor texts, often students stay silent. This is both related to the climate created by the teacher and the identity development process that high school students are experiencing. Ollin (2007) cautions teachers not to misinterpret these silences, noting that sometimes not speaking can be very productive to receptive learning. For example, Stauber (2017) documented a group of high school teachers working in social justice contexts who observed what they termed unsettling silences of girls, in particular, during classroom discussions. The teachers worked progressively to attune themselves to a balance of speaking and silence in their classroom. They realized that silences sometimes reflected students encountering, negotiating, and articulating their identities, and growing consciousness of themselves and the social issues being addressed.

In her dissertation, Gutierez-Schmich (2016) examined the role of identity-based, visibility pedagogies in high schools. She suggests that students should have opportunities for community engagement as a means of working against oppression and toward student-identified social goals, such as LGBTQ inclusion, advocacy, and civil rights. This form of public pedagogy is less about schooling predetermined skills or content knowledge and more about learning how education can empower youth to reflect, plan, research, and act.

Gutierez-Schmich (2016) further suggests that conflict pedagogy can be a component of this work: teaching young people how to discuss and learn through inter- and intragroup conflicts as a site of transformation. She cites Anzaldúa, a queer Latin social theorist and creative writer, who developed the concept of Nepantla:

> The place where different perspectives come into conflict and where you question the basic ideas, tenets, and identities inherited from your family, your education, and your different cultures. Nepantla is the zone between changes where you struggle to find equilibrium between the outer expression of change and your interrelationship to it. Living between cultures results in 'seeing' culture, first from the perspective of one culture, then from the perspective of another. Seeing from two or more perspectives simultaneously renders those cultures transparent.
>
> *(Anzaldúa, 2002, pp. 548–549)*

Building the classroom as a site in which we grapple with different, conflicting perspectives and histories through the lens of struggle and personal identity development will support not only active learning across disciplines but also ideological clarity. Students can take stances on oppressions and erasures, and learn to adopt allied stances toward who speaks during discussions.

When teaching about conflict, we must also be cautious about potentially triggering past traumas in our most vulnerable youth (see Chapter 9 for more on trauma-sensitive schools). Inclusion of narratives and images of violence against LGBTQ people, such as the Stonewall Riots, Harvey Milk's assassination, or the murder of trans women of color, may retrigger traumas for some of our LGBTQ youth. Our challenge is to actively include multiple queer and gender-diverse perspectives, experiences, and histories with caution, care, and a critical mind (American Institute for Research, 2013; Treatment and Services Adaptation Center, n.d.).

Historiography

In our pedagogical efforts to be LGBTQ inclusive, teachers can also utilize the social science principles of historiography to analyze the impact of oppressions during inter- and intracultural contact and conflict. Traditionally, schools have taught social histories as a "single, unified past" rather than as an interpretive craft in which historians produce narratives through their own subjective lens utilizing available, limited evidence (Westhoff, 2012). Postlewait (1991) suggests that "What historians see—or fail to see—depends not only on *where* but *how* they look, how they constitute both the field of study and the method of investigation" (p. 159). Oftentimes, in the construction of historical and social narratives that youth learn in school, there is a separation of facts from theory, of documentation from interpretation. Traditionally, textbooks teach that evidence speaks for itself and that history is impartial and objective. However, no story is unbiased, without ideological values and beliefs, or without impact on different communities. Stories are partial and open to interpretation based on the subjectivity of the storyteller and the reader.

As early as 1994, the National Writing Project has asked teachers to "do history" with their students: to utilize primary sources and opportunities for historical writing and build historical understanding, to think like a historian (Kawazoe, 1994). Through historiography, students can question what it means to be human, using tools like logs, journals, and diaries to share reactions and feelings. We can teach the debates that historians participate in as we grapple with the meanings and impacts of historical events on different communities and from diverse points of view. For example, Westhoff (2012) recommends including historiographic mapping in different disciplinary contexts. Students record historical questions that have been asked, the sources used to investigate those questions, the claims made, and the perspectives and sources that have not been used or considered. As Sawchuk (2017) notes, textbooks have systematically omitted LGBTQ history, including how gender identity and sexual orientation influence the work of public leaders. Students can examine the curricular exclusions of LGBTQ people's perspectives and influences on history and in history textbooks, such as by examining primary and secondary sources about the 1950–1960s civil rights movement and by comparing and contrasting these documents to the narratives presented in textbooks. Does the textbook, for example, include or omit the gay civil rights movement or one of its leaders, Bayard Rustin, who was also gay? Teaching historiography impacts LGBTQ high school youth. As students think like historians, they become active citizens of the world and build more compassionate ways of viewing history from diverse perspectives.

Youth Participatory Action Research

Another research- and citizenship-focused active learning pedagogy is youth participatory action research (YPAR). YPAR encourages young people to generate questions about social issues that are of importance to them, and then to engage in a research inquiry process of gathering and analyzing data in response to their questions. Then student research groups present their findings publicly in various ways, with the intention of impacting the public conversation by identifying action steps informed by research on their selected social issues. Substantial research has documented the empowering outcomes of this pedagogical research process (Cammarota & Fine, 2008; Fox et al., 2010; Wagaman, 2015).

After an introduction to the YPAR process, we provide several examples of how this research supports LGBTQ inclusion in learning. The YPAR process is outlined by University of California, Berkeley's YPAR Hub (2015). This youth-driven research inquiry cycle includes the following (note that within each step are actions that students take):

- Defining an issue of interest to them
  - Analyze bias and power in their communities
  - Develop indicators and questions about the issue
  - Identify community strengths and problems.
- Investigating the issue
  - Find and use existing data
  - Conducting focus groups and interviews
  - Mapping current conditions
  - Conducting observations
  - Utilizing photography (Photovoice) to capture conditions from a variety of participant perspectives.
- Taking action
  - Make a plan for disseminating findings
  - Evaluate impact of the research on the community.

Educators have worked with youth using YPAR in many capacities including, for example, in Richmond, California. High school youth learned about the impact of LGBTQ visibility during Pride Month and then advocated for city recognition of LGBTQ communities. They declared, "pride month is about being comfortable with who you are," and "It makes me feel like my city supports me when I see the rainbow flag being flown." Other Richmond youth learned about the health and wellness needs of young people and presented their findings at the Building Healthy Communities Free Our Dreams: Queer and Trans Youth Summit (Villa, 2016).

In New York, LGBTQ youth of color participated in the FIERCE organization to survey 62 LGBTQ youth organizations and programs, and then publish a report of their findings. In this report, they named the most urgent issues facing LGBTQ youth, such as gaps in service, and then provided recommendations for improved services such as "increasing access to political education and leadership development for LGBTQ youth, to better enable them to organize for structural changes that would improve conditions for themselves and their peers" (Powers & Allaman, 2012, p. 4)

In Sacramento, LGBTQ youth conducted research on mental health justice (Sanchez, Lomeli-Loibl, & Nelson, 2009). Their recommendations included increased mental health services for LGBTQ youth; training schools and institutions to be more responsive to and knowledgeable of LGBTQ youth; increasing transgender workshops and trainings; and increasing LGBTQ-specific programs, such as LGBT Big Brother/Big Sister, GSAs in high schools, parent support programs and organizations, LGBTQ sex education, and LGBTQ-specific youth activities.

We recommend that high schools increase their knowledge of the YPAR pedagogical process and brainstorm applications across the disciplines. As students
build collective knowledge about the world they live in and the histories that
came before them, they are disrupting singular narratives and norms that have
so often omitted LGBTQ lives. Further, through conducting collaborative research in their communities, they are building inclusive spaces for learning.
High school teachers can strategically use disciplinary classroom spaces to nurture belonging and critical thinking in ways that ultimately not only make it
safer for LGBTQ youth, but for all students. The following are stories of pedagogical practice from youth and teacher activists who work in their classrooms
and schools to provide safe spaces for LGBTQ youth.

STORY ONE: "(Trans)forming Education: How Transgender Youth Are Leading the School Justice Movement" by Eli Erlick

Being an openly transgender girl in a rural high school comes with
many difficulties. In an isolated small town in Northern California, I
experienced years of violence from students, teachers, and staff after transitioning. Instead of letting this hinder my involvement in the
trans community, I used my oppression as motivation to create systemic
change. While in the eleventh grade, I helped create a trans-inclusive
policy at my school. However, the harassment and intimidation did not
stop. This led me to realize that it is community-based education and not
policy or institutionalized inclusion that will help create safer schools for
trans students. I use this essay to educate organizers on generative ways of
creating healthier institutions for trans students coming from a personal
narrative.

In 2003, I opened up about being a transgender girl to my rural elementary school by announcing to my classmates and teacher that I was a
girl. Being a relatively conservative community, it was far from supportive. During this time, I spent years facing severe isolation, harassment,
and beatings from the other students. However, like many other resilient
transgender youth, this would not stop my involvement in the transgender community. Not wanting anyone else to experience what happened
to me, at age 16, I co-founded Trans Student Educational Resources
(TSER), a national youth-led organization dedicated to transforming
the educational environment for trans and gender-nonconforming youth
through advocacy and empowerment. Since then, TSER has made international headlines, created the largest leadership program for trans youth
in the world, and produced multiple model policies on transgender education. I write this chapter to chronicle the ways in which transgender

youth are leading the movement for creating a safer educational system from the inside using transformative organizing methods.

To fully know the issues transgender youth are facing in school, it is vital to be able to understand transformative versus inclusive organizing. Transgender youth are much more likely to utilize strategies for our liberation through transformative rather than inclusionary work. Transformative organizers understand the system is founded on the oppression of marginalized bodies. For trans youth, this means the segregation of program and facilities by sex assigned at birth and the frequent suspension and expulsion of trans students (particularly trans students of color). In all, 82 percent of trans students feel unsafe in school, over half have been physically attacked, and nearly all have stated they feel unsafe (Greytak, Kosciw, & Diaz, 2009). No amount of inclusion can fix these problems, and instead, we must look past the misleading goal of equality to the ability to fundamentally changing school discipline, buildings, and programs. While inclusion into programs and facilities with the correct gender will decrease harassment and isolation, the idea that we must segregate these programs by gender will always leave out students who identify outside the gender binary.

Additionally, transgender students are disproportionately targeted for disciplinary measures, and it is best to fundamentally rethink how we enact justice when students do not behave. The assumption that punishment is an educational tool is fundamentally anti-transgender. Partially due to harsh punishment and zero-tolerance policies—some of which are disguised as protections for marginalized youth—nearly half of transgender students have experienced school discipline, such as suspension or expulsion, with 3.5 percent having contact with the juvenile justice system as a result of this treatment. Transgender students are often targeted for suspension, with some states allowing this group to be disciplined for simply presenting a certain way due to it being "distracting" to cisgender students. Other trans youth will act out after being mistreated and, according to the 2015 US Transgender Discrimination Survey, 36 percent were punished for fighting back against bullying (GLSEN, 2016). With an exceptional lack of resources, we have very little to rely upon outside of policy.

Currently, Trans Student Educational Resources is the only national organization specifically focusing on transgender students. At age 15, I was reported to my school's principal for "spending too much time in the women's restroom," which made my cisgender classmates uncomfortable. Despite their report clearly being transmisogynistic, the principal said she "had to take these accusations seriously." She unofficially banned me from the women's room and told me I would have to use the single stall gender-neutral facility. I would have to get a key from the office every time I needed to pee and could not go into the same restroom with my friends. Shortly after, I learned about a model district policy for K–12 school districts for transgender and gender-nonconforming students through online research. At the time, I had much faith in policy advocacy and wanted to use this for the access to the women's room I should have been allowed as a woman. I decided to help establish a policy based upon this model at my high school's district. Proposing it to the school board was simple, albeit slow. It would take two monthly board meetings for it to be passed. While waiting for the policy to be officially passed with the second board meeting, I stood up for myself vocally to school staff instead and explained to them that it was unfair I was being excluded from the women's restroom as a woman. I began using the restroom again without the administration's permission, which actually proved to be much more effective than any policy itself. The lack of change following the passing of the policy was frustrating at best. While the changes did help establish guidelines for the teachers to follow, they were not immediately enforced, and I was still being misgendered by staff and faculty, harassed by other students, and excluded from gendered programs. It would take much more drastic action than policy to create change at my institution.

My junior year of high school, I co-founded Trans Student Educational Resources with Chicago-based activist Alex Sennello to make foundational change to the education system and to mobilize young trans people to advocate for themselves nationally. While we encouraged policy change, we also paved the way for long-term solutions to the issues we faced through organizing transgender youth. Like many young trans people, we had to take initiative for ourselves because nobody else would. We created a movement rather than a moment: a practice of long-term structural change rather than institutional adjustment. If trans youth are allowed a platform in which we can advocate for ourselves instead of being confined to the limitations of institutional policy, we could radically transform educational activism and the system overall. I was able to use my connections built through this organization to know my rights and speak out when I was not being treated fairly. Having access to an organization and group of like-minded young people was more powerful than any policy. I could be included in education completely but still would be isolated from my trans community members and not have access to the foundational knowledge I needed to succeed.

Now, over five years later, Trans Student Educational Resources has reached millions of people all over the country, established ongoing programs to develop the leadership of young trans activists, and created over a dozen different programs facilitated by our many youth members. One example resource is TSER's Gender Unicorn graphic, as featured in Chapter One. Our volunteers have spoken at hundreds of conferences and events around the country and contributed to the education of millions on critical issues trans youth face today. This is a process of both individual and collective growth. As program director and college student, Harper Rubin stated during an interview for the organization,

> Working at TSER has helped me understand the transformative power of youth movements. Being able to see the impacts of our collaborative efforts first-hand has inspired me to center activism in my life and push for more change than I thought imaginable.

Through the establishment of a group by and for our community, we have transformed education more than I ever dreamed was possible. To build a youth movement is to imagine a future in which we are all free from oppression, one where transgender people can thrive in education and our everyday lives.

STORY TWO: "Sustaining Queer Activism across Time as Teachers: Changing Pathways in Working toward Queer Friendly Schools" by Ryan Schey and Ariel Uppstrom

Introduction

In 2007, the two of us graduated together from our teacher education program and were fortunate to get jobs in the same high school. The community was predominantly white, working- and middle-class families with a mix of small-town, rural, and suburban elements, located an approximately 45-minute drive from a major Midwestern city. During our first year, we sought to do what our friend and mentor Caroline Clark (2010) has called *ally work*, advocating on behalf of LGBTQQ (lesbian, gay, bisexual, trans, queer, and questioning) youth in our new school as straight cisgender white teachers deeply committed to utilizing schooling practices as sites for social change.

As part of our efforts, we began to support and grow our school's GSA and work against homophobia and heterosexism (Schey & Uppstrom, 2010). Early in our teaching careers, we navigated the complexity of getting started with queer educational activism. We have since spent more time teaching in this school; Ryan taught there until 2014 when he left to pursue a doctoral degree and at the time of this writing, Ariel still teaches there. Throughout these years, we learned about developing and sustaining an activist pathway across longer time arcs. It's this learning that we focus on in this chapter.

We hope that by discussing the ways our activism changed, other educators might reflect on their own contexts and experiences in order to work toward schools where LGBTQQ youth and their allies can learn, flourish, and contribute to the enrichment of others. We discuss three changes—each focusing on teachers, students, and school practices—and then close by reflecting on their collective significance.

Supporting Teachers: Moving from Single Experts toward Collective Knowledge

When we started our careers, teachers in our high school generally didn't see the value of—much less the possibilities for—queer educational activism. While there were a few who supported our efforts, we generally felt isolated and on our own as the two educators who were visibly working to support LGBTQQ youth and families.

In some ways, our efforts became new resources that teachers and students didn't have access to before, and people didn't hesitate to call on our perceived expertise. For instance, we had experiences where our principal or a guidance counselor would ask us to stop by their office to talk about a student who was having some "trouble." We'd visit their office and listen to the story, confused about why we were being told about this student whom we had never met. Typically, by the story's end, we would understand why we'd been included: the student was gay and the principal or guidance counselor was hoping that *we* (meaning Ariel and/or Ryan) could "take care of" the situation—maybe working with the student in "that group you run" (euphemisms for the GSA abounded in these early years).

As new teachers, we were eager to act on our activist values and so immediately jumped in when we received these invitations. We were happy that finally an adult in the school was interested in helping rather than simply remaining passive or ignoring the situation. We were happy that, with our input, they were acting to benefit the particular needs of LGBTQQ youth at our school. However, after we experienced this cycle several times, we became critical. We wondered if it was ideal for strangers to work with a student rather than somebody who already had a relationship with them. We wondered if the most effective way for us to be activists was to take care of things for other people. When we identified some of these tensions, we attempted to shift our approach, moving away from being the sole so-called experts and toward developing knowledge and capacity that would be collectively shared among teachers.

This shift seemed to occur organically across the years. Our early actions had contributed a change in the high school climate where it was no longer unheard of for teachers to publicly support LGBTQQ youth. In turn, this precedent invited new teachers to immediately begin supporting LGBTQQ youth. Instead of battling against the long established heterosexist and cissexist status quo, newly hired teachers encountered encouragement, if not an expectation, of supporting LGBTQQ students. This shift helped alter our position from *the* supportive teachers to *one of the* supportive teachers. LGBTQQ students no longer needed to be directed to us as the GSA advisers, but rather were surrounded by a greater number of teachers who understood and developed relationships with them holistically, feeling comfortable discussing LGBTQQ topics in addition to academic concerns. In other words, these teachers supported them in both their *student* and their *sexual and gender* identities. This distribution of knowledge across many teachers enabled the two of us to become sounding boards for the staff and contribute to a shift in the school culture. Anecdotally, students across the years went from saying they felt safety and support in particular classrooms to saying they felt safety and support in the school more broadly.

Changing Language Practices: Moving from Working for LGBTQQ Youth toward Working with LGBTQQ Youth

When we began our careers, we entered a school where students commonly used homophobic language. We saw this as an immediate and obvious opportunity for working as queer activists. In this effort, we began each school year by talking with students about what language would and would not be acceptable in our classrooms, pointing to the posters displayed on our walls about our school's GSA and our "no hate speech" classroom rule. We specifically named homophobic language and gave examples of this. We also sought to intervene, whether inside our classroom or in the hallways, when we heard homophobic speech. One year during a school-wide assembly, we showed videos from GLSEN's "ThinkB4YouSpeak" campaign (www.glsen.org/participate/programs/thinkb4youspeak) and explained to students the importance of considering the impact—rather than the speaker's intent—when using language such as "that's so gay."

While we are proud of and value this work, we also see its limitations. Here, we, as adults with the institutional authority of teachers, worked *for* LGBTQQ (and primarily LG) students. We think it's crucial that teachers leverage both their power and responsibility in making such choices. However, we realized that we couldn't stop here and later came to work *with* LGBTQQ students—and trans and gender-nonconforming youth in particular—with respect to self-advocacy around language.

When some students started to self-identify as trans or gender-nonconforming, many teachers lacked basic knowledge about these identities. As a result, whether well-intentioned or not, teachers were seen by students as unsupportive, if not hostile and dismissive. Initially, we would talk with the teacher, attempting to educate them about trans people. We came to see that in doing so we were still making choices in a way that worked *for* LGBTQQ, specifically trans, youth. In an attempt to learn from our mistakes, we talked with self-identifying trans youth regarding ways they could advocate for themselves. This resulted in students approaching teachers individually to let them know their pronouns and/or name. Based on the frequency of these interactions and from the suggestions of trans youth, teachers and staff were encouraged to create gender-neutral student information sheets and gradebook coding from the counseling department to notify teachers of students' gender identities and other personal identifiers. We shifted the way we approached language practices from stepping in front of our students to trying to work *with* LGBTQQ youth in collaborative activist relationships.

Reframing School-Wide Practices: Moving from Making Space for Queer Individuals toward Queering School Traditions

During our first years of teaching, many school rituals were heteronormative, if not heterosexist and homophobic. For instance, our school, like many others, had homecoming festivities that included seniors running for homecoming court. Students ran in pairs as "couples," always one young woman and one young man, for the queen and king spots. Most of the time these couples were dating. One year a lesbian couple who were publicly out and dating were nominated. Whether someone intended their nomination as a joke or not wasn't clear, but the young women went with it, running for homecoming court as the queen and king. As their election campaign and the homecoming festivities unfolded, we were surprised and delighted. First, the sole instance of publicly expressed homophobia—graffiti on one of their campaign posters—was quickly addressed by the administration in collaboration with the two young women and other teachers. Next, the teacher over-seeing the homecoming festivities asked the couple about what language around "queen and king" they preferred, and he ordered homecoming flowers and sashes based on their choices. While the lesbian couple didn't win the vote, it was overall an affirming experience in their eyes.

Similar to our other early efforts, this story demonstrates important dimensions of queer activism. Our school community supported two lesbians in challenging the heterosexism of a school ritual in ways that the couple generally experienced as positive. However, we also understand that there were limits to our approach. We focused on supporting these two particular students once they found themselves navigating heteronormativity, if not heterosexism. In doing so, we didn't consider ways to queer, or disrupt and change, the traditions of the school rituals themselves so that the traditions offered more opportunities beyond (hetero)sexual courtship expectations.

After the lesbian couple ran for homecoming court, students disrupted other dimensions of the school traditions. In a subsequent school year during homecoming nominations, two boys, both identifying as cis and straight, were nominated as a senior homecoming couple. The boys had been nominated by their friends, not as a joke, but in admiration of their longtime friendship. The two young men, who knew nothing of the nomination until after the fact, decided to embrace it and campaigned for court. The student body didn't find this to be a joke or mock them, but rather normalized it and voted as they would ordinarily. LGBTQQ students didn't express that it was offensive or demeaning either but were positive about the friends running.

In light of these two events, homecoming nomination and voting ballots no longer have gender categories, meaning that anyone can now be a queen or king. So, while the lesbian couple challenged the **hetero**sexual dimensions of school traditions, the two boys challenged the hetero**sexual** aspects. In other words, the lesbian couple worked against school traditions only being about boys and girls as opposed to girls and girls, while the boys worked against the traditions only being about romantic and sexual relationships as opposed to friend relationships. However, all of the students collectively contested the range of possible relationships that were counted as part of the official school tradition, reshaping the practice itself. Where teachers' support of the lesbian couple initially was about supporting those two young women in their sexual identities, the result was that it enabled the student body to disrupt both the *hetero* and *sexual* dimensions of traditional school courtship rituals, queering, or disrupting and changing these traditions, and making space for more diverse ways of relating to one another in and through these traditions.

Conclusion

While at the beginning of our teaching careers we were focused on getting started with queer activism, we came to understand that developing and sustaining this work over time was a much different undertaking. Across each of the three changes that we describe (focused on teachers, students, and school practices, respectively), we see a common thread where our activist efforts broadened outward. At first, we focused on specific situations and our own actions. In hindsight, this approach makes sense. We were new teachers who were inexperienced and uncertain in many ways, still figuring out the myriad of things that new teachers learn. We were also new to the community, lacking the depth of insight and the school-community relationships that we would develop over time. We hadn't yet learned to see subtle patterns, so we focused on the obvious and highly visible singular situations. Across years, we became able to better understand patterns, and so our work spread outward.

On reflection, we believe that our experiences helped us learn the value of sustained queer activist efforts. Mentoring other teachers, developing trusting and collaborative relationships with LGBTQQ youth and families, changing schoolwide traditions—all of these changes take time. And along with time, teachers need patience, deep wells of emotional energy, and courageous resolve. We have also learned that queer activist teaching isn't a solo undertaking, but rather a collective action (as we believe that all social action and social change is). This means it's necessarily "messy." It's unpredictable and uncertain. It can feel tenuous. We are continually trying to learn to find peace and stability within this uncertainty. We won't pretend this is easy, but we will encourage others to embrace this.

We have also learned that change and flexibility are central to our queer activist work. While we've held onto the goal of cultivating queer-friendly schools, the pathways and our footing on them are always changing and shifting. We weren't able to recognize ahead of time what we have come to see in hindsight, but we always worked to listen to youth, families, and colleagues to make the optimal choice based on what we knew at the time. In the end, we believe that be(com)ing teachers engaged in queer activism means that we are continually striving and listening so that we can take actions that LGBTQQ people experience as meaningful, supportive, compassionate, and just.

STORY THREE: "The Story I Tell" by Polly Attwood

Sometime during the semester of "Culture, Equity, Power and Influence," an undergraduate course I teach for preservice teachers at the university, I tell a story of my high school teaching experiences related to the tensions of being a teacher and being queer.

I speak of fall 1986 in my first year of teaching high school history when I slowly came out to colleagues. Breaking that silence opened space for connection with two colleagues of color as we recognized each other's struggles in white- and hetero-dominant society. However, silence surrounded my classroom interactions with students. I taught for six years from "inside the closet" in Brookline, MA. No desktop pictures of my partner. No mention of co-parenting a stepson. Evasive answers about the ring on my finger. Stereotypes about gay men and lesbians who "recruit" young people, of "gay perverts," led me to keep my "private life" out of school and focus on being a "good teacher."

I tell of fall 1992 when during a year's leave and on a silent meditation retreat, it became clear that "silence would not protect me" (Audre Lorde, *Sister Outsider*). Coming out of that retreat silence in December, I learned that Brookline High had started a GSA, right behind Project 10 in Los Angeles, CA, and Project 10 East in Cambridge, MA. I also learned that students from Brookline, and communities all across the state, courageously testified at a series of five public hearings held by the first Governor's Commission on Gay and Lesbian Youth from November 13 to December 1, 1992. These students and their parent, teacher, and community allies marched, organized letter-writing campaigns, met in person with legislators, and made Massachusetts the first state to pass a "Gay Students Civil Rights Bill" (Rimer, 1993).

I tell of fall 1993, when I returned to classroom teaching and put a letter in faculty and staff mailboxes informing them I would no longer be silent. As a Quaker, feminist, and lesbian out in so many other contexts, this decision reflected an integrity I felt called to embrace. Like any heterosexual teacher who appropriately shared about family, children, their life beyond school, so would I. That fall, I became a GSA advisor alongside two other faculty, one lesbian and one heterosexual. Slowly, students learned that I was gay. I was no longer evading questions about the ring and sending mixed messages to students, some of whom told me later "they knew."

I tell of December 10, 1993, when then Governor Weld signed the Gay Students Civil Rights Bill into law. On that Friday, an administrator came to my classroom and asked to speak to me in the hallway. A TV reporter was on the phone and wanted to speak to faculty and students from the Brookline GSA. It felt awkward to leave my class. I let them know that I would be right back. I told the reporter that I and others from the GSA would talk to him after school. Ten minutes later, I walked back into the classroom, clear that I did not want students to learn I was gay from a news spot. This was the "organic moment" for which I had been preparing and to which my letter spoke—no more evading, side-stepping. I came out to my 20-plus students.

The following Monday, my department chair called me into his office to say that one of the students from that Friday class and her parents were upset. The student wanted to switch into a class with a colleague who, while respectful of me professionally, was known to be politically "conservative." My department chair and principal were clear: no student can leave a teacher's class because of who the teacher is. No longer attending class, the student was visibly upset when I met with her and her guidance counselor a few days later. He hoped that after a respectful listening between us, the student might choose to return to my classroom.

The student let me know that she was "not a homophobe," that she had "figured out I was gay," but that I "did not need to announce it," that what I had done was "wrong." More painful was her telling me that all my efforts to support her "more conservative views" in the classroom had backfired, that she felt "outside," not included or respected by her classmates. It was a long and layered conversation. In the end, her counselor asked if she could stay in my class. Through tears, she said no.

The student moved to another teacher's section, but not the class that her parents and she had requested. Another colleague taught the same course. Close curriculum collaborators, we occasionally combined classes for certain activities. Thus, the student and I saw each other a few times over the semester. All through December, much unfolded in difficult conversations with the parents. Seeing this as an issue beyond me, the department chair, principal, and superintendent took on these conversations with the parents. My colleagues had concerns that the parents had their own political motivations in mind, not just concern for their child. In late January, I learned that the student responded to the open-ended essay on the course's midyear exam with a long reflection on her experience with me. She left the school and began attending a local private Christian school.

I tell of 1996, when the family sued. My department chair's phone call on an early Sunday afternoon in March informed me that the family was suing me, the school administration, and the superintendent for "professional negligence." An election year, and time of another rise from the political religious right, positioned this family to challenge the new Massachusetts' Student Civil Rights law by claiming that I/we had "violated" their daughter's "heterosexual rights." They wanted payment for emotional stress "damages" and her parochial school tuition.

I knew that my strongest statement came through my teaching. If this was going to go to court, I would have my chance to speak. I did not want to cause her personal pain. It was difficult not to speak out, especially in the immediate aftermath. The political became personal as my name and the story played in local newspapers and on talk radio. The 1990s internet was in its infancy. No Twitter. No Facebook. I received hate mail, though nowhere near the volume of supportive letters and cards.

And then, silence. The case never went anywhere. The town did not accept the charges. The family never filed in court within the three-year statute of limitations. I was left to pick up the pieces, weave them together into my high school teaching and now as a teacher educator at the university.

I want today's aspiring teachers to know of the gay and lesbian students of 1992 who found each other and their collective voice, and then acted on their realization that their silence will not protect them. In doing so, they called teachers, administrators, and parents to break their silence and stand with them to bring changes that created more just and humane schools. And yes, this struggle continues.

New teachers want to be "classroom ready," yet this requires more than technical skills. It requires that teachers engage the intellectual, personal, and political. As teachers realize that they themselves are, or may be, "sites of contention" between competing ideologies of what it means to teach (and learn) and be a teacher (and a learner), they begin to see beyond a narrow search for a "toolkit" for teaching. They open to the possibility that ongoing political self-examination is essential to teaching and that they cannot do this learning alone. They need each other, mentors, and learning spaces that support deep inquiry into the political contexts of schools and classrooms.

Questions for Reflection

1. Reflecting on your own results from the LGBTQ Cultural Competence School Assessment tool, in which areas are you already competent? In which areas do you need to become more competent? How will you go about learning more in the needed areas? What about your school?

2. How might you use the teaching strategy of historiographic mappings in different curricular contexts?

3. How might you incorporate the active learning strategy of youth partici-
    patory action research (YPAR) across the disciplines?
4. Did you find traditions in your own high school that excluded a group or
    groups of students?
5. Does the school in which you teach hold traditions that exclude groups of
    students? How might they be changed or reimagined to be more inclusive?

References

American Institute for Research. (2013). *Practice guidelines for the delivery of trauma-informed and GLBTQ culturally-competent care.* Retrieved from www.air.org/sites/default/files/downloads/report/Trauma-Informed%20and%20GLBTQ%20Culturally%20Competent%20Care.pdf

Cammarota, J., & Fine, M. (2008). *Revolutionizing education: Youth participatory action research in motion.* New York, NY: Routledge.

Clark, C. T. (2010). Preparing LGBTQ-allies and combating homophobia in a US teacher education program. *Teaching and Teacher Education, 26*(3), 704–713.

Cooper, K. M., & Brownell, S. E. (2016). Coming out in class: Challenges and benefits of active learning in a biology classroom for LGBTQIA students. *CBE – Life Science Education, 15*(3).

Fox, M., Mediratta, K., Ruglis, J., Stoudt, B., Shah, S., & Fine, M. (2010). *Critical youth engagement: participatory action research and organizing, in handbook of research on civic engagement in youth.* Hoboken, NJ: Wiley.

GLSEN. (2016). *Educational exclusion: Drop out, push out, and school-to-prison pipeline among LGBTQ youth.* New York, NY: GLSEN.

Greytak, E. A., Kosciw, J. G., & Diaz, E. M. (2009). *Harsh realities: The experiences of transgender youth in our nation's schools.* New York, NY: GLSEN.

Gutierez-Schmich, T. (2016). *Public pedagogy and conflict pedagogy: Sites of possibility for anti-oppressive teacher education* (Doctoral dissertation). Retrieved from University of Oregon, ProQuest Dissertations Publishing.

Hawkins, R. (2017, June 23). Being non-binary. *Ygender.* Retrieved from www.ygender.org.au/being-non-binary

Kawazoe, A. (1994, Spring/Summer). Historiography? What's that? *The Quarterly of the National Writing Project & The Center for the Study of Writing and Literacy, 16*(2–3), 1–35.

Kulke, C. (2016, September 26). For LGBT students, history lessons often leave out a key chapter. *WBUR.* Retrieved from www.wbur.org/edify/2016/09/26/teaching-lgbt-history

Morgan, K. (2017, June 26). Pride for some? We need Pride4All! *The California Endowment.* Retrieved from www.calendow.org/pride-need-pride4all/

Ollin, R. (2007). Silent pedagogy and rethinking classroom practice: Structuring teaching through silence rather than talk. *Cambridge Journal of Education, 38*(2), 265–280.

Postlewait, T. (1991). Historiography and the theatrical event: A primer with twelve cruxes. *Theatre Journal, 43*(2), 157–178.

Powers, C. B., & Allaman, E. (2012, December 17). How participatory action research can promote social change and help youth development. *The Kinder & Braver World Project: Research Series.* Retrieved from http://cyber.harvard.edu/sites/cyber.harvard.edu/files/KBWParticipatoryActionResearch2012.pdf

Rimer, S. (1993, December 8). Gay rights law for schools advances in Massachusetts. *The New York Times*. Retrieved from www.nytimes.com/1993/12/08/us/gay-rights-law-for-schools-advances-in-massachusetts.html

Sanchez, J. S., Lomeli-Loibl, C. & Nelson, A. A. (2009, Summer). Sacramento's LGBTQ youth: Youth-led participatory action research for mental health justice with youth in focus. *Focal Point – Research, Policy, & Practice in Children's Mental Health, 23*(2), 6–8.

Sawchuk, S. (2017, September 5). LGBT history gets short shrift in schools. There's an effort to change that. *Editorial Projects in Education –Education Week*. Retrieved from www.edweek.org/ew/articles/2017/09/06/lgbt-history-gets-short-shrift-theres-an.html

Schey, R., & Uppstrom, A. (2010). Activist work as entry-year teachers: What we've learned. In M. V. Blackburn, C. T. Clark, L. M. Kenney, & J. M. Smith (Eds.), *Acting out!: Combating homophobia through teacher activism* (pp. 88–102). New York, NY: Teachers College Press.

Stauber, L. S. (2017). Turning in or tuning out? Listening to silences in education for critical political consciousness. *International Journal of Qualitative Studies in Education, 30*(6), 560–575.

Suicide Prevention Resource Center. (2018). *LGBTQ cultural competence school assessment*. Retrieved from www.sprc.org/system/files/private/event-training/6C%20 Handouts.pdf

Treatment and Services Adaptation Center. (n.d.). *Advocating for LGBT issues in schools*. Retrieved from http://traumaawareschools.org/articles/view/9628

UC Regents. (2015). *Young people empowered to change the world*. Retrieved from http://yparhub.berkeley.edu/

Villa, B. (2016, June 20). LGBTQ youth are reshaping their city. *The California Endowment*. Retrieved from www.calendow.org/lgbtq-youth-reshaping-city/

Wagaman, A. (2015). Changing ourselves, changing the world: Assessing the value of participatory action research as an empowerment-based research and service approach with LGBTQ young people. *Child & Youth Services, 36*(2), 124–149.

Westhoff, L. M. (2012). Historiographic mapping: Toward a signature pedagogy for the methods course. *Journal of American History, 98*(4), 1114–1126.

PART IV

Higher Education

11

UNIVERSITIES AND TEACHER EDUCATION

As higher education faculty across university disciplines, and particularly in teacher education, you may be keenly aware of how challenging social justice work is to include in your courses, in collaboration with fellow faculty, and in relationships with students. While higher education campuses have worked toward gender and lesbian, gay, bisexual, transgender and queer (LGBTQ) inclusion through climate initiatives like gender-neutral housing and bathrooms, LGBTQ History Month, and Resource Centers, we have yet to make deep strides in examining higher education courses, both in terms of ideological assumptions and curricular content that may be exclusionary and/or depend on biases and prejudices steeped in patriarchal and heteronormative binaries and stereotypes.

We begin this chapter with a case study that speaks to the impact of perpetuating unexamined curricula and pedagogy at the university level. In particular, we look at the effects of traditional, rigid constructions of gender using stereotypes and binaries that lead to a limited examination of the social structures and institutions impacting people's lives. This case study takes the form of a communication between the second author and an undergraduate student at the semester's end. The student is concerned about unexamined curricula and instruction, and its impact on the greater student body's conceptualization of gender.

UNIVERSITY STUDENT CASE STUDY

Student Complaint on Gendered Assumptions in Communications Class by Noemi Santillan

Hi Prof K,

I feel like this professor is only taking into account cisgendered people and not letting my class learn about the reality of the diversity that exists with gender today. I feel like I am being asked to dumb myself down and think with a micro-lens which is really REALLY bothering me. This seems like it is reinforcing the inaccurate, non inclusive, and harmful gender binary that exists today. The panels will consists of three guys and three girls from class, these will be volunteers. I just emailed him to volunteer to be on the panel.

I just really needed to vent, thank you professor. Hopefully I can get him to think about gender and this outdated assignment twice.

COMMUNICATIONS 101 ASSIGNMENT DESCRIPTION

Gender Panel Assignment

What: Interview a panel of students representing their gender. Write a story about how the gender views a variety of topics, such as relationships between the sexes or about the gender itself ("Why do men/women..."). You will write only about one of the panels, not both.

When: Tuesday, Dec 1. The two panels will take turns answering your questions.

Length: Your first effort (draft) will be produced on paper. About 2–3 pages. Double space. Use 12-point font.

Deadline: Draft is due Tuesday, Dec 8. Rewrite due Thursday, Dec 10 at noon via email.

Notes

- At the top of your story, write a 3- to 8-word headline (see examples on the web or newspaper).
- The story is about how the *gender* views the topics, not the particular panel member. Make sure your questions and story are clearly focused on this angle. <u>Do not ask questions nor write a story about gender equality.</u>
- Make sure your questions are specific. Are you asking a personal question or one specifically about gender?
- Come prepared with some questions and some possible follow-up questions.
- Digital recorders (or your phone's recorder) will come in handy—as a backup. Remember to make paper your primary source of note-taking.
- Listen carefully to other questions. You may use the responses in your story. You may also want to ask a follow-up question.
- You will be graded on how you consciously and deliberately apply what you have learned so far in your readings and in the discussions.
- Please refrain from women's magazines or *Teen Vogue* approaches to your story: "Hey, girls! Want to know what guys REALLY think?" That

kind of stuff. It pains me to read that stuff. Yes, the story can benefit from a light touch.

- Organization is king. If you have lots of good individual items that don't work well in the body of the story, you can do it one of two ways. One way is the bullet approach. Keep the sentence short and sweet. The lead-in graft might say, "The panelists also said..." A second way is by topic. Example: "Love stinks, the panelists said." Then you may have one or two examples. If more, then use the bullet format under the topic. Do what it takes to help your reader follow the story.

- Don't belabor the obvious. Once you identify the panelists, don't refer to them as the panelists. "John Smith, another panelist..." Or keep badgering the reader that there were three panelists: "The three women said..." "Of the three male panelists, one..." We get the point.

At the end of the semester, Naomi then sent this evaluation of the gender panel assignment to the communications professor:

Dear Professor,

I would really like to express my concern over the "Gender Panel Assignment." It seemed as though it was geared strictly towards the unrealistic gender binary that is extremely inaccurate these days. We know that not all men identify through masculinity and not all women identify through femininity. The idea that we were supposed to frame the questions in a "Why do men?" and "Why do women?" implies that because a person is a man they must do a certain thing or act a certain way. The same goes for the idea that because a person is a woman they must also do a certain thing or act a certain way. This is actually a harmful way of stereotyping gender. If someone doesn't feel that that their own gender doesn't match the societal expectations that are put on them, the result is extremely damaging to one's self identity and self esteem.

Biological Sex, Gender Identity, Gender Expression, and Sexual Orientation are all DIFFERENT THINGS. We can not assume all of these about someone and place them in a confined category in our minds and expect them to act accordingly. It is the ignorant disregard for the reality of someone's true self that has led to discrimination, hatred, and violence with homosexuals, transgender people, and people of different ethnic backgrounds. I watched all of the discussion videos and I learned some very important things in regards to being a journalist. I was very pleased to learn about the importance of diversity. It was great to hear that "Journalists have an ethical duty to report on ALL parts of their diverse community." This would have been such a better approach to the panel assignment. The truth is that

EVERYONE'S GENDER IS DIFFERENT and some people don't even identify with a gender at all.

I felt like you were insensitive to your students about this. Also, you expressed your opinion about how you think students today are "too sensitive." Also you pulled up an article titled "The Delicate Flowers of Today's College Campuses." Please know that the title is actually considered homophobic misogynistic rhetoric. It implies that men who don't identify though masculinity are weak. These kinds of titles are damaging and hurtful to someone who is struggling to come out as gay, especially to be seen inside of a classroom, from a teacher, and from their school. Professor, please ask yourself WHY DO STUDENTS FEEL THAT WAY? Perhaps it's because women are far from being treated equally to men in a social and economical aspect, perhaps it's because states such as Texas want to deport their citizens even when they are born IN THE UNITED STATES, or perhaps it's because the average lifespan of a transgender individual is 34. Professor, please ask yourself why. The diversity lecture gave tips on dealing with diversity. Some of these included getting out of your comfort zone, visiting ethnic neighborhoods, to finding experts. I encourage you to do the same. One last thing Professor, what I found was most important was that the Society of Professional Journalist have an ethical code. To Seek The Truth and to Report it.

Undergraduate student Noemi's experiences in the communications class' "Gender Panel Assignment" exemplifies the importance of increasing higher education faculty's awareness of and professional development about gender and LGBTQ issues, broadly across the university and specifically in teacher education.

Higher Education and LGBTQ Inclusion

In higher education, the increased number of negative experiences among LGBTQ students makes them four times more likely to attempt suicide. These negative experiences include harassment from peers, faculty, and staff (23 percent of LGBT students; 35 percent of transgender students); being referred to in a derogatory way (61 percent of transgender students); physical and sexual assault (respectively 5 percent and 3 percent of transgender students); and leaving school due to negative experiences (15 percent of transgender students) and due to financial hardship (11 percent). Referencing these statistics, in 2016, undergraduate student Destiny Caro introduced the Resolution in Support of LGBTQ Student Life at California State University, Fullerton (CSUF; see the full Resolution in Appendix G). The Associated Students, Inc. Board passed the resolution, which requests that supplementary education and training be provided for university faculty and staff, including training in the use of in-clusive language in classroom curricula, policies, and procedures; knowledge of the distinct challenges of LGBTQ students; and the building of safe and welcoming university spaces, including gender-inclusive restrooms and other facilities.

As referenced by the CSUF resolution, universities continue to provide in-adequate support and understanding of LGBTQ student experiences. Teaching in higher education requires teachers to build cross-cultural competence in order to improve these experiences, beginning with identifying and address-ing systemic barriers toward inclusivity. The National Education Association (2017) identifies five skill areas for faculty to develop in order to become more LGBTQ and gender inclusive: valuing and adapting to diversity (accepting and respecting differences), being culturally self-aware, understanding the dynam-ics of difference in cross-cultural communication and how to respond, learning about students' cultures, and institutionalizing cultural knowledge.

As universities increase efforts to adopt more inclusive language, policies, practices, and classroom climates, DiPietro (2012) of the American Association of Colleges and Universities offers these points of reflection to consider when creating LGBTQ-inclusive classrooms and campuses:

1. Students' prior knowledge can help or hinder learning.
2. How students organize knowledge influences how they learn and apply what they know.
3. Students' motivation determines, directs, and sustains what they do to learn.
4. To develop mastery, students must acquire component skills, practice inte-grating them, and know when to apply what they have learned.
5. Goal-directed practice coupled with targeted feedback enhances the qual-ity of students' learning.
6. Students' current level of development interacts with the social, emotional, and intellectual climate of the course to impact learning.
7. To become self-directed learners, students must learn to monitor and ad-just their approaches to learning.

DiPietro (2012) cautions,

> It is important for all faculty members to examine our emotions around these issues of identity: our anger at societal oppression, passion about righting wrongs, feelings of empowerment from gains achieved, fear of offending people, doubts about our competence in handling diffi-cult conversations, etc. Our pedagogical challenge lies in focusing these emotions productively while sharing our disciplinary mastery with students.

In other words, as educators, we must reflect on our own gender journeys; our preconceptions and assumptions about the relationship between gender and sexuality; and the impact of being socialized with rigid gender binaries and heteronormative social structures on our teaching, curriculum, and pedagogy.

To be LGBTQ inclusive, cross-cultural competence includes teaching beyond the gender binary, such as by improving faculty's fluency with gender nonbinary, genderqueer, and gender-fluid vocabulary (see Appendix A for a list of definitions); familiarity with and/or commitment to gender nonbinary topics; and the implementation of gender-inclusive pedagogical practices (Harbin, 2015). For example, faculty can incorporate gender nonbinary or genderqueer voices into course materials without exoticizing or tokenizing gender-nonconforming experiences and without focusing solely on negative or victimizing examples of LGBTQ lives and histories. DiPietro (2012) provides this example:

> I once worked with a transgender student who did not identify within the gender binary, and who was taking a statistics class where the instructor collected student data broken down by gender (male or female) in order to illustrate a statistical concept. While the practice of using student-generated data is generally desirable, in this case, the student remembers nothing from that class other than frustration at being asked to choose between two equally undesirable [gender] alternatives and disappointment at not having raised these concerns. The nature of statistics is to put people in boxes, count, measure, and compare them, but some students find this act of labeling oppressive.

The relationship between campus climate, instruction, and relationships is clear. University faculty must become more critically aware of our impact on LGBTQ students and the ways in which we position ourselves in relation to student concerns and experiences. In the remainder of the chapter, we explore how to become more inclusive, specifically in the field of teacher education.

Teacher Education, Gender Diversity, and LGBTQ Inclusion

As an illustration of the aforementioned concerns, colleges of education have historically spent limited curricular time on issues of gender, gender socialization and stereotypes, or gender and LGBTQ diversity and inclusion in teacher preparation. This is of particular concern given how central gender and sexuality are to human development and young people's socialization, and how important teachers are as mentors in the lives of youth. This issue is further compounded when we see resistance from school districts to providing professional development for current teachers on LGBTQ topics. As an example, across the San Francisco Bay Area, at least 73,000 students attend schools that don't educate teachers on transgender issues (Shaban, Campos, Rutanashoodeh, Villareal & Horn, 2017). If school districts and teacher education programs are not working with teachers to learn about LGBTQ inclusion, and gender and sexual diversity more broadly, who holds the responsibility for ensuring that schools are safe for our youth? Who will ensure that queer youth thrive?

Recent approaches in elementary teacher education have included limited teaching about gender socialization in child development; about sexual orientation in relation strictly to family diversity; and about the impact of gender stereotypes on children's achievement, such as stereotypes about girls and STEM (Curran, Chiarolli, & Pallota-Chiarolli, 2009; DePalma & Atkinson, 2006, 2009; Sanders, 1997). Most often, discussions of gender, sexuality, and LGBTQ communities occur in prerequisite courses on diversity in education or educational foundations, while these topics are less commonly, if ever, integrated into subject matter preparation classes.

However, subject matter courses can and should address the inclusion of gender and family diversity, such as through the contributions of LGBTQ individuals and communities, LGBTQ perspectives in society, LGBTQ histories, changing gender roles in society, and the role of LGBTQ struggles in civil rights in the regular curriculum (Flores, 2012, 2014; Hermann-Wilmarth, 2010; Naidoo, 2012; Phillips & Larson, 2010). Other approaches can include discussing LGBTQ topics in relation to inclusive family and community partnerships, bias-bullying prevention and intervention, restorative justice practices, and comprehensive sex and health education (Flores, 2014).

Some teacher education courses draw upon feminist and queer theory to assist in supporting teachers in their deconstruction of gender socialization and the hetero-normatization of children's relationships at schools (DePalma & Atkinson, 2006; Phillips & Larson, 2010). These critical theories call for the deconstruction and dismantling of rigid gender norms, binaries, and hierarchies (Atkinson & DePalma, 2008; Flores, 2014; Renn, 2010; Sears, 2009). Theorists focusing on queerness in education ask us as teachers and students to "lose our gender expertise" and allow discomfort and doubt to occur (DePalma, 2013) by asking questions like how do you know someone is male or female? "Queering" rigid gender norms and binary-based assumptions about gender identity and expression (DePalma, 2013) should also include determining how discussions about gender-creative children will serve to dismantle or reinscribe gender binaries by Othering gender-creative experiences (Kelso, 2015).

In the following stories, we share several university faculty's efforts to create safe, welcoming spaces for LGBTQ students; to reflect on the intersections of personal gender and sexuality identities and our identities as educators; and to raise awareness about gender binaries and stereotypes in curricula with preservice teacher candidates.

STORY ONE: "Gender Representations in a Mathematics Teacher Education Class" by Cathery Yeh

Diversity and equity are stated priorities in mathematics education research and practice. The talk surrounding diversity and equity is often framed around issues of race, socioeconomic status, sex, disability status, or language. Gender identity and sexual orientation are largely absent from these discussions (Esmonde, 2011). This story looks closely at my own journey as a teacher, mother, and teacher educator in connecting gender and sexual identity within my teaching of mathematics methods.

Teaching and Learning from Students, Families, and My Own Children

I started teaching in 2000 in the Los Angeles urban core. Most of my students had moved from Mexico, countries in Central America, or China. Immigration was our shared experience, and this helped to build common ground. As a classroom teacher, I made visits to every student home (over 300 households) and tried to integrate their lived experiences, knowledge, and histories into the curriculum.

I never examined gender socialization or gender oppression until I became a parent. Six years ago, when I learned I would have another girl, I felt a sense of comfort. My oldest now has a sister. However, Eliannah was distinctly her own being. By age 2, El gravitated toward what society has modeled as images of boyhood: swords, Nerf guns, and superhero shirts with capes. I once found El standing on the toilet seat squatting to pee "boy style." At age 3, El said to me, "When I grow up, I want to be a daddy. I want to be a boy."

El has taught me that gender is not something that we are or have; it is something that we do and perform (Butler, 2004); this gender socialization process takes place daily. El is learning about gender performance while watching the men and boys just as much if not more than the direct messages of how El *should* behave as a child who was assigned female at birth. Over time, I have come to admire El's nonconforming ways. How long have I attempted to conform to society's ideas of femininity? How often do I question my own worth as a mother, a wife, and a woman of color in the academy? El's realness is an amazingly endearing and laudable quality. If all people had the courage to just be themselves, wouldn't the world be a better place?

Queering Mathematics Education

My students, their families, and my own children shape my vision and goals as a mathematics teacher educator. As a university-based teacher educator, I have tried to foreground equity and social justice in my mathematics methods courses. Nasir, Hand, and Taylor (2008) describe mathematics classrooms as "inherently cultural spaces where different forms of knowing and being are being validated" (p. 206). Teaching mathematics is a complex endeavor. Teachers need opportunities to think critically about the social, political, and cultural spaces in which school mathematics takes place (Nasir et al., 2008; Weisglass, 2002).

My methods course starts with the mathematics reflexivity assignment. The teachers and I write about our mathematics learning experiences: the identities most salient to us (i.e., mathematical, cultural, linguistic, gendered), our personal history with mathematics, and the issues and factors that influence our learning and sense of self. The reflexivity essays are shared out loud to interrogate how our own and our colleagues' mathematics performances emerge as a product of the organization of our mathematics education, shaped by cultural and historical roots.

Paralleling inward reflection of self, the teacher-training course curriculum centers on children's voices and experiences. I've found that careful listening to children's rich mathematical thinking and to their lived experiences provides the most generative learning opportunities for beginning teachers. Starting on the fifth week of a 15-week course, my class moves off the university campus to a local community center. The first of the three-hour course is devoted to working with elementary-age students from a local school. The teachers interview students and families, listening to their stories, and then work in triads to design mathematics lessons that incorporate students' cultures, languages, and identities.

We begin to explicitly problematize genderism and heteronormativity during the weekly lesson planning, analyzing word problems in published mathematics curriculum materials. The use of contextualized problems is particularly important in mathematics education. A rich word problem allows students to connect school mathematics to real-world contexts, to utilize their daily experience to problem-solve, and to use mathematics as a tool to understand and solve problems in the world. However, all word problems are carriers of cultural values and each problem privileges particular worldviews.

Let's start with a series of problems in the fifth-grade *Math Expressions* fractions and decimals unit to share some of our observations:

1. Amie used 7/9 yard of ribbon in her dress. Jasmine used 5/6 yard of ribbon in her dress. Which girl used more ribbon? How much more did she use?
2. A fifth-grade class is made up of 12 boys and 24 girls. How many times as many girls are in the class as boys?
3. Ms. Hernandez knitted a scarf for her grandson. The scarf is 5/6 yard long and 2/9 yard wide. What is the area of the scarf?

What is normalized and valued in these problems? Beginning teachers made the following observations: normalizing gendered activities (sewing as "feminine" hobby or pastime); competition (more ribbon = more feminine?); gendered clothing (dresses as commonplace); conflation of sex and gender and binary opposition of the sex/gender categories.

We've found that the thread of inequity is woven throughout all mathematics curricula. The process of analyzing together has allowed us to expose "hidden" narratives of oppression—classism, sexism, heterosexism, racism, xenophobia, and consumerism. These new insights then allow us to undertake agentive activities to actively disrupt and challenge hegemonic narratives. The mathematics context can be reframed to create more relevant, socially just scenarios that better reflect the beauty and diversity of our students (e.g., "John used 7/9 yard of ribbon"; "Mrs. Hernandez knitted a scarf for her wife.") The contextualized problems themselves can serve as a vehicle for students to use mathematics to analyze privilege and oppression (e.g., by analyzing the gender pay gap or the differences in the rate of hate crimes and police brutality between transgender and cisgender populations).

Students often expect a math methods course to "just be about numbers." Every decision teachers make about how to present the relevance of mathematics in everyday life sends powerful messages about what is valued and whose knowledge and experiences are deemed important (Kumashiro, 2004, p. 96). As teachers, we must create learning spaces that are humane and liberating; this social justice work begins by allowing our children to see themselves and to understand and investigate the world mathematically through the tasks we assign.

STORY TWO: "Passing, Privilege, and Preservice Teacher Preparation: Queering the Conversation" by Alison Dover

I don't remember the moment I came out. It must have been sometime in college, when campus identity politics pushed me to claim my LGBTQ identity. For a while, I brandished my queerness as both shield and sword to combat the rigid androgyny of my campus' lesbian community—which welcomed neither my high femme self nor my butch and genderqueer partners—and the straight streets of the neighborhood where my skirts and heels triggered catcalls or worse. I found my home among other gender outlaws: Leslie Feinberg taught me I wasn't alone, and Boston's 1990s trans activist community welcomed me with open arms. I never came out because I wasn't ever "in." Being queer, and visible, was simply part of my daily reality. I used my gender as a weapon, called my partners by name, and had their pictures on my desk at school; it never occurred to me to do otherwise.

Fast-forward 15 years. I'm older now and far less flamboyant. I have a husband and two kids. We live in the suburbs and look straight. Coming out is now a choice and not always an easy one to make. I've been married a long time and don't especially want to throw open my bedroom door for the salacious voyeurism that emerges when we discuss sexual orientation and gender identity. I'm at the park with the kids: do I let the other moms assume I'm straight or find a way to casually mention sleeping with women? "Don't worry," I could tell them, "never women like you, and besides, I'm happily monogamous." Maybe we could reminisce about back episodes of *Will and Grace* while our children play on the swings. I'm in class: I come out as queer, and a student asks if my "sexual history" bothers my husband or when I grew out of it. (This really happened. Several times.) I'm at my kid's school, advocating for curriculum about LGBT families. "But we don't have any of those here," the teacher says. "Interesting," I say, "are you sure?"

These are the realities of being this queer educator in this moment in time. My students, colleagues, and fellow activists assume I'm straight. I have to decide how to handle it every time. What will it be today? Invasive personal questions, or passing as "that straight lady with a weird level of investment in queer stuff." Or, is today the day I get silent, allowing the privilege of passing to lull me into complacency? It's seductive to not to have to defend yourself at every turn (Dover, 2017).

This tension was cast into sharp relief a few years ago, when I was teaching a course on multicultural children's literature to preservice elementary teachers. It was our week to focus on LGBT children's literature, and my students were presenting standards-aligned lessons that featured books about diverse families, gender identities, and expressions. I was confident facilitating this content: after all, I used to run a statewide safe schools program and have trained thousands of educators about creating equity and social justice. At the time, I was one of only two out faculty members in my university's education program and had come out to this group of students at the beginning of the semester. I had examples of lessons from my own high school classroom and all the most current research from GLSEN. The inevitable question came: "So, what do we do when a child says his religion, or his parents, say homosexuality is wrong? Do we say his parents are wrong?" I had fielded this one many times. "It's simple," I said. "We just tell students that different families may have different beliefs at home, but in school we respect and welcome everyone." I turned to move onto the next group of students. "But wait," called back one of my undergraduates, "isn't that just condoning homophobia? Would you say the same thing if a student's parents said something racist? That they were entitled to their own beliefs, and you weren't going to challenge them?"

She was right; I'd never be complicit with racism in that way. But somehow, I had become willing to accept homophobia, especially when packaged in the trappings of religious freedom. I was taken aback, humbled, and more than a little ashamed. Somewhere along the way, it had happened: I had been lulled into complacency and allowed pleasant affirmations of diversity to stand in for justice. So, I told my student she was right and that my response wasn't good enough. We stopped class and brainstormed better answers. None were perfect, but together, we modeled what accountability can look like in the classroom: I made a mistake, and a student called me out; I showed up for the conversation, and together, we made something better.

Since then, I've used this example regularly in my teacher education courses, both to highlight the ubiquitous nature of our surrender to homophobic institutional practices and to underscore the imperative to grow as educators. It's not my students' job to teach me how to be a social justice educator, and neither my queerness nor my professional pedigree protects me from the covert pressures of heteronormativity. Schools can be hostile places, and too many teachers are lulled into letting pleasantries, compliance, and silence prevail. I share this story with my students to remind them to avoid complicity with unjust systems and ideologies. "Don't do it," I tell them, "you be the teacher who speaks out."

"Don't do it," I tell myself as I read the note scrawled at the bottom of a student's paper. She's a preservice teacher, enrolled in the required diversity class. "What is the bare minimum," she asks, "that I have to do to comply with state non-discrimination legislation?" "Everything," I think, as I look up the law. "You have to do everything."

STORY THREE: "Small Shifts, Big Changes: LGBTQ-Inclusive Professional Development for Elementary Educators" by Brittney Beck and Cody Miller

As teacher educators and practicing teachers pursuing doctoral degrees in education at a large research-one institution in the southeast, we have created and facilitated the first-ever LGBTQ+ professional development (PD) opportunities offered to teacher candidates and in-service teachers at both our university and within our local partnering school district. Navigating a largely conservative environment while seeking to provide professional development reflective of the realities of LGBTQ+ people has pushed our boundaries as well as the boundaries of our partners. However, with a multi-stakeholder approach to PD framed by national statistics and grounded in the lived experiences of local queer students, we have seen small shifts that have led to big changes in the practices of educators and the climates of schools.

Our Context

While we are embedded within a college town, which tends to foster more inclusive ideologies, the broader community and state in which we are situated harbor a social conservatism that places actual and perceived barriers on the civil rights and human dignities of LGBTQ+ populations. Historically framed by the purge of gay and lesbian educators at the hands of the Florida Legislative Investigative Committee in the 1950s–1960s (Graves, 2009) and the 2016 murders of queer and Latinx people at Pulse nightclub in Orlando, the state of Florida does not enumerate sexual orientation and gender identity within its antidiscrimination policies. Our partnering school district offers these protections, yet the policies are often practiced as radio silence on queer issues due to fears and mythologies surrounding identities that fall outside of heterosexual norms and male/female gender binaries. This is especially true at the elementary level.

Specifically, from our experience, three layers of distortion tend to limit elementary educators' inclusion of LGBTQ+ perspectives and discourses. Foremost, many elementary educators are accepting of LGBTQ+ identities, yet perceive elementary-aged children as "too young" to be exposed to LGBTQ+ issues, as if doing so would sully their innocence. For teachers who want to include LGBTQ+ identities in their classroom, their dominant barrier is focused on parent backlash or their own lack of knowledge. Lastly, for a multiplicity of reasons, there are a few who roundly protest against the inclusion of LGBTQ+ issues in any dimension of community life, with the classroom being no exception.

This context is significant in unpacking why and how we advocate for small shifts that may reap big changes for children of all genders and sexualities who are caught in the culture wars of adults. As much as we would like to dismantle the system of schooling and put it back together in a way that prioritizes inclusion of queer identities at all levels, we recognize that change does not always occur with protests or legislative victories that topple current regimes. Change sometimes occur and must always be supported by sustained dialogue and ongoing education within and outside of the classroom.

Our Shifts

We posit our professional development sessions as a shift away from standard ways of thinking about LGBTQ+ issues in education. Based on our own experiences as teachers and doctoral students, we believe the three shifts outlined allow us to take a broader view of LGBTQ+ issues in education, empower educators to make positive changes within their own contexts, and help create a multiplying force to ensure the work to create equitable schools for LGBTQ+ students and families is not isolated to our PD sessions. Specifically, we seek to shift the perspectives of multiple stakeholders in the school system:

- From considering antidiscrimination as silence to centering the voices of queer youth
- From focusing on queer identities alone to focusing on intersectional identities
- From individual-level thinking to community-level thinking regarding all dimensions of schooling that impact queer youth.

From Silence to Centering the Voices of Queer Youth

We recognize that fostering an inclusive climate for students demands the attention of all stakeholders who create the physical, emotional, and mental spaces of classrooms: students, families, teachers, administrators, support staff, district personnel, and community agencies. As a result, our workshops seek to have as many of these stakeholders at the table as possible in order to create a network of support, and, as one participant explained, "give us permission to talk about a topic with colleagues that we often felt was taboo." This quote is representative of how many participants feel as they are entering the PD—as long as they are not saying anything explicitly bad about LGBTQ+ youth or denying them opportunities based on gender identity and sexual orientation, they feel they are not discriminating.

Yet we pose questions such as: is it discrimination to only have heterosexual families on your bookshelves? Is it harassment to make a genderqueer student choose between a girls line and a boys line? To answer these questions, we seek to center the experiences of LGBTQ+ youth and let their lived needs guide our practice. Our PD is not designed to nurture debate (although we appreciate that debate signals the move from simple to more complex consideration of an issue), but to provide a space where the gritty realities and needs to LGBTQ+ students can be heard and addressed.

To ground the work in the needs of local students, we asked for middle and high school students who are part of Gay-Straight Alliances (GSAs) in our partnering district to tell us what they would like school personnel to know. Having the voices of these students is both a strength and a limitation. While we have brave middle school and high school students who are willing to speak retrospectively about their experiences in elementary school, there have been significant barriers to getting the perspectives of elementary-aged students. This same barrier is broadly reflected in scholarship on LGBTQ+ issues in Pre-K through sixth grade, which have not used the student as a unit of analysis (Wimberly & Battle, 2015). Nonetheless, the voices of these local students provide a potency and sense of urgency unmatched by more abstract calls to action.

We open the PD with a quote from a student compelling the district to prepare educators who will

> fight for our right to have equal educational opportunities as the student sitting next us. We need teachers and counselors to be able to advise us, and help us to grow as students and people, and to provide a safe learning environment. And from administrators we need to have support from the very top, regardless of personal opinion. Administrators must enforce protection against bullying, large and small, in order to give students a place to escape bigotry and discrimination.

Quotes of this nature are integrated throughout the PD, addressing the debilitating forces of heteronormativity and cisnormativity in schools as well as the need to demythologize the innocence of youth.

We also situate the narratives of our local students within national statistics from the Gay, Lesbian, Straight Education Network, emphasizing how not being inclusive of LGBTQ+ populations amounts to more than just hurt feelings or differing opinions, but can change the trajectory of their lives or even end their lives. Statics tell a broader story that a disproportionate amount of LGBTQ+ youth commit suicide (Consolacion, Russel, & Sue, 2004), experience depression, have a low self-esteem, and do not pursue post-secondary education (Kosciw, Greytak, Palmer, & Boesen, 2013).

Just as we center the experience of LGBTQ+ students, so too do we encourage our participants to provide space for students to share their stories and to, as one of our participants put it, "error on the side of child" even in the fury of adult debate and dissent. At the elementary level—although some students are very aware of their identities—many are not. Therefore, providing space for children to share their narratives looks a little different than a middle school or high school support system. We encourage elementary educators to normalize LGBTQ+ identities in their classrooms through books, historical figures, math word problems, letters home, and by not organizing students by gender. We emphasize that creating this space in the classroom is not about reacting to having a student with same-sex parents or to having a transgender child in their class, but to proactively making LGBTQ+ inclusion a part of their everyday practice.

From LGBTQ+ Identities to Intersectional Identities

The concept of intersectionality originated as a discourse that enabled women of color to share their narratives at the crossroads of the Feminist and Civil Rights Movements and operates on the assumption that you cannot dismember a person's identity into its component parts. A person is not black and a woman; a person is a black woman. This discourse has since expanded to include the intersections of class, sexuality, and ability.

In the interest of enabling students to share their full stories and recognizing that there is a hierarchy of oppression even within the queer community, which affords white, gay, cisgendered men privileges not accessible to transgender populations or queer populations of color, our PD seeks to shift participants' perspective from considering the LGBTQ+ community to considering how LGBTQ+ identities intersect with other marginalized identities to form matrices of oppression that can further limit a students' learning and life chances. To illuminate this reality, we share data that specifically speak to the intersections of identity. Specifically, people of color are less likely to be out to their families (Grov & Bimbi, 2006), less likely to have mentorship from queer people of color, are harassed for both their queerness and their race, and feel as if they must choose between their race and their gender identity/sexuality when choosing peer groups (Dube & Savin-Williams, 1999; GLSEN, 2009, 2016).

Knowing the lived experiences at the crossroads of identity brightens once-hidden corners of the LGBTQ+ student experience, nurturing questions and narratives that would have gone unspoken. As one queer middle school student of color expressed, "I didn't think there were words to describe who I was or how I was feeling. I thought I would only exist inside myself forever." As elementary educators begin building their classroom libraries, reworking their world problems, and choosing historical and contemporary leaders to discuss, we remind them of the danger of a single story and how LGBTQ+ inclusion is not just queer check-box, but is a constantly moving expression of human diversity with the classroom as a window, a mirror, and a door for students.

From Individual-Level Thinking to Community-Level Thinking

In both policy and rhetoric, a new focus on the social and emotional needs of students has entered our discourse. The framework of "Multi-Tiered Systems of Support" or "MTSS" has been adopted in states concerned with addressing the needs of students from multiple points and recognizing that academic achievement is more nuanced than simply a test score. While many educators should champion the inclusion of MTSS in their school systems, we want to caution that an MTSS approach that does not address issues of sexuality and gender identity can be detrimental to LGBTQ students and families. An MTSS approach that ignores LGBTQ concerns sends the message that sexual and gender identity do not factor into students' and families' lived experiences within schools; we know the opposite is true. Ergo, we position our professional development within the MTSS framework by claiming that being responsive to LGBTQ students helps "meet the needs" of *all* students.

TABLE 11.1 Analyzing Normativity in Curriculum, Policy, Procedure and Language

	Curriculum	Policies	Procedures	Language
Heteronormativity				
Cisnormativity				

By centering the needs of LGBTQ students and families on their sexual and gender identity, we allow educators to rethink LGBTQ issues as something superfluous or "not related to the curriculum." Indeed, we found that educators are more able to identify and challenge the often invisible hetero- and cisnormativity within their contexts by centering support for students around sexual and gender identities. As one participant in a session put it, "I never realized the way I have students line up for the bathroom could be harming my students."

We walk our participants through a "concept chart" to support our participants in unearthing the hetero- and cisnormativity within their contexts. We talk about heteronormativity as the assumption of heterosexual relationships, and cisnormativity as the assumption of alignment between gender identity, expression and sex assigned at birth. We provide a chart for our participants to trace these two concepts throughout their own contexts. Our participants work in groups often from similar contexts. For instance, a group of teachers and administrators will work on one chart together to get a holistic view of how hetero- and cisnormativity manifest within their school. A topic like "policies" will generate different answers depending on the participants' role in the schools. For instance, a teacher may think about how they line up students to go to lunch while a principal may think about how they organize parent conferences (Table 11.1).

We've found that allowing multiple stakeholders at a school unpack their school contexts is fruitful for making positive change. For one, educators take ownership of their own contexts, which is important considering that participants know their school contexts better than we do. Additionally, this type of PD does more than provide definitions without context. Instead, educators develop their ability to critically analyze their schools, which is essential for future change beyond the time limit of our session.

Our Changes

We ask participants to make pledges at the end of our sessions. These pledges are action steps educators can make within their own contexts to better serve the needs of their LGBTQ+ students and families. We inform our participants that broad, social change is not easily attained in one session or school year or administration, and we encourage our participants to share their pledges with their colleagues in order to amplify the changes made.

Here are some initial pledges that Elementary Educators and Administrators have made to challenge hetero- and cisnormativity in their contexts:

- No longer line up students based on a strict gender binary.
- Amending family forms to ask for preferred pronouns.
- Broadening classroom libraries to include intersectional LGBTQ+ voices within classroom literature.
- Moving from nondiscrimination as silence to including, affirming, and empowering LGBTQ+ youth
- Developing diversity clubs at school
- Rethinking Take Mom/Dad to School days
- Amending uniform policies that operate on a male/female gender binary.

Our PD sessions have shown that educators can be empowered to make small shifts resulting in positive impacts in their own contexts while acknowledging the work is never complete. However, if we can empower more educators to change their schools, then we can empower more stakeholders to change their districts, their states, and even their nation. To do anything less would be a disservice to our LGBTQ+ students and families.

As teacher education faculty, each decision we make about how we present curriculum tells students what we respect and value. We recommend reading this book's preceding chapters and reflecting on how to integrate critical, inclusive, humanizing curriculum and pedagogy, that is also gender diverse and LGBTQ inclusive, into your teacher education program. It is important that we examine our own assumptions and prejudices about gender and sexuality and become culturally self-aware so that we can begin to recognize and understand our students' gender and cultural identities. Self-reflection also enables us to discover how our teaching and course content are influenced by our own biases. We must ensure that students are able to see themselves reflected in the curriculum regularly and that these representations are infused within the curriculum rather than being restricted only to prerequisite courses on diversity and equity in education. Examining curriculum and instruction for bias and stereotypes is vital to creating a curriculum that is inclusive of gender and family diversity and which includes the important contributions of LGBTQ and other marginalized individuals in history.

Questions for Reflection

1. Upon reflection of your own assumptions and biases and how they affect your curriculum, what gender stereotypes and preconceived notions have you discovered? What issues of identity have you uncovered?
2. How do you describe your own cultural identity? How do your cultural identities, history and dispositions toward other identities impact you as a teacher educator?
3. What activities or assignments will you give in order to help you get to know your students' cultures and identities?
4. How will you examine your curriculum for heteronormative bias and exclusion? What modifications will you make in order to begin queering your course content, making it more inclusive and socially relevant?
5. What areas of your college or university system still remain biased in rigid gender binaries and heteronormative social structures?
6. What can be done to change these structures, in particular to support teacher candidates in their efforts to become more just, equitable and inclusive teachers?

References

Atkinson, E., & Depalma, R. (2008). Imagining the homonormative: Performative subversion in education for social justice. *British Journal of Sociology of Education, 29*(1), 25–35.

Butler, J. (2004). *Undoing Gender.* New York, NY: Routledge.

Caro, D. (2016). *Resolution in support of LGBTQ student life at California State University, Fullerton.* Retrieved at http://asi.fullerton.edu/downloads/government/resolutions/inSupportLesbianGayBisexualTransgenderQueerQuestioningStudentLife.pdf

Consolacion, T. B., Russell, S. T., & Sue, S. (2004). Sex, race/ethnicity, and romantic attractions: Multiple minority status adolescents and mental health. *Cultural Diversity and Ethnic Minority Psychology, 10*(3), 200–214.

Curran, G., Chiarolli, S., & Pallotta-Chiarolli, M. (2009). 'The c words': Clitorises, childhood and challenging compulsory heterosexuality discourses with pre-service primary teachers. *Sex Education, 9,* 155–168.

DePalma, R. (2013). Choosing to lose our gender expertise: Queering sex/gender in school settings. *Sex Education, 13*(1), 1–15.

Depalma, R., & Atkinson, E. (2006). The sound of silence: Talking about sexual orientation and schooling. *Sex Education, 6,* 333–349.

Depalma, R., & Atkinson, E. (2009). "No outsiders": Moving beyond a discourse of tolerance to challenge heteronormativity in primary schools. *British Educational Research Journal, 35,* 837–855.

DiPietro, M. (2012). *Applying the seven learning principles to creating LGBT inclusive classrooms.* American Association of Colleges and Universities. Retrieved from www.aacu.org/publications-research/periodicals/applying-seven-learning-principles-creating-lgbt-inclusive

Dover, A. G. (2017). Privileging the pragmatic: Interrogating stance in teacher preparation. In B. Picower & R. Kohli (Eds.), *Confronting racism in teacher education: Counternarratives of critical practice* (pp. 53–59). New York, NY and London: Routledge.

Dube, E., & Savin-Williams, R. C. (1999). Sexual identity development among sexual minority male youths. *Developmental Psychology, 35*(6), 1389–1398.

Esmonde, I. (2011). Snips and snails and puppy dogs' tails: Genderism and mathematics education. *For the Learning of Mathematics, 31*(2), 27–31.

Flores, G. (2012). Toward a more inclusive multicultural education: Methods for including LGBT themes in K-12 classrooms. *American Journal of Sexuality Education, 7*(3), 187–197.

Flores, G. (2014). Teachers working cooperatively with parents and caregivers when implementing LGBT themes in the elementary classroom. *American Journal of Sexuality Education, 9*(1), 114–120.

Harbin, B. (2015). *Teaching beyond the gender binary in the university classroom.* Retrieved from https://cft.vanderbilt.edu/teaching-beyond-the-gender-binary-in-the-university-classroom/

GLSEN. (2009). *Shared differences: The experiences of lesbian, gay, bisexual, and transgender students of color in our nation's schools.* New York, NY: Elizabeth Diaz & Joseph Kosciw.

GLSEN. (2016). *From teasing to torment: School climate revisited.* New York, NY: Emily Greytak, Joseph Kosciw, Christian Vilenas, & Nooren Giga.

Graves, K. (2009). *And they were wonderful teachers: Florida's purge of gay and lesbian teachers.* Urbana: University of Illinois Press.

Grov, C., & Bimbi, D. S. (2006). Race, ethnicity, gender, and generational factors associated with the coming out process among gay, lesbian, and bisexual individuals. *Journal of Sex Research, 43*(2), 115–121.

Hermann-Wilmarth, J. (2010). More than book talks: Preservice teacher dialogue after reading gay and lesbian children's literature. *The Reading Teacher, 87*, 188–198.

Kelso, T. (2015). Still trapped in the U.S. media's closet: Representations of gender-variant, pre-adolescent children. *Journal of Homosexuality, 62*, 1058–1097.

Kosciw, J. G., Greytak, E. A., Palmer, N. A., & Boesen, M. J. (2013). *The 2013 Gay, Lesbian, Straight Education Network National School Climate Survey.* Retrieved from: www.glsen.org/sites/default/files/2013%20National%20School%20Climate%20Survey%20Full%20Report_0.pdf

Naidoo, J. C. (2012). *Rainbow family collections: Selecting and using children's books with lesbian, gay, bisexual, transgender, and queer content.* Denver, CO: Libraries Unlimited.

Nasir, N. S., Hand, V., & Taylor, E. V. (2008). Culture and mathematics in school: Boundaries between "cultural" and "domain" knowledge in the mathematics classroom and beyond. *Review of Research in Education, 32*, 187–240.

National Education Association. (2017). *Diversity toolkit: Cultural competence for educators.* Retrieved from www.nea.org/tools/30402.htm

Kumashiro, K. (2004). *Against common sense: Teaching and learning toward social justice.* New York, NY: Routledge Falmer.

Phillips, D. K., & Larson, M. L. (2010). Preservice teachers respond to *And Tango Makes Three*: Deconstructing disciplinary power and the heteronormative in teacher education. *Gender and Education, 24*(2), 159–176.

Renn, K. A. (2010). LGBT and queer research in higher education. *Educational Researcher, 39*(2), 132–141.

Sanders, J. (1997). *Teacher education and gender equity.* ERIC Clearinghouse on Teaching and Teacher Education, Washington DC. Retrieved at www.ericdigests.org/1998-1/gender.htm

Sears, J. (2009). Interrogating the subject: Queering elementary education, 10 years on. *Sex Education 9*, 193–200.

Shaban, B., Campos, R., Rutanashoodeh, T., Villareal, M., & Horn, M. (2017). *At least 73,000 students attend Bay Area schools that don't provide teacher training on transgender issues.* NBC News. Retrieved from www.nbcbayarea.com/investigations/At-Least-73000-Students-Attend-Bay-Area-Schools-that-Dont-Provide-Teacher-Training-on-Transgender-Issues-451953973.html?_osource=SocialFlowFB_BAYBrand

Weissglass, J. (2002). Inequity in mathematics education: Questions for educators. *The Mathematics Educator, 12*(2), 34–39.

Wimberly, G. L., & Battle, J. (2015). Challenges to doing research on LGBTQ issues in education and important research needs. In G. L. Wimberly (Ed.), *LGBTQ issues in education: Advancing a research agenda.* Washington, DC: American Educational Research Association.

AFTERWORD

Lisa Richardson, Sharon Chappell, and Karyl Ketchum

You now have strategies and resources that will enable you to begin to create a more welcoming elementary, middle, and high school environment. In this book, you have read about inclusive curriculum, teaching practices, and resources to support gender diversity and LGBTQ youth. So… What next? How will the information, tools, and resources provided in this book affect and inform your actions? How will you begin to teach in order to support the gender diversity and intersectionality that exist in your classroom and school community? What next steps will you take?

We ask you to appreciate the impact that socializing and disciplining rigid binary-based gender norms has on all students. We hope that in your daily practice, you will interrupt binary concepts of gender where they are present in

FIGURE 12.1 Hands of the World. Photo by Michele Hatchell.

curriculum and when you witness them during the school day. We hope that you will recognize and celebrate the gender diversity and the intersectionality that exist in your students' identities, and that you will expand the representation of the marginalized groups in your classrooms and community accordingly.

TIPS FOR MAKING A SCHOOL SAFE FOR LGBTQ STUDENTS

1. Educate yourself.
2. Check your biases.
3. Teach inclusively.
4. Be visible.
5. Respond to anti-LGBT behavior.
6. Support students who come out.
7. Support a student GSA.
8. Revisit your school policies.
9. Educate your colleagues.

by Jennifer Gonzalez, Cult of Pedagogy, 2017[1]

We hope that you have been inspired to embrace inclusive practices and to have real conversations about welcoming diversity, preventing bias-based bullying, and understanding gender in support of transgender and non-binary students. You will find that you can start small, knowing that things will evolve as you begin to reflect, evaluate, and act. It will take effort and commitment, but once you begin, you will find that your classroom and your school will slowly become more inclusive, and thus more welcoming. Equity and compassion are contagious. On your journey—and it is a journey—to improve the inclusiveness of your classroom and curriculum, you will foster empathy and curiosity about others, along with teaching your students how to see the world from multiple perspectives. Students will begin to recognize and think critically and creatively about injustice and you will empower them to take informed action.

It is our hope that you are inspired to learn more about queer, gender-expansive, and transgender youth and families. We hope that you will examine state and federal laws and policies that support a more inclusive classroom and school community. We trust that you feel empowered to evaluate and adjust your curriculum and teaching practices in terms of inclusions and exclusions, in support of the intersectionality of your students' identities. Set goals for yourself as an educator and become an advocate for this important work. With courage and compassion, you have the power to act! You can prevent and intervene in bias, stereotyping, and discrimination when you observe it at school. You can help normalize gender diversity.

The world is changing. It is becoming more accepting of those perceived to be different. The world is opening and expanding. Although not fast enough, we are moving in the right direction. With self-reflection and critical analysis of literature and curriculum by you and your students, by ensuring that all groups and identities are represented, by normalizing an expansive concept of gender, and by providing safe spaces for students to be their authentic selves, you will be teaching your students that the world is ready for them. As an educator, parent, or advocate, what greater legacy or impact could you desire?

Note

1 For more, see https://www.cultofpedagogy.com/lgbtq-students/.

CONTRIBUTOR BIOGRAPHIES

Polly Attwood teaches both undergraduates and graduates in Northeastern University's (Boston, MA) teacher education programs. She brings her experience as a former high school social studies teacher to courses on the history of education; the sociopolitical context of education; issues of inclusion, equity, and diversity; critical pedagogy; and teaching secondary social studies/history.

Brittney Beck is an Assistant Professor of Teacher Education at California State University, Bakersfield. For over 12 years, she has led teaching and research initiatives on civic engagement, democratic education, and activist-centered pedagogies, with specific emphasis on intersectional identities in education. She has developed and facilitated professional development in partnership with K-12, university, and community stakeholders regarding how to develop and sustain empowering curriculum and instruction for lesbian, gay, bisexual, transgender, queer (LGBTQ) youth and allies. She serves as an affiliate faculty member for the Kegley Institute of Ethics and a faculty liaison for the presidentially appointed campus-wide LGBTQ outreach committee. Brittney can be reached at bbeck4@csub.edu.

Brett Bigham is the 2014 Oregon State Teacher of the Year and a recipient of the National Education Association (NEA) National Award for Teaching Excellence. He filed state and federal complaints against his school district after they ordered him not to say he was gay and was fired for refusing their orders. He now speaks around the globe for the rights of LGBT students and teachers. Bigham was named an NEA Foundation Global Fellow for 2018 for South Africa and was a 2015 Peru Fellow.

Mollie Blackburn is a Professor in the Department of Teaching and Learning at the Ohio State University. Her research focuses on literacy, language, and social change, with particular attention to LGBTQ youth and the teachers who serve them.

Sharon Verner Chappell is an Associate Professor in the Department of Elementary and Bilingual Education at California State University Fullerton. She specializes in social justice in curriculum, youth-centered schooling, and arts education. Trained as a Welcoming Schools facilitator with the Human Rights Campaign, she conducts professional development workshops on gender diversity and LGBTQ inclusion for teachers and other school professionals throughout Orange County and Los Angeles. She is a practicing poet, and her book *Wet Wings*, poems on thriving through breast cancer, can be found at https://schappel2.wixsite.com/wetwings.

Alison G. Dover is an Assistant Professor in the Department of Secondary Education at California State University, Fullerton. Her teaching and research examines literacy education; social justice-oriented teacher agency in K-12 and higher education; and strategies for promoting equity and justice in school curriculum, policy, and practice. Her recent publications include *Preparing to Teach Social Studies for Social Justice: Becoming a Renegade* (Teachers College Press, 2016) and articles in *Teaching and Teacher Education, The Educational Forum,* and *English Journal.*

Lori Duron is the award-winning author of the best-selling book *Raising My Rainbow: Adventures in Raising a Fabulous, Gender Creative Son* (Random House, September 2013). The first parenting memoir to chronicle the journey of raising a gender-nonconforming child, the book is based on her blog of the same name. Duron is an advocate and often-quoted source on parenting gender-creative, gender-nonconforming, protogay, and prehomosexual children.

Jey Ehrenhalt, M.Ed., has taught English and Special Education in Portland, OR. They currently work as the Social Justice Educator Grants Manager at *Teaching Tolerance.*

Eli Erlick is the Director of Trans Student Educational Resources, a national youth-led organization dedicated to transforming the educational environment for trans students. She is also a PhD student in Feminist Studies at the University of California, Santa Cruz, where she researches the political philosophy of the transgender movement. Her broader research focuses on contemporary transgender/queer studies, necropolitics, rural studies, self-determination, depathologization, suicide, youth politics, and neoliberalism. You can learn more about Erlick at www.elierlick.com.

Emily Freeman holds an MFA from the University of Texas at Austin in Drama and Theatre for Youth Communities and a BA in Theatre from Northwestern University. She worked for theatre companies around the country, including

The John F. Kennedy for Performing Arts, Imagination Stage, and Asolo Repertory Theatre. She works at Orlando Repertory Theatre as the Community Engagement Director and is an applied theatre artist, playwright, and educator. Her play *And Then Came Tango* was named Outstanding TYA (Theatre for Young Audiences) Play by the Kennedy Center American College Theater Festival and premiered at The Growing Stage in New Jersey.

Salvador Andrés González-Padilla has a BA in Communications from Loyola Marymount University and an MS in Education from California State University, Fullerton. He would like to dedicate his essay to the people of every continent who act in the name of social, environmental, and economic justice and, in particular, to the people of his native México who, with courage and integrity, labor tirelessly against impunity and for the promotion and protection of human rights.

Michele Hatchell works with the Welcoming Schools program as an expert trainer and curriculum developer. She has been a public school elementary art teacher for over twenty-three years in Chicago, IL, and Madison, WI. She is also a professional artist and has created individual and public art with folks of all ages in communities, schools, museums, and college campuses.

Karyl E. Ketchum is an Associate Professor at California State University, Fullerton. Her research emphasis is on critical and theoretical analysis of technology, visual culture, and new media forms as these intersect with gender identity/expression, desire, race, class, and nation. She also publishes and is a frequent speaker on topics related to K-12 education reform through principles of social justice, critical theory, and transformative pedagogies. She is a founding member of the Orange County Equality Coalition School Compliance Task Force and has partnered with the American Civil Liberties Union of Southern California on several projects centered on supporting LGBT students, including producing a public service announcement informing students and their families of new rights afforded to them by way of evolving state education codes.

Daniel A. Krack is a PhD candidate in the Composition and Teaching English to Speakers of Other Languages (TESOL) program at Indiana University of Pennsylvania. He currently teaches high school just outside of Pittsburgh, PA, and is interested in exploring the ways that composition can help empower LGBTQ+ high school students.

Emily Maeda graduated from Cal State Fullerton with her bachelor's degree in Child and Adolescent Development in May 2016. She is currently in a combined credential and master's program at Cal State Fullerton with the plan of becoming an elementary school teacher. As an educator, she hopes to foster a safe and welcoming classroom environment where all of her diverse students can share their unique perspectives and ideas.

Cody Miller teaches ninth-grade English language arts at P.K. Yonge Developmental Research School, the K–12 laboratory school affiliated with the University of Florida's College of Education. In addition to teaching, Cody is also a PhD candidate in English education at the University of Florida.

sj Miller is a transdisciplinary award-winning teacher/writer/activist/scholar; is Deputy Director of The Center for Research on Equity in Teacher Education at the New York University (NYU) Metro Center; and is Research Associate Faculty in NYU's Steinhardt School of Culture, Education, and Human Development. sj has a combined 22 years of teaching secondary English Language Arts and undergraduate/graduate courses in Literacy and Urban/English Teacher Education. sj has written and published over forty articles in peer-reviewed journals as well as over twenty book chapters and six books, and has presented widely in state, national, and international conferences on a variety of topics, including anti-bullying pedagogy, challenging the gender binary and LGBTQ topics, and disrupting the school-to-prison pipeline. sj is Advisor for The National Council Teachers of English LGBT Issues in Academic Studies Committee, GLSEN's Educator Advisory Committee, Consultant for the College Board, and Senior Advisor working with teachers about transgender issues for Public Broadcasting Station (PBS). sj is Coeditor of two book series, *Social Justice Across Contexts in Education* and *Queering Teacher Education Across Context*, and United Nations Educational, Scientific and Cultural Organization (UNESCO) representative for the United States to develop education for peace and sustainable development in India with the Mahatma Gandhi Institute. sj recently appeared in a feature documentary on CBS, *Gender: The Space Between*, and is a frequent contributor to the Huffington Post, CBS, and PBS. sj was awarded the 2017 American Educational Research Association (AERA) Exemplary Research Award for *Teaching, Affirming, and Recognizing Trans and Gender Creative Youth: A Queer Literacy Framework*.

John Newman is an Associate Professor of theatre at Utah Valley University (UVU) and Director of the Theatre for Youth and Education (TYE) Center at UVU. He taught and directed theatre at Highland High School in Salt Lake City, UT, for 18 years. He is an author, playwright, director, play developer, and solo performance actor.

Andrew Pegan has numerous years of experience teaching secondary Social Studies and Language Arts, having taught everything from fifth-grade Humanities to eleventh-grade US History. Andrew is particularly interested in social justice education and the integration of 21st-century literacy skills into the classroom.

Veronica Reinhart has taught English, History, Journalism, and Speech & Debate at Spurgeon Intermediate in Santa Ana for the past eleven years. She is also the advisor for Rainbow Warriors, Spurgeon Intermediate's Gay–Straight Alliance (GSA). Mrs. Reinhart received her BA in Sociology from the University of California, Irvine, and her MA in Education at Azusa Pacific University.

Mindi Rhoades is an Assistant Professor in the Department of Teaching and Learning at the Ohio State University. Her research focuses on interdisciplinary arts-based research, teaching, learning, and activism inside and outside of school. Her research often addresses issues related to LGBTQ+ students and educators with regards to educational, arts, and visual culture contexts.

Lisa Richardson is a Veteran Teacher with over thirty-five years of classroom experience. She recently retired from teaching in Irvine, CA, and was a member of the district's Curriculum Leadership team. She was an Instructional Strategies Mentor Teacher, a Literacy Presenter, and a Coach. She is a past president of the South Orange County Parents and Friends of Lesbians and Gays (PFLAG) chapter and is actively involved as a member of the Long Beach/ Orange County PFLAG Speaker's Bureau, advocating and educating others about LGBTQ experiences. As a School and Community Outreach Coordinator, she enthusiastically advocates for students and the integration of inclusive curriculum and anti-bullying programs in schools. She meets with school district administrators, counselors, and teachers to provide resources and assistance in creating more welcoming schools for LGBTQ students.

Melissa Rivers has worked in education for over 20 years in many different roles. She has taught in P-12 settings; served as a high school principal; and taught dual enrollment, undergraduate, and graduate education courses. Her research interests are educational leadership, teacher preparation and professional development, and the P-22 pipeline.

Ryan Schey is Assistant Professor of English Education in the Department of Curriculum and Teaching at Auburn University. His research explores literacy and language practices, and social change in schools, focusing on LGBTQ and gender-diverse young people. He is currently analyzing data from a year-long literacy ethnography in an urban public high school where he collaborated with a teacher and her students in English language arts classrooms and the school's Genders and Sexualities Alliance. Before working on his doctorate, he taught high school English and co-advised his school's Gay–Straight Alliance (GSA).

Veronika Shulman is a lover of everything magical and surreal. In addition to writing and marketing for plays and films, she is currently the director of content & communications for Get Lit, a performing arts organization that works with youth all over California. In the words of Alejandro Jodorowsky, "I sold my devil to the soul." More @ bambinobranding.com.

James Shultis is a Poet and Social Activist who divides their time between creative writing, speaking engagements, and nonprofit work. Some of their most recent work was with the YWCA of Western Massachusetts (Springfield, MA) as Director of Parent & Youth Support Services; at the Pride Center of the Capital Region (Albany, NY) as Director of Programs and previously as its Youth Programs Manager; and as Cochair at the New York Capital Region Chapter of GLSEN. James holds an MFA in Creative Writing from Queens College (2010) and a BA in English Literature and Gender Studies from Hunter College (2008). Their poetry has appeared in print and online journals, including *Hematopoiesis Press*, Up the River, Mud Luscious Press, The Scrambler, Women Studies Quarterly (through *Feminist Press*), AlexZine, Farmhouse Magazine, and *Next Door Magazine*. You can reach James at www.jamesshultis.com

Deb Smith is a High School Principal at Daniel Pearl Magnet High School in the Los Angeles Unified School District. Deb has 40 years of experience as an educator, including teaching all grades and working with special needs students, primarily students with serious emotional disturbance.

Sarah Tyler is the proud single mother of two wonderful children and an activist for the LGBTQ community, especially for the rights of transgender people. She is also the Co-founder of Shift Happens, a support group for family and friends of transgender people in Orange County, CA. Sarah and her family have been featured in the award-winning documentary "Trans, the Movie" and have appeared on the Anderson Cooper and Ricki Lake shows discussing raising a transgender child. Sarah is currently working on a book about her life and the privilege and struggles of raising a transgender child.

Ariel Uppstrom is currently a High School English Teacher and was a Co-advisor of her school's Gay–Straight Alliance (GSA) in Delaware, OH. During her 11 years of teaching, she has worked to cultivate an atmosphere of activism and equality in her classroom. Focusing on minority representation in literature and history, she has taught courses from English 10 to CCP Honors World Literature as well as Film and Literature. She is currently working towards a certificate in composition studies.

Cathery Yeh is an Assistant Professor in the School of Education at Chapman University. Cathery studies how people learn, with an emphasis on how systems of power and privilege play out in learning contexts and the opportunities for transformative pedagogy when teachers place their attention on students, families, and communities.

APPENDIX A

IMPORTANT GENDER, SEXUALITY, AND LESBIAN, GAY, BISEXUAL, TRANS, QUEER (LGBTQ) DEFINITIONS

Ally: A term used to describe someone who is supportive of LGBTQ people. It encompasses non-LGBTQ allies as well as those within the LGBT community who support each other: for example, a lesbian who is an ally to the bisexual community.

Asexual: A term used to describe individuals who do not experience sexual attraction.

Bisexual: A term used to describe individuals who are physically and emotionally attracted to both the opposite and same sexes.

Gay: A generic term used to describe individuals who are physically and emotionally attracted to someone of the same sex. Sometimes used just to refer to gay men. It is also used as a derogatory slur to describe anything, anyone, or any behavior that does not meet the approval of an individual or a given group.

Gender: The socially constructed roles, behaviors, activities, and attributes that a given society considers appropriate for men and women. Gender varies between cultures and over time. There is broad variation in which individuals experience and express gender.

Gender binary: The idea that there are only two distinct and opposing genders (female/male).

Gender continuum/spectrum: The idea that gender identity and expression is often experienced through a continuum or spectrum.

Gender-expansive: Conveys a wider, more flexible range of gender expression, with a range of interests and behaviors. Expanding beyond traditional gender stereotypes. It reinforces the notion that gender is not a binary, but a continuum; and that many children and adults express their gender in multiple and changing ways.

Gender expression: How one expresses their gender to the world (clothing, dress, mannerisms, speech).

Gender identity: How one feels inside. One's internal, deeply felt sense of being girl/woman, boy/man, somewhere in between, or outside these categories.

Gender-nonconforming: A term used by the California Department of Education to describe students whose gender expression does not fit into the socially constructed gender binary of male/female.

Heteronormative: The expectation that all individuals are heterosexual. Often expressed subtly through assumptions that everyone is, or will grow up to be, straight. Can also refer to the social, political, and economic system that supports and rewards heterosexuality and, the institutionalized belief that heterosexuality is the superior and singular mode of sexual organization for society.

Intersectionality: Describes the ways that people's multiple identities are formed and forming in relation to systems of power and oppression. The whole of one's identity is complex and informed by the component identities in relation to social institutions impacting those component identities.

Intersex: A general term used for a variety of conditions in which a person is born with a reproductive or sexual anatomy that doesn't seem to fit the typical definitions of female or male.

LGBTQ or LGBTQIA: Acronym for lesbian, gay, bisexual and transgender. Q can stand for questioning or queer, I stands for intersex, and A stands for ally or asexual. Also abbreviated as GLBT and LGBT.

Lesbian: A woman who is sexually and romantically attracted to other women.

Queer: Historically a negative term for LGBT people. More recently reclaimed by some LGBT people to refer to themselves. Often used to reference a more flexible view of gender and/or sexuality. Some people still find the term offensive. Others use it as a more inclusive term that allows for more freedom of gender expression. Also used in academic fields, such as queer studies or queer pedagogy, indicating an interest in how norms and difference are constructed and maintained.

Queer theory: A theoretical approach to analyzing lived experiences used in academic fields like queer studies and queer pedagogy. This approach challenges either/or essentialist categories about gender and sexuality and includes a critical and historically grounded inquiry into normative social and cultural processes.

Sex: One's biological and physical attributes—external genitalia, sex chromosomes, hormones, and internal reproductive structures—that are used to assign a sex at birth.

Sexual orientation: Who you are attracted to—physically, romantically, or emotionally. Current research indicates that sexual orientation exists along a continuum of emotional and sexual attractions and, in some cases, can change over the course of an individual's lifetime.

Transgender: An umbrella term that describes a wide range of identities, expressions, and experiences. It includes those whose gender assigned at birth does not match their internal sense of gender identity. A child who is transgender will often assert firmly, over time, that their gender identity is the not that which was assigned at birth. They will often insist that they are in the wrong body. Not all gender-nonconforming individuals consider themselves transgender. Some transgender individuals do not assert their identities until they are adults or even seniors.

APPENDIX B

ANTI-BIAS LEARNING STUDENT OBJECTIVES

- <u>Objective One (seeing self)</u>: Teachers will engage each student in their demonstration of self-awareness, confidence, family pride, and positive social identities.
- <u>Objective Two (being in relation to others)</u>: Teachers will engage each student in their expression of comfort and joy with human diversity; accurate language for human differences; and deep, caring human connections.
- <u>Objective Three (understanding bias)</u>: Teachers will engage each student in their recognition of unfairness and bias, their use of language to describe unfairness and bias/stereotypes, and understanding that unfairness/bias hurts.
- <u>Objective Four (taking action)</u>: Teachers will engage each student in their demonstration of empowerment and the skills to act, with others or alone, against prejudice and/or discriminatory actions.

—Objectives developed for teacher candidates at California State University Fullerton, based on Derman-Sparks, L., & Edwards, J. O. (2010). *Anti-bias education for young children and ourselves*. Washington, D.C.: National Association for the Education of Young Children

APPENDIX C

INSTEAD OF... TRY THESE CLASSROOM PRACTICES

As a teacher, you might wonder, what practical strategies you can use when you are working to make your classroom and interactions more just, equitable, and inclusive for all students.

TABLE 16.1 Inclusive language and actions (Try these ideas instead of these)

Try These Ideas	Instead of
Gender	
Line up as you arrive.	Using boy/girl lines.
Line up by number or table group.	
Line up by interest.	
Use gender-neutral language in class.	Calling the group together saying, "boys
e.g.: Call your class "scholars" or "friends."	and girls."
Use parents and guardians or families.	Only using mother/father language
Survey and learn about families. Include diverse family structures in literature and examples.	when describing families verbally or in written communication.
Set the classroom norm that books are for everyone. Materials (like colors, role-play items) are for everyone. Subjects are for everyone. Roles (like in class plays) are for everyone.	Assuming boys or girls want particular books, toys/manipulatives, colors, or activities based on their gender.
Language	
Ask for pronunciation of children's and families' names. Practice and use that pronunciation.	Mispronouncing a name or renaming a child without their permission.

(Continued)

Try These Ideas	Instead of
Post multilingual greetings in the classroom. Learn to say hello and welcome in the languages of your families, and greet families that way. Ask students to share their languages in class. Read bilingual and multilingual books. Talk about the ways languages have been discriminated against in CA and the USA.	Encouraging exclusive use of English. Discouraging use of other languages. Ignoring students' bilingualism.

Race and ethnicity

Help your students use accurate language to describe themselves and others, and to talk about race and racism (e.g.: With younger kids, talk about hair, eye, and skin color. Reframe language and assumptions. With older kids, talk about the way skin color was/is used to categorize and oppress particular groups of people).	Ignoring your students' race/ethnicity or your students' talk about race/ethnicity (e.g.: "I don't see color, I see children").
Discuss the impact of racism against people of color in history and contemporary society. Identify strategies to help student combat racism.	Ignoring that racism exists.

Diversity in curriculum and pedagogy

Supplement adopted curricula to ensure multiple perspectives and experiences, diverse contributions, and multiple interpretations of events. Include ethnic studies, disabilities studies, and gender studies approaches.	Solely using scripted recommendations for books and curricula that have single perspectives or ignore particular experiences (e.g.: texts that talk about families but omit same-sex families or families with adopted or foster youth).
Reflect on what children you talk to and in what context. Ensure that you have high expectations and interest in each child. Ensure you develop a personal, asset-based relationship with every child.	Being unaware of whom you are calling on in or talking to in class. Using lower expectations for particular children. Assuming that only particular children want to participate in a certain activity, role or responsibility in class.
Research ways to talk about current events. Utilize resources through respected organizations like the National Education Association: Human and Civil Rights. Ensure you know the antidiscrimination laws and policies that govern schools in California and the USA.	Not addressing current events that impact children's lives (immigration raids, racial violence, same-sex families, and transgender child discrimination).

Try These Ideas	Instead of
Bias, bullying, and bystanders	
Talk to your supervisor and/or mentor teacher right away. Practice what you will say to express your concerns.	Not addressing negative or discriminatory talk you hear in the teacher lounge or other school staff spaces.
Work on prevention and intervention. Prevention work includes the four department objectives above. Use resources on addressing bias-based bullying, like those from Welcoming Schools and Teaching Tolerance.	Not addressing negative or discriminatory talk on the playground or in the classroom.
Families and family diversity	
Ensure your library and book selections have diverse experiences (use the Fair, Accurate, Inclusive and Respectful (FAIR) Education Act and resources from Welcoming Schools and Teaching Tolerance).	Using literature that have narrow, assumed, normative experiences of children and families.
Use tools like family surveys, family events, family volunteering, and family collaborative assignments to bring family lives into the classroom. Use your knowledge of families as reference points in class activities.	Ignoring or not utilizing the assets and resources of your students' families and communities in the classroom.
Teach about the world's religions. Don't assume your students all share the same family religious beliefs and traditions.	During holidays, only referencing a single religion's holiday or only using symbols for that religion's holiday for school activities (e.g.: Santa, reindeer, *The Polar Express*).
Classroom climate	
Post images of people defying gender stereotypes in expression and occupation, people with a range of physical and cognitive abilities, people of different ethnicities, people in different family structures, a range of home structures we live in.	Having limited representations of human diversity on classroom walls.
Use restorative practices and trauma-sensitive practices, including community circles, small group discussions, and collaboration.	Creating limited classroom community.
Use interactive exercises to help students understand bias, bullying, and how to be an upstander.	

(Continued)

Try These Ideas	Instead of
Teach about words like *bias, discrimination, oppression, civil rights, equity, tolerance, acceptance.* Use examples from literature, history, and school experiences, such as from Teaching Tolerance and Teaching for Change.	Omitting a discussion of bias and discrimination when talking about classroom and school values.
Reflect on how families gain access to information about your class. Discuss strategies for increasing access with other teachers and your mentor teacher.	Not addressing equity concerns around family access to school materials and resources.
Every child and family has strengths, assets, and resources. Notice, engage, and celebrate them every day. Reflect on terminology that is deficit versus asset-based. Use asset-based strategies (such as emergent bilingual students, students with differing abilities).	Using deficit thinking when thinking and talking about or planning for a child's learning and interaction with families.
Discuss differing abilities. Discuss how bias and discrimination impact people with disabilities as well as this community's civil rights struggle. Use "people first" language and teach students to use this language. (e.g.: a person with special needs, a person with autism) Use asset-based strategies.	Ignoring differing abilities in society and in school.
Celebrate cultural, linguistic, family, and gender diversity in your Back to School messages.	Omitting mention of diversity from Back to School welcomes.

Resources:

www.tkcalifornia.org/teaching-tools/

www.edutopia.org/

www.adl.org/education-and-resources/resources-for-educators-parents-families

www.welcomingschools.org/

www.nea.org/home/64654.htm

www.teachingforchange.org/

www.tolerance.org/

www.faireducationact.com/about-fair/

APPENDIX D

SUGGESTED TALKING POINTS: WHAT TO SAY IN DIFFICULT CONVERSATIONS ON GENDER, FAMILY, RACE/ETHNICITY, LANGUAGE, IMMIGRATION

It is always best to intervene in discriminatory language and bias-based bullying, and then follow up with individual conferences, restorative practices, and educational experiences. Here is some intervention language that you can use to stop the bias as it is happening.

Discriminatory Language

When you hear a homophobic term (such as hey faggot, that's so gay)
> **SAY: "We don't use put-downs in this class. Being gay is part of who some people are, and that is OK."**

When you hear a sexist term (such as pussy, you hit like a girl)
> **SAY: "It is never OK to use being a girl (or boy) as a put-down. Being a girl (boy) is wonderful."**

When you hear a racist term (such as anti-Semitic, anti-Muslim, anti-Black, anti-Latino, anti-Asian, anti-Immigrant)
> **SAY: "Using that word to put someone down is unacceptable. Someone's race/ethnicity is part of who they are and should be celebrated."** Then explain why it isn't funny.

When you hear an ableist term (such as lame, retarded, retard, slow, freak, what are you—deaf)
> **SAY: "You are putting someone down when you use that word. There are people with differences, and it is hurtful to them."**

When you hear a classist term (such as cheap, your mom shops at the 99-cent store)
> **SAY: "We don't use words to hurt people. And we don't make fun of the amount of money people make or the jobs that they have."**

When you hear a body-shaming term (such as fatty, fatso, skinny, shrimp, shorty)

SAY: "We don't use words to hurt people. People are all shapes and sizes, and all bodies are beautiful."

When you hear emotion-shaming term (such as cry baby, scaredy cat; what are you, scared)

SAY: "We don't make fun of someone's emotions. It is ok to cry or be afraid. It is natural. I am afraid sometimes, and I cry too."

Community Concerns

After discussing hate speech and racial violence in the classroom, a parent might say you have a political agenda.

You can say, **"We care about every child at school and in the world. Talking about how to ensure the safety and well-being of people in the US is about inclusion and is part of the curricular standards."**

When supporting a transgender child's right to access the bathroom or locker room of their gender identity, a parent might express concern and discomfort with the transgender child being in that space with their child.

You can say, **"I hear that you feel uncomfortable. We can accommodate your child with a different restroom if that would help you. However, under California and US, we cannot discriminate against any child because of their identity in public schools. All children have the right to access the bathroom of their gender identity."**

When talking about families and including stories of diverse family structures, a parent might say that it is against their religion for people to be gay and that they don't want their child learning about gay people.

You can say, **"We are learning about the range of human diversity in society, including many types of families. We are teaching about the importance of love, care and human relationship in families. We will provide many examples through stories of many families. We respect your personal and religious beliefs. However, under California and US law, we are required to teach about this range of family diversity in public schools."**

After talking about immigration raids in the classroom, a parent might express that their child shouldn't have to go to school with illegal children.

You can say, **"At public school we are required by law and the Constitution to teach every child. We do not discriminate based on national identity or citizenship status."**

You are working in multiple languages in the classroom. A parent comes to you and says that English is the official language of this country, and they want their child to speak only English at school.

You can say, **"At our school, we are so fortunate to have families who speak many languages. Utilizing home languages as part of learning helps develop the brain and supports academic success. I would be happy to share resources with you if you are interested."**

A child has confided that they are gay and/or trans. Later, the parent approaches you and asks you to tell them what their child said. Additionally, other teachers ask you to tell them about the child's conversation with you.

Discuss this situation with your school leadership. Then you can say, **"The law requires that school personnel may only share this information on a need-to-know basis or as the student directs. Every child has the right to their privacy at school by the FERPA law."**

APPENDIX E

LGBTQ AND GENDER DIVERSITY INCLUSION RESOURCES FOR FAMILIES AND K-12 SCHOOLS

Organizations and Resources

GLSEN
Advocacy, research, and curriculum development on LGBTQ topics.
www.glsen.org

> *Ready, Set, Respect! Elementary Toolkit!*
> Offers educational tools, lessons, booklists, and resources for elementary schools grades K-5
> www.glsen.org/readysetrespect

Gender Spectrum
Support for organizations and individuals in creating gender-inclusive environments with articles and information on legal and school-related gender issues.
www.genderspectrum.org

> *Annotated Booklist for Children*
> *Annotated Bibliography of Teen Books About Gender Diversity*
> www.genderspectrum.org/resources/parenting-and-family-2/#s7

> *Schools in Transition: A Guide Supporting Transgender Students in K-12 Environments*
> www.genderspectrum.org/studenttransitions/

HRC (Human Rights Campaign)
Advocacy, state laws, curriculum, and current events on LBGTQ topics.
www.hrc.org

Welcoming Schools
Offers professional development tools, lessons, resources for elementary schools on:

- Embracing Family Diversity
- Creating LGBTQ-inclusive Schools
- Preventing Bias-Based Bullying
- Supporting Transgender and Gender Expansive Students.

www.welcomingschools.org/get-started/

Bibliographies of books on LGBTQ topics
www.welcomingschools.org/pages/bibliographies-books-to-engage-students

PFLAG South Orange County and Long Beach Chapters
Support for families, allies, and people who are LGBTQ
http://lbpflag.org

Olweus: Bullying prevention programs
www.violencepreventionworks.org/public/index.page

Rethinking Schools

Trevor Project: Provides crisis intervention and suicide prevention with LGBTQ youth
www.thetrevorproject.org 866-488-7386

Teaching TOLERANCE: Over 470 K-12 lessons and curricular resources on a variety of diversity topics, including LGBTQ.
> *Lessons*: Classroom lessons, spanning essential social justice topics, and reinforcing critical social emotional learning skills.
> www.tolerance.org/classroom-resources

> *Perspectives of a Diverse America*: Antibias literacy-based curricular materials, grades 3–12.
> www.teachingtolerance.org

Additional Resources

American Library Association: Provides LGBTQ book lists and resources for LGBTQ youth. www.ala.org/glbtrt/publications.

Bornstein, K., & DiMasa, D. (1997). *My gender workbook*. New York, NY: Routledge.

Derman-Sparks, L., & Olson Edwards, J. (2010). *Anti-bias education: Young children and ourselves.* Washington, DC: NAEYC.; *Welcoming Schools*, Overview Module; *Perspectives for a Diverse America*, Anti-bias Framework.

Duron, L. (2013). *Raising my rainbow: Adventures in raising a fabulous, gender-creative son.* Portland, OR: Broadway Books.

Videos and Blogs

Film: Creating Gender Inclusive Schools. *The Youth and Gender Media Project and Gender Spectrum.*
www.genderspectrum.org/creating-gender-inclusive-schools/

Video: What children learn from the things they aren't told | Chris Tompkins | TEDxCSULB.
www.tolerance.org/magazine/why-heteronormativity-is-harmful

APPENDIX F

GENDER SPECTRUM'S GENDER INCLUSIVE SCHOOLS FRAMEWORK

Gender Inclusive Schools Framework

When someone with the authority of a teacher describes the world and you're not in it, there is a moment of psychic disequilibrium, as if you looked into a mirror and saw nothing.

--Adrienne Rich

Gender inclusive schools...
- Recognize that gender impacts all students
- Interrupt binary notions of gender
- Acknowledge and account for gender diversity
- Question limited portrayals of gender
- Support students' self-reflection
- Teach empathy and respect

Entry Points

When focusing on the intentional development of gender inclusive school settings, it is helpful to think in terms of four discrete approaches, or entry points: **Internal**, **Institutional**, **Interpersonal**, and **Instructional**. Through deliberate work in each one of these areas, gender inclusive practices can be woven into the fabric of the institution.

Internal entry points focus on educators' own knowledge and experiences of gender. It involves reflecting about how each person's understandings and beliefs about gender impact the work they do with students and applying the lens of gender to their professional practices. This entry point is crucial for the others to be effectively implemented; this foundation of gender literacy should be solidly in place before schools move to the other entry points.

Institutional entry points are structural steps that create a foundation for gender inclusive practices to take hold. Institutional entry points demonstrate to your community that the school/organization recognizes and honors gender diversity and actively works to reflect a more complex understanding about gender. Such approaches include:

- Policies/administrative regulations emphasizing gender as an area of diversity protected and supported by the school
- Systematic staff training that builds the capacity of teachers and other staff to honor the gender diversity of all students
- Student information systems allowing families to specify a child's gender marker, name and pronouns
- Identified staff members functioning as leads around gender diversity work or issues
- Systems and procedures for working with transgender and other gender expansive students
- All gender restroom/facilities that provide options for privacy without stigmatizing any students
- Readily available written materials and information about gender diversity
- Signage/imagery celebrating gender diversity
- Procedures/forms that demonstrate a non-binary understanding of gender

Interpersonal entry points are the interactions, intentional behaviors and communications that reinforce the school's commitment to gender inclusion for all. They are designed to interrupt simplistic notions about gender by providing a "counter narrative" to many of the binary assumptions being made about it. Educators operating from this entry point:

Use language that challenges binary messages about gender and "de-genders" objects
- ○ *Colors are just colors. They don't have a gender. You can like any color you want to.*
- ○ Rather than "boys and girls," "ladies and gentlemen," etc., refer to pupils as "students," "children," or another non-gendered term for the group.

gender **spectrum**

Help students understand the difference between patterns and rules
- *That may be true for some people, but not for everyone.*
- *More common and less common; frequently but not always*

Question limited portrayals of gender
- *Who decided what things are for boys and what things are for girls?*
- *Sometimes this stuff is confusing. We get messages that some things are for boys and some things are for girls. But these messages are just some people's ideas. They may not be right for you.*

Validate choices people make associated with their personal gender
- *That looks great! If you like it and it makes you feel good, that's what matters.*
- *You sure are good at that; I wish I could do it as well as you do!*

Teach empathy and respect
- *How do you think you would feel if people were always asking you about your own gender?*
- *Have you ever been teased? How does it feel when you are teased or treated as an outsider?*

Acknowledge gender diversity
- *Ideas and expectations about gender are changing all of the time.*
- *History is full of examples of gender diversity! There have been gender diverse people in every culture and religion, from all over the world and throughout time.*

**Instructional entry points** are specific ways in which teaching and learning are used to instill greater awareness and understanding about gender. Whether standing alone or integrated into other aspects of instruction, these approaches are the most direct way to impact students. In some ways, instructional approaches are the most easily accomplished. At the same time, in an era of increasingly scripted curricula or environments in which controversial subjects are highly scrutinized and regulated, instructional methods for creating gender inclusion can have the highest stakes for teachers and other educators. Instructional approaches include:

- Designing lesson plans to expand understandings of gender diversity
- Exploring curriculum areas or units for inserting gender diversity issues or topics
- Using literature that has themes raising gender diversity issues
- Utilizing the arts to explore gender
- Using the social-emotional curriculum to surface gender related themes
- Examining the media and popular culture for gender related messages
- Assigning open ended projects that include gender related topics, readings, or news

- Highlighting transgender or other gender expansive people in the news or from history
- Analyzing data about various trends related to evolving understandings of gender
- Inviting guest speakers who work for greater gender equity in education, law or other fields
- Using video or other media that present specific ideas about gender
- Creating space for students to articulate their own understanding and beliefs about gender
- Integrating gender into curriculum areas through story problems, writing prompts, readings, art assignments, research projects and more

RESOLUTION IN SUPPORT OF LESBIAN, GAY, BISEXUAL, TRANSGENDER, AND QUEER/QUESTIONING STUDENT LIFE AT CALIFORNIA STATE UNIVERSITY, FULLERTON

CALIFORNIA STATE UNIVERSITY, FULLERTON • 800 N. STATE COLLEGE BLVD. • FULLERTON, CA 92831-3599 • ASI.FULLERTON.EDU

A Resolution in Support of the Lesbian, Gay, Bisexual, Transgender, and Queer/Questioning Student Life at the California State University, Fullerton

WHEREAS, The Associated Students, Incorporated (ASI) of the California State University, Fullerton (CSU Fullerton) is the official voice of the students of the campus; and

WHEREAS, The role of ASI at CSU Fullerton is to facilitate participation across a spectrum of fields relating to the promotion of student life on the campus; and

WHEREAS, The increased number of negative experiences among LGBTQ students who are of college age makes them up to four times more likely to attempt suicide than their non-LGBTQ peers[1]; and

WHEREAS, 23% of LGBTQ students experience harassment, 61% of transgender college students are referred to in a derogatory way, 35% of transgender students experience harassment by peers, faculty, and staff, 5% of transgender students are physically assaulted and 3% are sexually assaulted, 15% of transgender students leave university due to severity of harassment, 11% leave university due to financial hardships of being transgender, and 44% are denied service or equal treatment for public accommodations, and 41% of transgender people attempt suicide at some point in their lives[2]; and

WHEREAS, Goal 3 of CSU Fullerton 2013-2018 Strategic Plan seeks to develop a Diversity Action Plan to "cultivate an environment that honors differences in various forms – race, ethnicity, gender, age, disability, sexual orientation, religious or political beliefs and status within the University."[3]; and

WHEREAS, The staff of the Division of Human Resources, Diversity and Inclusion at CSU Fullerton have not had complete and inclusive training on LGBTQ issues on campus[4]; and

WHEREAS, The CSU Chancellor's Office issued an executive order which established a systemwide policy prohibiting discrimination, harassment, retaliation, sexual misconduct, dating and domestic violence, and stalking against employees and third parties, along with a systemwide procedure for addressing such complaints[5]; and

WHEREAS, The current mandatory orientations on Title IX training are created by the Chancellor's Office and mandated by the Executive Order of the Chancellor's Office[6]; and

---

[1] http://www.thetaskforce.org/, retrieved February 18, 2016
[2] http://www.thetaskforce.org/, retrieved February 18, 2016
[3] http://planning.fullerton.edu/_resources/pdf/CSUF-Strategic-Plan.pdf, retrieved February 18, 2016
[4] Interview with CSU Fullerton Division of Human Resources, Diversity and Inclusion
[5] http://calstate.edu/EO/EO-1096.html, retrieved February 18, 2016
[6] Interview with CSU Fullerton Title IX Program Administration

WHEREAS, The current mandatory orientations for faculty, staff, and student employees currently implemented by the Division of Human Resources, Diversity and Inclusion includes Title IX training, but not training specific to LGBTQ issues[7]; and

WHEREAS, The current Title IX Program Administration at CSU Fullerton offers some supplementary education on LGBTQ issues relating to Title IX, however lacks funding resources for the supplementary training to be updated and implemented[8]; and

WHEREAS, Several CSUs including California State University, Long Beach, California State University, Northridge, San Francisco State University and San Diego State University have completed and been published in the Campus Pride Index which demonstrates a university's inclusiveness of the LGBTQ community[9]; and

WHEREAS, ASI Titan Recreation, CSU Fullerton Athletics, and the Club Sports program currently do not have a policy statement describing LGBTQ students' respective rights and incorporation; and

WHEREAS, The use of inclusive language is not actively encouraged by any specific part of the University; and

WHEREAS, The Office of Admissions and Records has recognized the need for self-identification of gender for students, faculty, and staff and will therefore be updating part of the system to reflect that in the 2016 Fall semester[10]; and

WHEREAS, The Office of Admissions and Records currently has a system in place that allows students to choose their preferred name, however it is not implemented in all systems throughout CSU Fullerton[11]; and

WHEREAS, Renovations in the Titan Student Union have begun to create facilities such as gender inclusive restrooms in order to accommodate the diverse student, faculty, and staff at CSU Fullerton; therefore let it be

RESOLVED, ASI and its constituents, the students of the CSU Fullerton, recognize and support LGBTQ students; and let it be further

RESOLVED, in accordance with ASI's Goal 2 of the ASI 2013-2018 Strategic Plan, ASI encourages the CSU Fullerton President's Commission on Equity and Inclusion to specifically address diversity and inclusion on campus as it relates to LGBTQ students, and to advise the Division of Human Resources, Diversity and Inclusion and the Title IX Program Administration in their efforts to support and provide LGBTQ supplementary training within the Title IX program; and let it be further

---

[7] Interview with CSU Fullerton Title IX Program Administration
[8] Interview with CSU Fullerton Title IX Program Administration
[9] https://www.campusprideindex.org/searchresults/display/105122, retrieved February 18, 2016
[10] Interview with CSU Fullerton Office of Admissions and Records
[11] Interview with CSU Fullerton Office of Admissions and Records

RESOLVED, ASI recommends that the staff of Division of Human Resources, Diversity and Inclusion be trained formally and annually by an LGBTQ professional on the LGBTQ community and their distinctive challenges in order to maintain their commitment to LGBTQ students; and let it be further

RESOLVED, ASI recommends that the CSU Fullerton ASI President, University President, Division of Human Resources, Diversity and Inclusion, Title IX Program Administration, CSU Board of Trustees, and California State Student Association encourage the CSU Chancellor's Office to include LGBTQ specific training in the mandatory program administered and created by the Chancellor's Office; and let it be further

RESOLVED, ASI recommends that the CSU Fullerton Title IX Program Administration be given increased funding and support from the University to provide inclusive and updated training for faculty, staff, and student employees on LGBTQ issues pertaining to Title IX, as well as to update the Title IX web page so that it may reflect LGBTQ issues and trainings; and let it be further

RESOLVED, ASI encourages the Division of Student Affairs and the Office of Diversity Initiatives and Resources to complete the Campus Pride Index and submit a report to the Campus Pride Index and CSU Fullerton ASI Board of Directors; and let it be further

RESOLVED, ASI encourages ASI Titan Recreation, CSU Fullerton Athletics, and the Club Sports program to adopt the statement, "California State University, Fullerton is committed to creating a welcoming and diverse climate for all participants. As such all Titan Recreation, Athletics, and Club Sports staff are encouraged to participate in Safe Space training. This training familiarizes individuals with the LGBTQ population, how to be an ally, and how to create a safe and welcoming space for LGBTQ individuals to participate in the athletic and recreation community. Recreation is a vital part to a healthy lifestyle for all people and these groups are committed to diversity and inclusion of all types of students."; and let it be further

RESOLVED, ASI encourages ASI Titan Recreation, CSU Fullerton Athletics, and the Club Sports program to complete the Campus Pride Sports Index and submit a report to the Campus Pride Index and the CSU Fullerton ASI Board of Directors; and let it be further

RESOLVED, ASI encourages that the CSU Fullerton ASI President, University President, and representative of Title IX Program Administration to work closely with the Senators of Academic Senate to encourage the chairs of each department to hold in-person training of faculty to be conducted by the Title IX Program Administration regarding LGBTQ education and challenges; and let it be further

RESOLVED, ASI encourages the Senators of Academic Senate to further promote inclusive and diverse language in classroom curriculums by introducing inclusive concepts to faculty members; and let it be further

RESOLVED, ASI recommends that a policy be administered by the CSU Fullerton Office of the President that requires both the Office of Admissions and Records and the Division of Human Resources, Diversity and Inclusion to integrate the option for students, faculty, and staff to use their preferred name and self-identification of gender in all systems; and let it be further

RESOLVED, ASI encourages the inclusion of gender inclusive restrooms in the future renovation of all CSU Fullerton buildings to insure that LGBTQ students are free of the stigma associated with their perceived gender, and if gender inclusive specific facilities are not feasible, ASI encourages the exploration of alternative solutions including but not limited to the reassignment of existing facilities; and let it be further

RESOLVED, In order to ensure that adequate progress is made on the expectations outlined in this resolution, the ASI President shall provide two status updates to the ASI Board of Directors per semester and continue until no further action is required; and let it be finally

RESOLVED, that this resolution be distributed to the California State University Board of Trustees, California State Student Association, and the following CSU Fullerton departments, divisions, and/or entities for their support and consideration: Office of the President, the President's Advisory Board, the Academic Senate, Office of the Vice President for Student Affairs, Office of the Vice President of Administration and Finance, Office of the Dean of Students, Division of Human Resources, Diversity and Inclusion, Office of Government and Community Relations, Office of Student Life and Leadership, The Title IX Program Administration, Office of Admissions and Records, and the Office of Diversity Initiatives and Resource Centers, and the CSU Fullerton Auxiliary Service Corporation (ASC).

Adopted by the Board of Directors of the Associated Students, California State University, Fullerton, Inc., on the first day of March in the year two thousand sixteen.

Joseph Valencia	Michael Badal	Gabriel Sedeño II
Chair, Board of Directors	President/CEO	Vice Chair, Board of Directors

INDEX

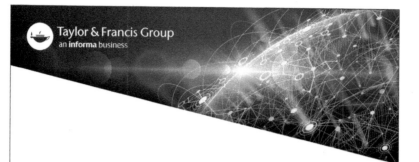